VISIONS OF KEROUAC
by
Charles E. Jarvis
University of Lowell
Lowell, Massachusetts

ITHACA PRESS
LOWELL, MASSACHUSETTS

D1496331

Published by Ithaca Press - Lowell, Massachusetts.

I gratefully acknowledge permission to reprint passages from the following material:

Dr. Sax by Jack Kerouac, copyright © 1959 by Jack Kerouac, reprinted with permission of Grove Press, Inc.

Visions of Gerard by Jack Kerouac, copyright © 1958, 1959, 1963 by Jack Kerouac, reprinted with permission of Farrar, Straus & Giroux.

'Once God Moves the Hand, You Go Back and Revise, It's a Sin!" Essay by Paul Jarvis, March 1972, reprinted with permission.

"The Art of Fiction LXI" by Ted Berrigan, copyright © 1968, reprinted with permission of *The Paris Review*, No. 43, Summer 1968.

The Town and the City by Jack Kerouac, copyright © 1950 by John Kerouac, reprinted with permission of Harcourt Brace Jovanovich, Inc.

Vanity of Duluoz by Jack Kerouac, copyright © 1967, 1968 by Jack Kerouac, reprinted with permission of Coward, McCann, & Geoghegan, Inc.

Sports Article by Jack Kerouac, *The Lowell Sun,* February 19, 1942, reprinted with permission.

Letter to Pertinax (Mary Sampas) by Henry Beaulieu, *The Lowell Sun,* April 17, 1973, reprinted with permission.

"Dialogues in Great Books" by Charles E. Jarvis and James T. Curtis, Radio Station WCAP, Lowell, Massachusetts, September 1962, reproduced by permission.

Howl and Other Poems by Allen Ginsberg, copyright © 1956, 1959 by Allen Ginsberg, reprinted with permission of City Lights Books.

Kerouac by Ann Charters, copyright © 1973 by Ann Charters, reprinted with permission of Straight Arrow Books.

On The Road by Jack Kerouac, copyright © 1955, 1957 by Jack Kerouac, reprinted with permission of The Viking Press, Inc.

Letter to Charles G. Sampas by Jack Kerouac, December 27, 1949, reprinted with permission.

"The Life and Loves of Allen Ginsberg: An Interview" by Allen Young, copyright © 1973, reprinted with permission of *The Real Paper,* March 28, 1973.

The Subterraneans by Jack Kerouac, copyright © 1958 by Jack Kerouac, reprinted with permission of Grove Press, Inc.

Desolation Angels by Jack Kerouac, copyright © 1960, 1963, 1965 by Jack Kerouac, reprinted with permission of Coward, McCann & Geoghegan, Inc.

The Dharma Bums by Jack Kerouac, copyright © 1958 by Jack Kerouac, reprinted with permission of The Viking Press, Inc.

'In Loving Memory of Myself" by John Ciardi, copyright © 1959, *Saturday Review,* reprinted with permission.

Letter to Joe Chaput by Jack Kerouac, November 15, 1968, reprinted with permission.

"Jack Kerouac Comes Home" by Dan Wakefield, copyright © 1965 by *The Atlantic Monthly,* reprinted with permission.

iii

ISBN: 0-915940-00-0

Library of Congress Catalog Card Number: 75-24815

ITHACA PRESS
P.O. BOX 853
LOWELL, MASS. 01853

iv

To my son, Paul — whose insight led me to the precious touchstone of the Kerouac psyche.

CONTENTS

FOREWORD

My close friendship with Jack Kerouac was the major fount from which this book sprang. Yet there were other founts that provided me with rich reflections of Kerouac. These were the people who had also been touched by Jack Kerouac's life and who generously responded to my myriad questions about this man.

I express my sincere gratitude to the following:

Charles G. Sampas, Executive News Editor of The Lowell Sun and a brother-in-law of Jack Kerouac. The publication of this book would have been almost impossible without him. His earnest entreaties, his tireless efforts to bring my manuscript to print, his enthusiasm for my work — all spell out for me the image of a decent man, a concerned older (though he is not old) brother. Many thanks, Charles.

Paul Jarvis, teacher of psychology at Northern Essex Community College in Haverhill, Massachusetts. Paul is my son and I feel a special joy in thanking him. If I have succeeded to any degree in capturing some truth about Jack Kerouac, I owe this success to him. Though Kerouac, in his "on the road" existence, met many meaningful people, the most significant relationship of his life was with his brother, Gerard. This concept was originally delineated for me by Paul. The evidence of this is focused in the first chapter which is based on Paul's essay on Kerouac. The essay effectively defines the impact of Kerouac's family dynamics, especially his relationship with Gerard, and the way these emotional needs found expression in Jack's writings. Moreover, the essay in the appendix is authored by Paul in an attempt to focus on how Jack's personal life related to his political visions of America. My indebtedness to Paul is graced with my sense of pride.

Sammy "Sampati" Sampas. Sammy was a school chum of mine, and in the writing of this book, my remembrances of him were "pure gold". Sammy's friendship with Jack Kerouac was one of the great chapters in Kerouac's life. Sammy died as a soldier in the United States Medical Corps in World War II. Yet I believe that Sammy somehow knows about my expression of thanks.

Telemachus DeMoulas, a true friend who had faith in my work.

Each of the following people made a distinct contribution:

Stella (Sampas) Kerouac, Jack Kerouac's wife who gave him love and dignity; Aspasia (Ziavras) Welch, my sister, a longtime friend of Stella who confirmed for me the beauty of her character; Tony Sampas, a brother-in-law of Jack Kerouac who was a real buddy to him; Oddyseus "Duke" Chiungos, Kerouac's Lowell High School football buddy; George Apostolos, the "G.J." of Kerouac's growing-up-in-Lowell novels who focused for me a significant facet of Jack's character; Attorney James T. Curtis, who dug Kerouac with me; Joe Chaput who stayed with Kerouac to the end; Mary Sampas, feature writer for The Lowell Sun, who always reported Kerouac's doings with admirable grace and objectivity.

Finally, I thank Kerouac's Lowell High School track companion in Heaven, John Koumantzelis (who died in the service in World War II but whose memory lingers), Greg Zahos, Henry Mazur, James Alexakos, Hugh Seiffert, Xenophon "Zenny" Sperounis, Henry "Scotty" Beaulieu, John W. P. McHale, Gregory Corso, Allen Ginsberg, Stanley Twardowicz, John Clellon Holmes, Ann Charters, Mico Kaufman, Peter Schell.

Charles E. Jarvis
Lowell Mass.

CHAPTER 1 - GERARD

Few writers have written so autobiographically as Jack Kerouac has. Besides the physical facts of his life, Kerouac recorded every spiritual nuance that his vast prehensile mind could ensnare. Select randomly any page of the thousands of pages that Kerouac wrote and you will inevitably find a feeling, a sensory sound that will come through. His characters are real, yet in the hands of Kerouac, they become something more than mere flesh and blood; they become extensions of Kerouac; they become great heroes who walk the land and make the earth tremble, and all the "feats" they perform are Kerouac's.

It matters not who the characters are: Neal Cassady, the perennial protagonist with the transparent pseudonyms; Zaza, the French Canadian moron masturbating again and again on Lowell's Moody Street; Gerard, his brother-saint releasing a thrashing mouse from a trap and taking it home to nurse it — Jack Kerouac sculptured them all in his own grand ideal image. By his own admission, Kerouac preferred to look on his books as chapters comprising the Duluoz (Kerouac) Legend. Yes, Legend, no less. He was Jack Duluoz ranging the land, disguised as everybody, a twentieth century Everyman.

Yet, despite Kerouac's ongoing artistic autobiography, it is not enough — obviously. His volcanic subjectivity must be chastened by calmer objectivity. If Kerouac devoted his life to "digging everything, everybody," digging himself really, then it is only fair that some of us "dig him" in return.

It's a fact that Jack Kerouac was born in Lowell, Massachusetts on March 12, 1922. It's also a fact that he plopped into this world squalling fitfully — like all normal babies. But to Kerouac, it wasn't merely facts; it was something more. He writes: "It was in Centralville (a section of Lowell) I was born. . . . Across the wide basin to the hill — on Lupine Road, March 1922, at five o'clock in the afternoon of a red-all-over suppertime, as drowsily beers were tapped in Moody and Lakeview saloons and the river rushed with her cargoes of ice reddened slick rocks, and on the shore the reeds swayed among mattresses and cast-off boots of

1

Time, and lazily pieces of snow dropped plunk from bagging branches of black thorny oily pine in their thaw, and beneath the wet snows of the hillside receiving the sun's lost rays the melts of winter mixed with roars of Merrimac — I was born. Bloody rooftop. Strange deed. All eyes I came hearing the river's red; I remember that afternoon, I perceived it through beads hanging in a door and through lace curtains and glass of a universal sad lost redness of mortal damnation . . . the snow was melting." [1]

Kerouac romanticizes his birth and the significance of this is that he romanticized everything else that he confronted from that day on. It makes no difference to Kerouac that from his vantage point on that day he had no way of knowing what kind of a day it was; or whether the Merrimack River "rushed with her cargoes of ice reddened slick rocks, and on the shore the reeds swayed among mattresses and cast-off boots of Time . . ." No, it makes no difference, and we can not blame him for that because the creative artist need not be concerned with weather reports or meteorological conditions. And Kerouac was first and foremost a creative artist.

And literature abounds with the artist's free spirit. Witness Bret Harte's "The Luck of Roaring Camp" and his treatment of the scene depicting the birth of the child in the brutal, godless mining town: "Above the swaying and moaning of the pines, the swift rush of the river, and the crackling of the fire rose a sharp, querulous cry — a cry unlike anything heard before in the camp. The pines stopped moaning, the river ceased to rush, and the fire to crackle. It seemed as if Nature had stopped to listen too."

Both Kerouac and Harte appear to have the same purpose in mind, and that is to personify nature and to make the birth of a child an immortal event. Yet it quickly becomes evident that Kerouac succeeded, whereas Harte got lost in a slough of sentimentality. We can hardly be expected to believe that Harte's river stopped dead in its tracks and the fire suddenly stopped crackling — just because a baby was born. Yet we should not find it too difficult to accept Kerouac's view of the Merrimack River on his natal day, even though it might not have been quite that way. What matters is that Kerouac gives us a sense of time-

2

lessness about the day, the river, and about man. Nothing was different on the day I was born, he is saying; yet this idea, re-nurtured in the deep wells of Kerouac's emotion and insight, this idea becomes a fresh burst of sound from time's immemorial echo. And that, after all, is the true artist's worth.

So Jack Kerouac began his autobiography from the day of his birth. And he didn't miss recording a single day of the rest of his life.

"For the first four years of my life," he writes in *Visions of Gerard*, "while he lived, I was not Ti Jean Duluoz, I was Gerard, the world was his face, the flower of his face, the pale stooped disposition, the heartbreakingness and the holiness and his teachings of tenderness to me, and my mother constantly reminding me to pay attention to his goodness and advice." [2] These "first four years of my life" never ceased for Kerouac. Despite his vast travels, his many relationships, his mad, frenzied efforts to "dig everybody," Kerouac kept reliving those first four years, kept replaying them like a television segment.

The first four years of anybody's life are necessarily dim, shadowy, though it is possible to bring moments of them under a glaring microscope. Jack Kerouac was not satisfied with just moments; he re-created every second through the apotheosized image of Gerard. "I was Gerard," he writes, and so he was throughout his entire life. Gerard was always there, hovering over him, his angelic face forever smiling on him.

"Since the beginning of time I've been charged to take care of this little brother, my Ti Jean (Jack Kerouac), my poor Ti Jean who cries he's afraid — ." [3] This is Gerard speaking in a dream sequence, and Gerard never relinquished his mission: to take care of his little brother. No, not even death could abort this mission; Kerouac "confirms" this in his elegy to this long lost brother. Through the mind of the four-year-old who worshiped Gerard, Kerouac refuses to believe that his brother is forever gone from him. "Gerard is dead!" he writes . . . "But I thought it had something to do with some holy transformation that would make him greater and more Gerard like — He would reappear, following his 'death', so huge and all powerful and renewed —". [4]

The concept of transmigration was monumentally worked out by Jack Kerouac in the Gerard syndrome. Yes, Gerard did not

3

die; he passed on to the body of his brother and there he inspired Jack to create his pristine literary revelations. ". . . And I'm grown sick in my papers," he says, "(my writing papers, my bloody 'literary career' ladies and gentlemen) and the whole reason why I ever wrote at all and drew breath to bite in vain with pen of ink, great gad with indefensible Usable pencil, because of Gerard, the idealism, Gerard the religious hero —." [5]

Somewhere along the line, Kerouac went one step further, the last step: Gerard Kerouac was the author of every word that had appeared under Jack's name. Jack was merely a moving hand; Gerard was the brain and soul of every thought that reached the page. It's possible that Kerouac had followed through on all this by concluding (in his mind, logically) that he had plagiarized every syllable. "He's (Gerard) the one that's doing all *this!*" he had said to me in a Lowell radio broadcast in 1962. He had been visiting his hometown for a few days and I had persuaded him to talk with me on a local radio station. But more of this broadcast later.

It's incredible that Gerard could have entered the life of Jack Kerouac to the extent that he did. Kerouac was four when Gerard died; what could he remember? He remembered what his parents told him, and every word that came from their lips was rendered into Holy Scripture by Kerouac's hunger for sanctifying the pale, suffering, angel-image of his dying brother. Why? Why this need, this devastating need to constantly remind himself of a child that was cut down by rheumatic fever?

Guilt. Guilt? Possibly. In the book about Gerard, Kerouac tells us that he ran down the street to tell his father the news about Gerard's death. "Gleefully I'm yelling 'Gerard est mort!' (Gerard is dead) as tho it was some great event that would make a change that would make everything better . . ." [6] Out of context, this idea sounds as if Kerouac were happy that Gerard was dead; now *he* would get all the attention that had been lavished on Gerard; now *he* would come out of the shadows of Gerard's privileged, suffering image; now *he* would be Number One.

Yes, out of context it sounds almost banal: sibling rivalry. Yet there are times when the banalities of life, the "seeming"

4

banalities, are the most revealing. It's true that Kerouac wrote this scene years and years later and if one reads the next few lines that follow the above quoted segment, he will see that Kerouac attributes to Gerard the powers of a Jesus-Resurrection. So, first he gleefully shouts the news of Gerard's death; then he will wait for Gerard to reappear, a greater hero than ever. A rather well balanced schizophrenic ambivalence. Maybe the whole episode is not out of context after all.

In the previously mentioned radio talk that I had with Kerouac in 1962, he was asked by James T. Curtis, who did the show with me, what the book *Big Sur* was about. Was there a message? Kerouac affirmed that there was, but rather than elaborate on the book he commented on what his job as a writer was. "My job is to describe heaven just a little bit. But, there are a thousand guys from this town (Lowell) who know more about heaven than I do."

Whoever heard of a writer who devoted his career to describing heaven? I suppose we could point to someone like Dante and the Paradiso wonder of his *Divine Comedy;* but there was also the Inferno and Purgatorio. Kerouac was concerned with heaven, that realm of shining firmament where dwell the beautiful spirits. Yes, he was going to tell people about it because that was his mission in life. But he had never been there and he admitted that "a thousand guys" from Lowell knew more about it than he did. So from where did he get his revelations? Ah yes — Gerard. Gerard was the great fount of religious knowledge and religious ecstasy, and Kerouac received it all in a miraculous way.

I remember one cloudy day about a year or so before Kerouac died; my son Paul and I were sitting with him at a cookout that one of his neighbors was giving. Voices, laughter, food aromas — all floated around us. We were bantering with Jack and he was rolling along in his splendid free manner. He had been drinking (when *hadn't* he been drinking?) and he was laying himself on us with bursts of thought that were monuments of superficiality: his cats (he had two of them), T.V. commercials, movies, sports; this was his way. My son and I were enjoying him hugely and, for us at least, an otherwise dull gathering was shadowed into the background. Then almost in mid-sentence, Kerouac stopped talking; he fixed his gaze at the sky; we

5

looked up with him thinking that a plane or something had diverted his attention; there was nothing but pure, sun-streaked, twilight-flashing clouds.

"What's the matter, Jack?" my son asked. He ignored the question, or he didn't hear it; then tears filmed his eyes and we heard him saying, "I am seeing my Brother, Gerard; he is in heaven; I see his face behind those clouds." In the middle of a somewhat raucous, inane, prosaic backyard gathering, Jack Kerouac was looking for Gerard. The sudden desperate need for him shattered Kerouac for the remaining hour that he stayed with us. The cataract of thoughts which he had been spewing, suddenly ran dry. He retreated into a little boy's corner — sad faced and confused. Yes. Gerard.

Much has been written about Kerouac's literary style. The term, "spontaneous prose" seems to be the most commonly used in describing it. Allen Ginsberg has given us "bop prosody" as the proper designation for Kerouac's artistic creations. Jazz and its wild, liberating forces come into constant play whenever Kerouac is discussed. What it all seems to focus is that Kerouac did little or no revision — emphasis on no revision. Kerouac claimed that once he got started on a book, he wrote in vast bursts of 18,000 (why not 17,000 or 19,000?) words a night until the book was finished. If this is true, then revision (of even a comma) would be impossible. If this is true, then Kerouac's writings are an improvisation on the theme of life, a pure sound drawn from the purest, deepest part of him, and which sound begins to acquire another morphe only when it reaches the surface atmosphere of the world around him. Or another way of putting it: Kerouac is a saxophonist in an orchestra; the orchestra plays the music, reading the arrangement that is on the music sheets in front of it; the orchestra plays on, together, in pre-conceived fashion; then at a certain juncture of the arrangement, one of the musicians is allowed to break the bonds, chains that are the written notes on the music sheets; this musician (Kerouac) rises and begins to blow his own music; each note that comes from him is pure born; it is impossible to separate the moments of conception and birth of these notes; in a convulsion of ecstasy, the musician blows his own sound; he rises to his own element and the rest of the orchestra dims in the shadows. What I have

6

been talking about, of course, is the riff, the musical riff, that span of time when the performer impels his powers towards spontaneous expression, spontaneous creation.

One of the well known musicians of the 1930's was Bunny Berrigan, trumpet player. He's probably best remembered for his rendition of the song, "I Can't Get Started." He both sings and plays the song, but it's his trumpet that fleshes out the melody into an unforgettable musical experience. Yet this performance is not the only contribution that Berrigan made to the music of his time. As a member of the Tommy Dorsey orchestra, he sculptured two riffs, one for "Song of India" and one for "Marie", that are considered classics; they have been accorded the rare honor of being reproduced for whole trumpet sections. Thus we have examples of creativity in its most savage, most beautiful form. There was no music sheet in front of Berrigan; he rolled with the tidal wave that thundered within him.

Is it unreasonable to suggest that Jack Kerouac's prose spendings are great musical riffs of life? (He loved Charlie Parker, the supreme saxophonist) Great flashes of insight? Great escapes from the day-by-day shackles of society?

And is it unreasonable to suggest that Kerouac was tortured by the incessant volcano within him and that relief (momentary) came only when it would erupt and he had to tell everything to everybody. "I'm going to tell you what happened," he stated in our Lowell broadcast, "because it's all true stories . . ." And finally, is it unreasonable to suggest that every time he would tell one of his stories, he would look over his shoulder and thank Gerard and ask Gerard to forgive him because Jack's name would be under the story's title? No, Kerouac never doubted that Gerard fashioned the great riffs that are Kerouac's novels.

"Once God moves the hand," he had said, " you go back and revise it's a *sin*!" This idea was expressed somewhat angrily in our Lowell broadcast when Kerouac was asked how much revision he did with his work. Notice the emphasis on the word, sin. Notice also the depersonalization quality of "once God moves the hand."* It is not Kerouac who is doing the writing, but the

---

*This premise and others discussed in this chapter stem from the essay by Paul Jarvis, "Once God Moves the Hand, You Go Back and Revise, It's a Sin!" (May 1972).

hand, and this belief reinforces for him the self-abasement of his literary accomplishments since his thoughts come from heaven. Here, Kerouac is dealing with the ever present sensitivity that his writing is monitored from heaven rather than himself. Heaven is God, heaven is Gerard. Thus if you change (revise) what Gerard intended, revealed, flashed forth from the pure heights — "It's a sin!"

If one accepts all or part of the Jack-Gerard Kerouac concept, he could probably build up a good case study delineating Jack Kerouac's hallucinatory propensities. But would it make any difference? Would it diminish Kerouac's mountainous literary thunder? Would it shrink or blight his unceasing, roaring, kaleidoscopic spirit? Would it pale, darken the rare light of understanding that he leveled on the human psyche?

"For the first four years of my life . . . I was Gerard," he writes. He could easily have revised it (just once) to read, "For the *whole* of my life . . . I was Gerard."

CHAPTER 2 - JACK KEROUAC'S FATHER

So Gerard's spirit would live on; Kerouac would see to that. But there was another spirit superimposed on Gerard's — Jack Kerouac's. And what a spirit it was! Ceaseless, unyielding, multi-tentacled, reaching out for every atom of existence that was within his reach. He would never be satisfied, he would never be at rest. The term, curiosity, is mute when applied to him. This was not curiosity but a demonic compulsion to touch everything, to be everything.

One can only imagine the bewildering frustration and conflict that would bedevil him at times in his early childhood. He found himself born in a monumentally Catholic home; he found himself in an environment roiling in French-Canadian Catholics; he found himself in a storm of poor, hard-working people whose ethic was to obey, to accept. In short, he found himself in a section of Lowell, Massachusetts known as "Little Canada" whose main thoroughfare was Moody Street, or "Mouji Street" as the natives expressed it. It was a complete, French-Canadian world — school, church, language, customs. But as it turned out it was not enough for Kerouac. In his reminiscences, some of which I heard personally, he spoke of his ever nagging desire to "break out." But he would have to wait.

He began his school life at a Jesuit school, St. Joseph's Parochial School in Lowell. The teachers were not the Jesuits of today's flexible, malleable cant; they were awesome, inviolable (especially to school children) purveyors of God's mighty laws; they were constant reminders that deviation from these laws brought one into a horror filled abyss of sin and its inevitable punishment. Jesus was jammed deep into Kerouac's brain.

In an interview given in 1968, Kerouac was asked: "How come you've never written about Jesus? You've written about Buddha. Wasn't Jesus a great guy too?"

Kerouac became annoyed. "I've never written about Jesus? In other words, you're an insane phoney who comes to my house . . . and . . . all I *write about* is Jesus. I am Everhard Mercurian, General of the Jesuit Army"

9

"What's the difference between Jesus and Buddha?" came another question

"That's a very good question," was the reply. "There is no difference." [7]

In Kerouac's mind, not only was there no difference, there was no Buddha. "Don't get me wrong," he said to me one night while discussing *The Dharma Bums,* "I owe Gary Snyder a great deal for his great teachings of Buddha to me; for his just being there to give me the chance to learn something about all that." He then shook his head. "But I never really took it seriously. Nah. I never ever thought about Buddha becoming any real part of my religion." He then threw a quick look at me. "I was born a Catholic, and what I was taught as a Catholic is all that has ever mattered to me. Jesus is the only one that I've ever been interested in." Certainly the Jesuit teachers at St. Joseph's Parochial School had done their job well.

Not that the teachers needed help, but Kerouac's mother limned out the collosal Catholic spirit that remained imbedded in Kerouac. She was a woman sprung from French-Canadian pioneers whose religious faith was all they had to sustain them in the primitive world they found themselves. God, the great spirit that both punishes and rewards, was one of Kerouac's first perceptions. Then after God, came the shining network of saints that hovered everywhere; saints with miraculous powers. Kerouac's mother brought him into a world of sad-faced statues, white and candle-graced.

"We had a statue of Ste. Thérèse in my house," he writes in *Dr. Sax,* "— on West Street I saw it turn its head at me — in the dark. Earlier, too, horrors of the Jesus Christ of passion plays in his shrouds and vestments of saddest doom mankind in the Cross Weep for Thieves and Poverty — he was at the foot of my bed pushing it one dark Saturday night (on Hildreth and Lilley second floor flat full of Eternity outside) — either He or the Virgin Mary stooped with phosphorescent profile and horror pushing my bed." [8]

The devastatingly powerful combination of an early Jesuit schooling, a home Christmas-treed with Catholic decorations, and the sainthood of Gerard — all burned searingly into his child brain — made Kerouac into a rock of faith, a rock that the

10

later mountainous waves of his Beat storms would fail to erode. To be sure, there were other storms that heaved about Kerouac long before he traveled the Beat ocean. They were the storms blowing in the streets of Lowell, of "Little Canada," of the Merrimack River. His Catholic faith came up against the realities of poor people, wild with the desperation of making a living, wild with the desperation of seizing some pleasure in life.

It didn't take Kerouac long to discover the raw winds that whistled in his childhood Lowell planet. In his Huck Finn Merrimack River, he caught the early lights of man's existential writhings. In *Dr. Sax* he provides a touchstone of his half-fearful, half-exhilarating sense of discovery. "We found fat lovers disentangling huge dimpled lady legs and hairy manlegs out of an intercourse in a litter of movie magazines, empty cans, rat rags, dirt, grass and straw . . . they were delightfully engaged in a field dump by the river . . . jiggling hands, sucks, furtive listens to the Sound of Time in the river, the mills, the bridges and streets of Lowell . . . wildeyed in heaven they screwed, and went home." [9] If Kerouac had ever walked with his brother Gerard along the banks of the Merrimack River looking for Jesus, the walks he took with friends after Gerard's death had a different goal.

And if Kerouac's mother (and Gerard) was the constant link with his faith and its mystical powers, Kerouac's father was the channel to the more immediate world of people struggling and battering themselves against the rough hewn wall of life. His father was a short heavy man who seemed to go through life demanding honesty from everyone about everything. The trouble was that his honesty was occasionally victimized by an easily unleashed temper. The result inevitably was a fast mounting collection of enemies. It should also be noted that Leo Kerouac's honesty — like all men's — was subject to human failure: he was not always right.

"My father wouldn't take any bullshit from anyone," was the way Jack expressed it to me one day. "He was the first honest newspaperman that Lowell ever had." Kerouac was referring to the short lived weekly paper that his father put out. It was barely a cut above the maturity of a high school paper, though its contents were concerned with corruption in the city government.

Pathetically, this little publication was more ludicrous than effective. Nobody, save its publisher, printer, writer, editor (all in the person of Kerouac's father) nobody took it seriously.

It appears that Leo Kerouac fancied himself destined for more significant events in life than the simple boredom of being a printer — which was his chief means of feeding his family. There is a continuous thread of mission that follows him, a mission that focuses on the idea that the City of Lowell was controlled by a rapacious oligarchy and that he, Kerouac, was one of its few citizens that had the guts to speak out.

Whenever Jack Kerouac spoke to me of his father, the word, tough, always came on. The first time he used it in this context, I thought he was indulging in metaphorical language. He quickly corrected me. "No, no," he said. "My father was a physically powerful guy. He was short and pudgy, but there was a lot of steel under that beef. He would take on anybody, no matter who he was." A child's adulation of his father as a strong man.

In *Vanity of Duluoz,* Kerouac provides examples of his father's toughness. He gives us a "partial" list of the victims he roughed up: a wrestler who threw a match; a Greek clergyman who argued about the price of a printing job; a movie house owner who also questioned the value of his work. One can see a kind of spectrum here; obviously, Leo Kerouac's wrath and sense of righteousness did not distinguish between its targets.

In one of his earliest sandlot football exploits, Kerouac speaks of his father raging up and down the sidelines shouting at any opposing player who he felt was fouling his son. Clearly the man never did anything half-heartedly.

As regards his football career, Jack Kerouac unwittingly portrays his father as a person who constantly bellowed about the blindness and prejudice of those who coached his son. A perusal of the Lowell sports pages during the football season of 1938 will show that Jack Kerouac was primarily used as the fifth man in the Lowell High backfield. Leo Kerouac fiercely believed that his son was the suppressed genius of that team.

In his first book, *The Town and the City,* Kerouac captures the one-time thrill of the high school hero who comes home to the Thanksgiving dinner after emerging as the star of the game. It's true. Kerouac did star in the Lowell-Lawrence game of

12

1938, scoring the only touchdown. In this Wolfean novel, Kerouac portrays his characters against a sad, twilight backdrop. But he cannot resist a few harsh strokes. The hero's father complains that the radio report of the game did not give due recognition to his son's brilliance.

"I'll wring his scrawny neck!" he shouts of the announcer. ". . . This is the crummiest town anyway!" [10]

More than twenty-five years after the writing of *The Town and the City,* Kerouac wrote *Vanity of Duluoz.* In the latter book he recounts among other things his high school heroics, but here there is no idealization; here there is a backdrop of bitterness. Kerouac's father comes on much stronger in this book. Leo Kerouac believes that some parents were paying the coaches to keep their sons in the starting lineup to the exclusion of his own son. "Typical of stinktown on the Merrimack," he is saying. The bribery charge is egregious, because the starting lineup was composed of "poor people," immigrants' sons whose every earned penny was used to buy food and clothing. In Depression-buried Lowell, few could afford to indulge their vanity.

Evidence easily piles up that Kerouac's father was naggingly interposing his presence in his son's football life. "My father was afraid of nothing and nobody," Kerouac loved to say. One night, in the last few years of his life when he had returned to Lowell, we were sitting in his home on Sanders Avenue. By "we," I mean Attorney James T. Curtis, myself, and Kerouac. At that time, Kerouac was working on *Vanity of Duluoz.* "I'm really telling it like it is,"he was saying to us."Not that my other books are not true. *Everything* that I've written is true, every blooming word of it. But in this one, I've got the wisdom of age to go with my soul." He laughed, as he usually did whenever he thought he was taking himself too seriously. He volunteered that the first half of the book was pretty much about his "Homeric football deeds" (his words). When we pressed him to expand on this thought, he somewhat quickly, strangely focused on his father. "He was my greatest fan and he was the only one that really knew what I could do — if given a chance. But it seems that everywhere I went, I found weirdo coaches looking at me sideways. I could always sense it — and so did my father."

"How do you mean, Jack?" I asked.

13

He paused. He gave me a disgusted look. "Well, I just said that my father and I could sense it. I don't think anybody else could understand." He paused again. "But you must know — Professah Jaahvis — (Kerouac loved to act) the story of *Billy Budd*." I nodded. "Well, you remember Claggart and the fucked up, mysterious glooms that he would get whenever he'd clap his eyes on Billy. Well, that's about as close as I can get to answering your question. It was my fate — ah yes, my destiny — to always have a Claggart for a football coach."

"That's an intriguing analogy, Jack," I said.

"Yes, *you* would think so, you professor weirdo!" He laughed again, "But no, really," he went on, "my father knew all about guys like that. And he didn't hesitate to let them know how queerly fucked up they were."

I began to wonder, and probably so did Jim Curtis, when Kerouac would drop his father as a subject and go to other revelations about *Vanity of Duluoz*. The end was nowhere to be seen.

"You remember the famous Columbia football coach — Lou Little?" he drove on. "My father twisted his nose, ah that is, metaphorically he did. And by God if he had to do it physically he would have done it. He told Little he was wasting me on the bench and the next thing I know, I got my ass out of Columbia."

The Columbia episode reveals more than the frustration of a father and his athlete son. It can also be regarded as a classic study in motivational behavior. It can go something like this: when Jack Kerouac was a sophomore on the Lowell High School football team, one of the senior stars was Henry Mazur. (Later, Mazur went on to achieve national fame as a member of the Army football team). An incident which over the years has become shadowy and by its very wispiness has acquired distortion and a touch of legend, an incident, I say, took place between Mazur and Kerouac. In talking to people here in Lowell who might focus this incident, I discovered that there were a a number of versions. Actually, it doesn't matter; what is significant is that there was a confrontation between Kerouac and Mazur — and not on the football field. Everybody who claims knowledge of this confrontation agrees that it happened in the locker room. The most common account is that Kerouac, as a sophomore up-

14

start, invaded the showers while the varsity was using them. (In those days, the shower facilities were limited). Henry Mazur, so the story goes, assumed the job of physically evicting this tyro with unwarranted boldness. And he did so with what we can presume to be a superior attitude and force.

In *Vanity of Duluoz*, Kerouac, writing of his football days at Columbia, speaks of it this way: "Lu Libble (Lou Little) won't let you (Kerouac) start this year, not even in the Army game against your great enemy Art Janur (Henry Mazur) — (who pushed me out of the showers when I was a kid in Lowell High . . .)"

The matter appears to be so banal, so prosaic: a couple of high school kids — one a little older — tangling briefly. Yet Kerouac, and of course his father, saw it as anything but that. What comes through from them is that the concept of honor was involved; the dignity of the Kerouac character had been maligned; further, they saw the brief combat as outrageously unfair because Jack Kerouac was a mere boy going against a nearly fully matured man.

Though I, personally, never heard Kerouac speak of this episode, there is evidence of its rankling force in his literary thoughts. About his ephemeral experience as a member of the Columbia football team, he writes with rancor of the precious chance that was denied him in the Army game. The precious chance was to finally meet in *equal combat* his rival from his hometown, Henry Mazur, then a star of the Army team. "Because in the Army game," he writes, "I coulda gone out there and scored at least two touchdowns and made it close and incidentally *I would have smeared their best runner, from Lowell, Art Janur, (Henry Mazur) right smack dead ahead* . . . If you can't be allowed to play then how can you play anything?" [11] Kerouac quit the team after this game.

Soon after the publication of *Vanity of Duluoz*, Kerouac was interviewed in *The Paris Review*. The words he chooses to delineate the aborted Kerouac-Mazur duel are even stronger. Moreover, the words are put in his father's mouth. "Lou Little was my coach at Columbia. My father went up to him and said you sneaky long-nosed finagler. . . . He says why don't you let my son, Ti Jean, Jack, start in the Army game so he can get back at

15

his great enemy from Lowell?" [12] Why not indeed. It was a question that was never satisfactorily answered; and it was the kind of question that Kerouac's father seemed to ask all of his life. It was the kind of question that seemed to have as its purpose the exposing of all the wicked, sinister people in this world.

Kerouac was proud that his father had been asked by a group to run for mayor of Lowell. He records this in *Vanity of Duluoz* and he had spoken of it to me a couple of times. "He would have washed this shit town clean with the strongest detergent available!" was the way he put it one day. I never could call up enough courage to ask him who was in this group that introduced the idea of running for mayor to Leo Kerouac. Was this an official committee representing a political organization or was it a bunch of guys shooting out the idea over a game of pool at the Pawtucketville Social Club?

There was a wild wind of ego that blew through this man and no doubt gusts of it blew through Jack Kerouac. We can almost hear Leo Kerouac's French-Canadian etched tirades bouncing around the Kerouac home. (As a native of Lowell, I can say with some conviction that a Lowell French-Canadian accent is one of the devastatingly beautiful sounds in the English language). "Dose crooks downtown are stealing everyting," we can hear him, "and da mayor is da biggest crook of all. Dis town is nuteeng but a shit pile. 'Alf da people are starving and de udder 'alf are stealing from dem." We can hear him on Jack's Lowell High football career: "Dose coaches don' know shit. Dey gut da best runnerr right under deir fat noses (that would be his son) and deir using a midget and a horse of a slowpoke. Dey'll find out when dey give you a chance, Jackie, dey'll find out."

The word hate, rambles through Kerouac's later reminiscences of his hometown. His father was hated because he was honest; he, himself, was hated because he tried to top everyone. These are Kerouac's claims and today they sound like a belated paranoia. In the twentieth century, Lowell's population has hovered around 100,000 — certainly not a huge metropolis, but not a hamlet, either. There were times when Kerouac made it appear that 99,900 pairs of eyes were looking askance at his father and later at him.

I caught up with Henry Mazur a few days ago (April, 1973).

16

He is a retired U.S. Army colonel now living in the Lowell area. We discussed the "incident" between himself and Kerouac. The discussion was over in five minutes. Colonel Mazur was unable to recall any physical confrontation with Kerouac. He admitted that he had heard about it from others and that he sincerely had tried to retrieve his high school football annals. He recalled some interesting moments, he confessed, but none involving Jack Kerouac. Obviously, there were something fewer than 99,900 pairs of eyes watching Jack Kerouac — and his father.

It is sadly ironic that Kerouac's father did not live to experience his son's literary fame. He died before Kerouac's first book was published. Leo Kerouac, writhing and struggling in the dark, Depression Lowell streets, stirred and nagged by the thought that he was different from his thousands of prosaic fellow townsmen, throwing himself at any adversary and more often losing than winning — Leo Kerouac sired Jack Kerouac upon whom more, much more, than 99,900 eyes have gazed.

Chapter 3 - A Drive to New Hampshire

Jack Kerouac liked to say that he had a beautiful childhood. He was raised in a French-Canadian-Catholic-American home. He bounced back and forth between a saint-revering mother and a pell-mell, wordy, vibrant father who kept shouting that the world was a pigsty. Completing the family circle was his sister, Caroline (Nin) who ever remained a shadowy image.

"I want everybody to know what a crazy kid I was." He was talking to me and Jim Curtis one day on a drive up to New Hampshire. This was in 1968, the second year of his final return to Lowell. "But I also want everybody to know," he went on, "that my childhood years were fantastic flights of beauty into a world populated by saints and incredible monsters. *Dr. Sax,* you know, tells about that. But there was even more. When we moved from Centralville and came further into the city, to Pawtucketville and to "Little Canada," I felt like I had landed on a new planet. I guess I was about six. I took one look and one listen to all the faces and sounds of my new world and I said — or I must have said — Jesus Christ, I've gotta dig every inch of this place. And, believe me, I did.

"When I started elementary school, St. Joseph's, I was at first shit scared of those Jesuit teachers. They looked like great big black angels with huge fluttering wings beating over us and swooping down on us whenever we dared look them straight in the eye and ask a stupid question. But it didn't take me long to get over that. I just decided that they knew what they were doing — they got it from heaven didn't they? And I still believe that — yes, I decided they knew what they were doing, so I began to relax."

The drive that we were taking to New Hampshire was to stay a few hours at Mallophora, Jim Curtis's country lodge. It was mid-September, summer's end, but it was a gray kind of day that was trying to rush the Fall season. We were all sitting in the front seat (Kerouac in the middle) and our conversation was boiling, with Kerouac sizzling. He had his omnipresent bottle with him, a half-filled pint, and he kept nipping as he spoke.

19

We got him reminiscing quite unexpectedly, although more accurately, no topic in a dialogue with Jack could be considered unexpected. His was a buckshot approach that eventually wore down his listener. What got him on his early years in Lowell was a remark of mine about Lowell High School football, present day vintage.

"Hey Jack," I said, "have you seen your old alma mater, Lowell High, in any football games since your return to Lowell? You know they were undefeated, state champs, last year." (This was true).

He nipped away, and after emitting a huge belch he gave me a haughty stare and said British actor style: "No, my good man, I have not, which I regret extremely."

"Well, the new season is ready to start," I said. "You ought to take in a couple of games."

He dropped his British role. "I have seen all the football games that Lowell High has played since the first day I went out for the team as a scared sophomore." Curtis and I weren't sure of his meaning. He went on. "Besides the games that I actually played in, I have played in all the rest of them, right up through last season — undefeated, state champs, as you say. Yes, I have played in all the rest of them. My ghost has been in that Lowell High backfield for lo these many years." Then he elbowed me in the side and cackled briefly; he had changed his mood again. "You've heard of the Galloping Ghost haven't you?" he practically shouted. "Well, I'm the Lowell Ghost, and I don't only gallop in the Lowell football stadium, but in all the wailing sandlots and parks of the city. North Common, South Common, Walker Street, Shedd Park, empty Acre lots — you name them — I've been howling in all of them all these years."

"Well I've seen a few Lowell High games the past few years," I needled, "and I saw no ghost-driven number 35 halfback booming out there."

He fixed me with his favorite smile: a subtle coyness. "Of course you wouldn't see me." He picked up his British accent again. "How could you? You're a professor, and it's common knowledge my dear man that professors are a scurvy lot who spend most of their time in their private studies beating their meat eight to the bar!" We all broke up. Kerouac lifted his bottle of booze high and whacked down another portion.

After a few seconds of silence, he came on again. "No, but I want everybody to know what a crazy kid I was." I wasn't certain what avenue his mind was going on now. But this was something I had come to expect, to live with, to accept smoothly — this sudden shift, this lack of transition, this precipitous break-off in any dialogue with Kerouac. However, in this particular dialogue, his "crazy kid" remark was not a completely new departure in subject matter; it was a return to what he had said some minutes earlier.

"You mean you were a juvenile delinquent, Jack?" I fenced with him.

"Me? A delinquent? Why, I've never broken a law in my life. Every time I'd see a cop on Moody Street, I used to practically shit in my pants. Nowadays, these fucken kids make the *cops* shit in their pants!" Curtis and I waited. Kerouac seemed to be musing. "Ah shit," he mumbled. He worked on his whiskey cough. "I'm telling you," he resumed, "that I used to walk the streets of Lowell as a kid and I was everything — everything. I was the greatest athlete that ever lived, I was the greatest scholar that ever lived, I was the greatest adventurer that ever lived. And I'm not talking about a Walter Mitty; I'm talking about a crazy, fantastic child of milltown Lowell, U.S.A."

"How often did you venture over to the Greek section, Jack? You know, Market Street, Dummer Street, the North Common?" This was Curtis's question. "You know, of course," Curtis went on, "that Jarvis and I were raised there. We might have seen you a number of times around Market Street without realizing that we were close to the future internationally famous Prophet of the Beat Generation." Curtis finished his words with a smile. I was staring at Kerouac, amused, waiting for his reaction. Kerouac began singing Vaughn Monroe's old theme song, "Racing With the Moon." I joined him for a moment or two.

He suddenly stopped and said, "Now I can understand why you two fucken guys changed your Greek names to Jarvis and Curtis — excuse me — Jaahvis and Currhtis." Continuity in our dialogue appeared to have collapsed; but it hadn't, really. Kerouac was merely rebelling at the idea of a professional image

21

as now delineated by Curtis. Not that he refused the diadem, King of the Beats; this was a fact. What he resisted was adulation by people in his company; he could never quite cope with this; he always felt a hollowness about it all and would go out of his way to smash it. "Aah yess, Jarvis and Curtis," Kerouac repeated. He had now shifted from a British accent to a W. C. Fields intonation. I do believe that Curtis' remark was laced with a mild sarcasm, but this had made no difference to Kerouac. "Oh yeah," he resumed, "I used to go down to the Greeks. Man, they were something — jabbering away and running around like Mack Sennet's Keystone Cops. They were beautiful. And when I tell you that I was a crazy kid, I mean it. I mean I used to cross over from Pawtucketville, down Moody, and over to Market Street just to hear the Greeks speaking Greek, and I used to stand there and hope and pray that I could learn their language so I could understand all the holy, divine thoughts they were speaking."

"You must have learned *some* Greek, Jack," I suggested.

"Oh, I learned the choice words that anybody learns in a new language." And here he exaggerated the syllables that followed. "I learned 'ah gamisou' (go fuck yourself), 'skata' (shit) and other great thoughts like that. But it was all beautiful, all heavenly."

From the moment we had gotten in the car in Lowell and started for Curtis's lodge in Lyndeboro, New Hampshire (about an hour's leisurely drive), Kerouac had continually pecked at his pint. By the time we had reached Milford, New Hampshire (about halfway to our destination) his bottle had run dry. He appeared suddenly stricken. Fortunately, there was a liquor store in Milford Square. I ran in and, being no connoisseur of liquors, I came out with a moderately priced pint of whiskey. Kerouac screwed up his face in disdain and said, "Jarvis, that's the kind of stuff that corrupt government agents used to sell to the Indians." I went back in and returned with the best that the store had. Kerouac seemed to go back in his seat and relax. I had paid for the whiskey. Kerouac didn't offer to reimburse me, but I didn't mind. He was soon gurgling away as we resumed our trip. I wanted to get him back to "Little Canada," Lowell, 1920's, 1930's, but it wasn't easy. He was bent on giving a full

22

rendition of "I'll Never Smile Again." He was Frank Sinatra and he was singing his heart out. It all came out slurred. He went through the entire song and Curtis and I applauded him. The song proved a good bridge to the past.

"I'm telling you I was a crazy kid," he repeated for about the fourth time. "I dug all the words to all the songs that were written in those days."

"That was no big deal, Jack," I challenged. "I dug all the words and so did millions of other kids."

"Yeah, but did you ever go home and stand in front of a mirror, and pretend that you were Frank Sinatra and that every chick in the land was oozing come over you?"

"Yeah, I did," I said blandly.

He gave me one of his mock angry looks. "You must have been my shadow," he said, and then released a Shadow laugh.

"You know when you think about it, Jack," Curtis said, "our childhoods were not too different. We all lived in the Acre (core of Lowell) and only a street or two separated the Greeks from the French."

"Man, I was separated a whole galaxy away from you," he went at Curtis. "I had the great spirit digging me, while you were beating your bishop in some back alley." Then he started to laugh, reached over and touched Curtis and said, "Curtis, I'm always pecking at you, but that's because I dig you well, I *see* you well. I'm *with* you, okay?"

Curtis was amused. "Okay Jack," he said.

Kerouac then turned to me. "Jarvis, why don't you have some of this juice. It'll put some hair on your professorial chest."

"No thank you," I said, "there's plenty there already."

He responded with a hoarse laugh. "I ain't met a professor yet who has hair on his chest, and you don't look like no exception. Every professor I've ever met couldn't fight his way through a wall of tissue paper."

I decided to have some fun with him. "Okay, big hotshot ex-halfback of Lowell High, Dracut Tigers and Olympian Giants, I bet I could take you in arm wrestling without even working up a sweat."

"You? A Charles Atlas-advertised 98-pound weakling?" He

23

tried to effect disdain, but broke up into a smile. I am no 98-pound weakling; just an average man.

I tried one of the oldest tricks in the world on Kerouac. "I could take you left-handed, Jack," I said. "That's what I think of your vaunted Columbia halfback strength."

He was sitting to my left; he immediately put up his left arm and tried to look fierce. "You're going to regret this, gringo," he warned, breaking out unexpectedly into a Mexican accent.

Curtis, who was driving, heckled, "Watch out you two old men. Don't bust a gut." (All three of us were about a year apart in age).

It was awkward trying to arm wrestle in the front seat of a moving car; but we did. Three times we went at it and three times I won — somewhat embarrassingly easily. While we went at it, Kerouac kept throwing the word lucky at me. When it was all over, he seemed momentarily shattered. Then he decided to take a new approach.

"It is eminently clear, Sir," he said, in a British accent, "that you are descended from great Greek warriors who fought at the pass of Thermopylae. You are at least a demigod; so what chance does a poor mortal like me have against you."

If Kerouac were momentarily shattered by the ease with which I beat him, so was I. Then I felt guilty because the trick I was playing on him was that I am left-handed. (Kerouac was not). But then my guilt gave way to a feeling of great compassion for him. I almost revealed my left-handed secret and thought of giving him a chance with his good arm; but I didn't. I didn't because I realized that the man I had arm wrestled was not Jack Kerouac, the pile driving halfback from the Acre, but an inflated hulk, gutted to the core by the fires of booze, and now slowly rotting away.

We reached Curtis's place, a miniature Swiss Alps structure sitting on top of a large hill. The view reached beyond the New Hampshire border into Massachusetts — thirty to forty miles. We got out of the car and Kerouac immediately began walking around trying to suck it all in. "Man," he was saying, "this ain't no Desolation Peak, but it'll do for now." After months of Lowell and its crumby, smoky bars, Kerouac obviously felt resurrected.

"See any fires, Jack?" I said, alluding to his one-time job as a fire spotter, a job he deals with at length in his books, *The Dharma Bums* and *Desolation Angels.*

He turned and looked at me queerly. "The only fire I see is the one that's burning inside me."

"Hey, that sounds like a line from 'Night and Day'," I quipped. He chuckled.

We got into the house and soon we were being entertained by Kerouac versions of old songs. He was not even a good amateur singer, though his voice was pretty clear. He reminded me of Walter Huston's delivery of "September Song," a kind of meditative punctuating of precious thoughts. Kerouac's repertoire was extensive, and he really knew all the words. I remember some of the songs he floated out: "Always In My Heart," "Fools Rush In," "Imagination," "Blue Moon," "Wishing." As we listened, Curtis and I exchanged a few glances; we were asking each other how long we would have to sit there and play the role of audience.

Our role ended when Kerouac suddenly concluded his concert and blurted, "The sonumbitch who did that should be put on a medieval rack and stretched till his balls become peanuts!"

"Who did what, Jack?" Curtis reacted.

"That!" he said, pointing to a deer head that was looking at us dolorously from above the fireplace. "There's nobody in this world that has a right to kill anybody or anything," Kerouac added. "Look at that poor thing up there. How can anybody destroy such beauty? I can just see the guy that shot him: a fat slob stomping around the woods looking for a trophy." Kerouac trailed off his tirade in French-Canadian.

We did not ask for a translation, yet he surprised us because he rarely spoke this language in our presence.

"I agree with you, Jack," said Curtis mechanically.

"Then why the hell do you keep it up there? What are you, some kind of a ghoul?" Curtis looked stymied. "I used to bring home pets when I was a kid," Kerouac went on. "I learned that from my brother, Gerard."

I jumped in. "On the way up here, Jack, you kept saying what a crazy kid you were. Now, bringing home pets is not craziness, man. A lot of kids do it."

25

Kerouac smiled at me with a touch of disdain. "Yeah, Charley," he said (he rarely called me Charley; I was mostly Professor to him), "but how many kids do you know who would sit down and write a story about it. I mean a story that would appear in a newspaper, a newspaper that *I* would write, *I* would edit, *I* would publish. *I*, Sir, was the youngest publisher in the land! You didn't know that did you?" I'm sure that Curtis and I looked impressed. "You should have seen some of the newspapers I published. And where would I get the news? From Me!"

"You must have been a regular Horace Greeley, Jack," I said.

He threw a stern glance at me; then, smiling, he said, "Horace Greeley, my arse. Why I'd walk the streets of Lowell and I would perform Herculean feats. I would rescue every maiden that was in distress. I would beat the crap out of every bushy haired bully that pushed little kids around. I'd walk the streets of Lowell in disguise and everytime anybody needed help, I'd find the nearest phone booth, slip on my Superman outfit, and off I'd go on my mission of mercy."

"Then it must have been you that rescued me from drowning in the Merrimack River, Jack," I interposed. "When I was a kid, we went swimming one day in the Merrimack, just above the public bath house. I soon got into trouble and like a miracle some guy happened by and he jumped in and pulled me out." I paused briefly. "Now that I think of it, I swear he was wearing a blue body stocking, and spoke with a light French accent."

Kerouac tilted his head and fixed his gaze on me. I was trying to maintain my serious pose. Then Kerouac let go with a rasping, shaking laugh. "If I'da knowed it was you," he finally said, Rebel accent and all, "I'da let you drown, boy."

"You wouldn't do that, Jack, would you?" Curtis joined in.

"Ah sure would. And then ah'd go home and put out a newspaper extra."

"Did you really do that, Jack?" I asked. "Did you really make up newspapers?"

"Did I *really*?" Kerouac came back reflecting disbelief at my doubting tone. "By Jesus, I wish I had saved some copies. They were the greatest newspapers ever published, because they were published in heaven. They had the greatest circulation anywhere because they were read by heavenly people."

"You know Jack," I said, "the idea just came to me that all of your books could be considered later editions of your childhood newspapers. If *you* were the chief source of these early newspapers, then how about many of your books, especially books like *Maggie Cassidy, The Town and the City, Book of Dreams, Dr. Sax, Satori In Paris,* even large segments of *On The Road.* They're all so autobiographical."

"You trying to say that all I write about is myself?"

"Well, yeah mostly," I stood firm.

"Well, for a goddam professor, you're right for once. But I ain't alone in this type of genre. As far as I'm concerned, twentieth century literature is a lonely monologue. No, I'm not alone in this. Wolfe, Proust, Joyce — what the hell do you think *they* were doing? They were writing in a single voice. Joyce, spilling out his guts in a stream of consciousness; Wolfe translating the American scene and mood; Proust recording ever so delicately remembrance of things past. They were talking to themselves. Man, if Dostoievsky were alive today, he'd be writing true stories; he wouldn't have to invent a single character."

"Do you think that one of the reasons for this kind of writing is the so-called twentieth alienation of the individual?" I prompted.

"What do you mean, twentieth century?" Kerouac threw my question back to me. "The twentieth century didn't invent loneliness. Man, it's been around since the first caveman took a look at the stars one night and realized where he stood in the scheme of things. No, I think that the monologue literary form is just another step in the development of literature. Maybe by the next century nobody will be writing books anymore. Maybe everybody will learn ESP and all they'll have to do is to *read* each other's minds."

"Hey, that's a wild idea, Jack," Curtis said.

Kerouac feigned annoyance. "You think that's wild, you meatball member of the bar — and I'm not talking about Nicky's Cafe; that's a *real* bar. You think that's wild?" Kerouac tried to emote impatience but succeeded only in looking amused. "Let me tell you about a bar," he resumed. "When I was about twelve, I thought that the greatest man that ever lived was Jack London. Yeah. To me he was the great union of the adventurer and the writer. I wanted to be just like him. I would sail the seven seas by day and write about it by night."

"What about the bar, Jack?" I asked.

"Ah yass, the bar," he responded. He loved to use a W. C. Fields voice. "Ah yass. Now there's something that I can tell you about. I saw enough of them in Lowell as a kid — I mean from the outside. Man, I think that Lowell had more bars per square foot than any other Christian community on the face of this earth. Maybe it still does." He paused and seemed to be chuckling to himself. "One of the first stories I ever wrote as a kid was about how I had a cabin in the Rocky Mountains. I was a great mining engineer and I would tramp the great open spaces dressed in jodhpurs, great laced boots, and a jacket with a thousand pockets on it. I had a beautiful German shepherd and he was always by my side as I walked the trails. I also had a pipe made of the finest wood in Turkey. As for the bar, it was hidden away where nobody but me could find it. After a long day's work, I would come to my cabin, clean up, and after my supper I would press a magic button and the old wall would slide away and in its place would emerge a magnificent bar sparkling and dazzling with the great scotches of the world." As if reminded by his words, Kerouac took a few more swallows from the bottle in his hand.

"Jack," I said, "that story reminds me of an old Richard Arlen movie."

He drew back as if shocked by my words. "Sir, would you be accusing me of plagiarism? How dare you!"

"Would *I* do that, Jack?" I reacted. "Would *I* accuse the King of the Beatniks of plagiarism?"

He gave me the middle finger and said, "Up your ass with Mobil gas."

"I always knew you were a great poet," I came back quickly.

He laughed. "So you remember those Richard Arlen movies, huh?" He appeared to be musing rather than talking to me. "Man," he continued, "I saw enough of those at the Royal Theater till I began thinking that *I* was Richard Arlen."

"You know what, Jack?" I said, getting a bit excited. "I'll bet you there was many a Saturday afternoon when you were in the Royal Theater at the same time that Curtis and I were."

"I wouldn't be caught dead in the same theater with you and Curtis!"

"As a matter of fact," I went on, "you write in *Dr. Sax* about the usher who had a hand missing and a wooden stump in its place. As I recall, you write that he was a fine fellow. I always thought he was a no-good bastard. He used to slap us around up in the balcony. Now that I think of it, he must have been some kind of a pederast who got his kicks out of sadistically rapping kids around."

Curtis, who had followed the dialogue between Kerouac and me with a pleasant smile on his face, now laughed raucously at my remark. "I've got to go along with the Professor, Jack," he said. "Roland — that was his name wasn't it? — Roland was a mean man. He used to swing that stump of a hand and God help the kid that was on the other end of it."

"Well I hope he dented both of your skulls," Kerouac said, laughing and coughing. "Ah yass, the Royal Theater," he pursued his thoughts. "I remember seeing a movie there once about a young kid — I think it was Frankie Darro — who became a jockey and won great fame and fortune. And you know what? For a whole year after that I lived and breathed the ambition of becoming a jockey. No, really. All my home newspapers were great big scads of race results. And all the feature stories were about Jack Kerouac booting home eight winners every day. Great big headlines boomed out and I was the greatest jockey the world had ever seen."

"Too bad I didn't know you then, Jack," I teased ."I'd have become a millionaire betting on every horse that you rode."

"You couldn't bet on the races I rode in," he said, dismissing me. "Only those in heaven had that privilege." He threw his head back and looked up at the ceiling; he seemed to be reaching for an idea. "As a matter of fact," he came at us again, "I used to go to church and pray that I wouldn't gain weight. I was then around twelve and weighed about one hundred and ten pounds. I'd be in church on Sundays and send up huge fervent prayers, and after church I'd run down to Bailey's Drug

Store on Merrimack Street and weigh myself. We had no scales at home and Bailey's was the only place that I knew where you didn't have to drop a penny in to weigh yourself. You know, in those days a penny was a *penny*. Is that place still around?" We assured Kerouac that it was. "Well, by golly, I'd barrell ass down there and jump on the scales, and for weeks I stayed the same — one hundred and ten pounds. Everytime I'd see that pointer stop at one-ten, I knew my prayers were being answered. I'd fast like crazy. I was probably the youngest holy man in the universe."

"That's a fascinating story, Jack," I said. I then tried to look suspicious. "But something tells me that if you ran from church — that would be St. Jean Baptiste Church, right? — to Bailey's Drug Store, that's a half-mile run, and at top speed that's quite a run for a kid of twelve. I think that if you had put on any weight during the week, you'd sweat it off sprinting down to Bailey's!"

Kerouac raised his right arm in a grand gesture. "Oh meatball of little faith," he orated.

"Well what happened when you went past one-ten," I persisted.

"It was God's will, you infidel," he snapped. "By the time I was thirteen, I weighed about one-thirty and I knew that the Almighty had other things in store for me. And it didn't take long to prove this. *I* became the Reg Grange of the Lowell sandlots. Everytime I scored a touchdown I knew that it was getting me closer to my true ambition — which was to be a great athlete in college, a great scholar, and a great adventurer. One of the greatest thrills of my life was the first time I hitchhiked to Boston; must have been around thirteen. I remember I started walking and got all the way out past Gorham Street, past the Edson Cemetery (where Kerouac is now buried) and was halfway through Billerica when an old Greek farmer from Dracut in a manure-smelling old Ford truck picked me up."

"It seems like you can never get away from the Greeks, Jack," I interjected.

"This guy was a *real* Greek," he taunted. "He was no watered down, diluted, nickel-brick Greek like you two guys are.

30

He had a Cretan mustache and a face like the mountains of Greece."

"You know, Jack," I said, "I got relatives who are farmers in Dracut. I have an uncle out there who looks just the way you describe him."

"This guy was no uncle of yours. This guy had heart. He took me practically all the way into Boston and I remember how concerned he was about whether I had any money to buy a meal, and how I would get back to Lowell. As a matter of fact, when he dropped me off, he gave me a dime; he said he didn't want to see me go hungry all day." Kerouac suddenly became wistful. "I've never forgotten that old guy, that old Greek."

"I guess you could say that this was your first *On The Road* adventure, Jack, right?" I suggested.

Kerouac looked surprised. He looked at me queerly. "Yeah," he muttered.

He seemed to be receding within himself. I pulled him back. "So where did you go in Boston that day?"

"I went down to the ships," he answered, emerging. "I walked around the harbor all day, and I looked at all the ships and for at least one hundred times I almost talked myself into becoming a stowaway. Then for another hundred times I kept hoping that I'd be shanghaied on one of those ships and that I'd wake up in mid-ocean heading for Bangkok or some such place."

"Maybe that's why you joined the Merchant Marine later on," Curtis said.

"I joined the Merchant Marine because I wanted to do something for this country, and because I wanted to prove to those naval shit-kickers in Newport that I was a better seaman than they were." (Kerouac was referring to his abortive, brief stint in the U.S. Navy; he was discharged on psychiatric grounds).

"The money wasn't bad, either, Jack," I threw in.

He pretended anger. "Are you suggesting that I was nothing but a crass mercenary?"

"I'm suggesting that when you got back to Boston, you had a hunk of dough in your sock that must have made you feel like Rockefeller."

31

"Most of that dough went home," he said in an admonitory tone. "I was the dutiful son, and I never forgot what my parents did for me. My mother worked in the garbage shoe factories of Lowell to keep my sweet little child body healthy so that it could later develop into an Apollo miracle." Kerouac then looked down and it took Curtis and me a few seconds to realize that he was surveying himself, his now bloated body. He refocused us and there was a sad, confused light in his eyes. But he went on. "My Merchant Marine money went home." Then he suddenly blurted, "But I kept just a bit of it for some sailor fun in Boston. Scollay Square, the Old Howard. You guys ever go to the Old Howard? Naw, you wouldn't. They wouldn't let creeps like you in there." (The Old Howard was a famous burlesque house, now gone).

"Jack, you're full of shit," I said crisply. "I'll bet you that Curtis and I went to the Old Howard dozens of times before you ever realized there was such a place." I was not angry with him. I merely got a sudden impulse to test his real mood.

Kerouac smiled at me. It was what he always did with Curtis and me whenever he felt the slightest sense of having really annoyed us. He always enjoyed satirizing us, but always stopped short with a congenial smile and laugh whenever either of us indicated that his comments were touching a nerve. His basic kindness never failed to act as a brake.

Well, as I said, after I told him he was full of shit, he smiled. He altered his tone abruptly. "Then you guys must remember Georgia Southern, the greatest stripper of them all!"

"We sure do," Curtis prompted him.

Kerouac then stood up and began a shaky rendition of a song called "Flamingo." Then he attempted a gliding motion about the room. Obviously, he was trying to recreate a Georgia Southern dance production. Curtis and I choked in our laughter. Kerouac ended his song with a bump and a grind and we applauded. He flopped back on his chair and he began coughing. When he stopped coughing, he cleared his throat and said, "I got a slight bronchial condition. I've had it for years and once in a while it kicks up on me."

I suddenly felt compassion for him. He looked battered, sadly pathetic. Then before I could control the flow, the words came out. "Jack," I said, striving for a tone of kindliness and concern, "why don't you ease up on that booze? I don't mean for you to cut it out altogether but a little moderation would help. You know what the Ancient Greeks said about the Golden Mean. You've been with Greeks all your life — you finally smartened up and married one — so why don't you take a page from them and practice some of their philosophy."

I hadn't really intended to string together so many words. While I was doing so, he stared at me blankly. When I finally stopped, he turned his face away and said evenly, "Don't bug me, man, don't bug me." Then he looked past me and said, "I'd like to get the guy that snuffed out that little deer. He'll never get to heaven, that's for sure." I glanced behind, at the deer head on the wall. Kerouac's sudden shift, or seeming sudden shift, diverted me momentarily. I then looked at Curtis and back at Kerouac. An idea flashed through me, one that I managed to keep from articulating. It was this: "Jack, if you're weeping over this deer that was murdered by some guy with a gun, and you're certain that this murderer will go to Hell, then *you* will also go to Hell because *you* are murdering yourself with this booze." The idea was gone, and Kerouac was lifting his bottle again and wondering if he could write in such surroundings.

"I would be happy to have you stay here, Jack," Curtis offered. "But if you wrote a book here, you'd have to dedicate it to me."

"The only people I dedicate books to are holy people," he responded fast. "That leaves you out and that goes for this corruptor of young minds here." He tossed me an exaggerated stare of admonition.

"If I'm corrupting young minds," I retorted, "then I'm doing it by teaching your books." (I was giving — and still am — a course at Lowell Tech in Beat Literature), "In essence then, Mr. Jacques Lebris de Kerouac, *you* are the corruptor. I am merely a tool." He cackled.

"Your French pronunciation stinks," he said, referring to my delivery of his name. He turned to Curtis. "Curtis, if I were to write in this place, the first thing you'd have to do would be to take that head of the deer down from the wall. I'd break into tears everytime I'd look at it." Kerouac shook his head slowly.

33

I have no reason to doubt that he was truly affected by that object.

"You say the word, Jack," Curtis asserted, "and I'll get this place ready for you in a hurry."

"I couldn't write in this place," he suddenly rebelled. "It's too much like a Swiss chalet. I'd be expecting guys in short pants to be coming in and out of this phony retreat." Jack Kerouac never did write in Curtis's lodge; and we never had occasion to revisit the place with him.

On the way back to Lowell, Kerouac managed to empty his bottle, and in between gulps, he foisted on us a medley of old Crosby-Haymes-Sinatra-Como songs. The melody was occasionally flat but the words were perfect and complete.

Chapter 4 - An Old Football Buddy Remembers

"He hurried on home, and gloated because no one noticed him. He wished suddenly that no one would ever notice him again and that he would walk through the rest of his life like this, wrapped in his own secret mysteries and glories, a prince disguised as a pauper, Orestes returned from distant heroisms and hiding within the land, stalking unknown within the land under powerful autumnal skies. But why was it they did not notice him any more than before?" [13]

This passage is from the early pages of Kerouac's first novel, *The Town and the City*. It portrays Peter Martin (Jack Kerouac) the high school football hero returning home in triumph from the Thanksgiving Day game. He has emerged as the star of the game and as he heads for home, passing people, he is entranced in an autistic flight. He is walking along the streets of Galloway (Lowell) and he is deep in his own drama of the wonder of his existence. He is thrilled by the idea that thousands of people had seen him earlier in the day, in his battle uniform, Number 35 — had seen him climb the heights. Yet now, after the game, he is in street clothes and as he goes by people, he is not recognized. He is thrilled even more by this; he glories in this secret disguise, in being "Orestes returned from distant heroisms and hiding within the land."

Yet this is not the Jack Kerouac that we see in his other novels depicting his early years in Lowell. In *Dr. Sax* and *Maggie Cassidy*, we see no hero in disguise, no inward, closed spirit that ranges silently through his adolescence and his late teens. In these books, Kerouac obviously idealizes G. J., Lousy, Vinny and Scotty. These are the four who with Jack Duluoz (Kerouac) explore the planet that is Lowell. There seems to be no leader of the gang, but Kerouac occasionally emerges as the inventor of games, the thrust behind much of the action.

In *Dr. Sax*, he describes a sandlot track meet that he had organized; then he adds, "I was always giving orders and called the 'big punk' by both Billy Artaud . . . and Dicky Hampshire . . . Dicky wrote, 'Jack is a big punk' in chalk on the board fence of a French Canadian Salem street alley as we walked home for noon recess from Bartlett Junior High —" [14] It is true that Billy Artaud and Dicky Hampshire were not considered as part of the "original four," but the thoughts that Kerouac attributes to them are intended to portray him as intensively gregarious and involved with his buddies. We see him rushing in a tidal wave of words into the constant swirl of his friends' lives. It is all outwardness, all mad crazy action and language. Jackie Duluoz is wildly intertwined and screaming in the glee of his mates as they confront each Lowell day — each "Little Canada," Pawtucketville, Acre Lowell day. Kerouac tells us that *he* was as raucous and free as any of them.

The first sentence of this work says, "Few writers have written so autobiographically as Jack Kerouac has." I see no reason to revise it. Yet in his ecstasy of desire to put down everything that Kerouac saw, felt, and did, there comes through at times a fuzziness as to what *his* role was in the spree of dramas that he articulates. Still, one can claim that the distinction between the *doer* and the *observer-narrator* would be less shadowy in his Beat novels than those set in Lowell. Certainly characters like Dean Moriarty, Carlo Marx, and Japhy Ryder were sculptured from monumentally powerful models, giant silhouettes that spoke for themselves and all that Kerouac had to do (though I'm not minimizing his literary skills) was to shove a microphone in front of them and tape record their lives. There was no confusing Neal Cassady, Allen Ginsberg, or Gary Snyder with Jack Kerouac.

But in his novels of Lowell, though Kerouac is unmistakably Jackie Duluoz and the other four that made up the gang are clearly delineated, there appears to be a valid doubt as to just exactly what Kerouac was like in his early youth. Was he really the free talking open youth that he portrays himself to have been?

There are still in Lowell today people who remember the young Jack Kerouac. His "gang" is scattered, but what has surfaced in my investigations is that this group did not have the *durable* Musketeers solidity that Kerouac reflects in his books. When Kerouac returned to Lowell in the last years of his life, the only one of the group that he saw again (and this only a couple of times) was George Apostolos (G. J. Rigopoulos). Further, there were other individuals who appear in these early books that come on stronger in real life as forces that influenced Kerouac, both as a personality and as a writer; stronger than the "original four." There was Odysseus "Duke" Chiungos, a boyhood chum and later fellow athlete on the Lowell High football team. There was Sam Sampatacacus, high school companion who was his literary, esthetic link. There was John Koumantzelis, a track star with Kerouac on the Lowell High team.

The latter two died in the service during World War II; Duke Chiungos is today head of a large dairy firm in Lowell. Sam Sampatacacus and John Koumantzelis I knew very well as we all attended the same schools in Lowell. We graduated from Lowell High School in 1940. (Kerouac finished a year earlier). Duke Chiungos I have known all my life. The point of all this is that Kerouac's portrayal of himself in these Lowell books comes in conflict with the image that people like Duke Chiungos have retained and that people like Sam Sampatacacus and John Koumantzelis would befriend.

In the last book that Kerouac published while he was alive, *Vanity of Duluoz,* he writes fondly if not emotionally of Duke Chiungos. He is at the point where he is enumerating the Lowell High football line of his senior year; he dwells almost ecstatically on Duke Chiungos: "Telemachus Gringas (Chiungos) at right tackle, nicknamed Duke and brother to great Orestes Gringas, both of them the toughest, boniest and most honest Greeks to meet. Duke himself actually a boyhood buddy of mine in the short month's duration at age twelve or so we'd decided to be friends, Saturday nights walking a mile and a half leaning on each other's arm over shoulders from the glittering lights of Kearney Square, Duke now grown into a quiet fellow but a 210-pound blockbuster with merry black eyes."

At the time that Kerouac was rambling through Pawtucketville and Little Canada with the "original four," he was also "a boyhood buddy" of Duke Chiungos. The latter's remembrance, perception of Kerouac in these years is startingly antithetical to what we see of Kerouac-Duluoz in *Dr. Sax* and *Maggie Cassidy.* It almost seems as if Kerouac were Jekyll and Hyde — with Duke Chiungos allowed to see only the Jekyll in Kerouac. But then again there may have been no Mr. Hyde in Kerouac at all despite the glees and howls that he acts out in *Dr. Sax* and *Maggie Cassidy*.

Odysseus "Duke" Chiungos has been a lifelong resident of Lowell. After his football days at Lowell High, he joined his two brothers in developing one of the largest dairy firms in Massachusetts. He has always been well regarded in the Lowell community and despite the more than thirty years that have passed since his high school days, he still stands in front of you in a big, physical way and looks as if he could easily assume the football crouch of a lineman and go through you and five other guys that may be standing behind you without needing an extra breath. He speaks easily and his young voice flows naturally from his remarkably young face.

As I have indicated, I've known Duke Chiungos practically all my life and though we were not boyhood chums we went to the same schools and came from the Greek community of Lowell. The insularity of this community precluded any of its inhabitants from being strangers to each other. This is why I've always known Duke Chiungos and he has always known me.

Recently, for the better part of an afternoon, I sat down with him and talked at length about Jack Kerouac. Over the years, I had chatted with Duke about Kerouac, but our remarks were always brief exchanges. On this day, however, we had agreed by pre-arrangement to sit down and really try to focus Jack Kerouac.

"You know, Chuck," Duke got right into it, "I've got to tell you that the last years that Kerouac came back to live in Lowell were really heartbreaking to me. I had always remembered him as a really handsome kid who had a perfect build. He was never very big but he was as strong as anybody I ever knew. And he was really a bug on physical conditioning. He used to follow the Olympics and the great track stars of those days and talked about energy foods and all that."

We were sitting in Duke's office and his workday was pretty much over. However, at this point in his commentary the phone rang. There was a brief dialogue on the phone concerning yogurt. When Duke hung up, he smiled. "Now *there's* a food product that Jack would have discovered quickly," he said. "That was his way. Whenever he got on to something he wouldn't let go until he had squeezed out the last drop. And if yogurt were

38

around in *those* days, Jack would have stocked a ton of it — or better yet, knowing Jack, he would have found out how to make it and fill up a whole freezer of the stuff."

"I have no doubt of that," I said. "Kerouac, I'm sure, was never the sort of person who was satisfied with the surface of things."

Duke shook his head in a gesture of regret. "No, he wasn't" he said, his voice suddenly becoming quiet. Duke Chiungos' normal voice is a powerful, clear sound. At this particular moment, it became almost a whisper. "No," he went on, "Kerouac never did anything halfway — and *that* I'm sure included his drinking." Duke shook his head again. "How in the hell did he ever get that way?" he said rhetorically, his voice once more reaching its normal volume. "As I started to tell you, it was heartbreaking to see him again when he returned to Lowell. It was at a downtown cocktail lounge. I was there with a couple of friends having a quiet drink when three or four people came in and sat near us. Right away, one of them started talking loud and the others were trying to quiet him down. He was polluted. I just glanced over."

Duke stopped and effected an expression of disbelief. "Believe me, Chuck," he continued, "I didn't recognize Jack. He looked like a piece of silly putty that some kid had been fooling around with. At first I kept staring at him, because something told me that I should know this guy. But he was so bombed and banged out of shape that I couldn't put him together."

"How long had it been since you had last seen him, Duke?" I asked.

"Well, I'm not sure really. Let's see, it must have been at least twenty years. As a matter of fact, after our high school days, I don't think I saw him more than four or five times. I can't be certain of it, but I believe that I last saw Jack — that is, until I saw him again at this cocktail lounge — I last saw Jack at the old Plaza Lunch at the Square. (Kearney Square in Lowell.) It was during the war. Jack was back from one of his merchant marine trips and I happened to be at the Plaza around two in the morning. Well, in comes Jack and for the next couple of hours we really caught up with each other."

"This was before Jack had started to write seriously," I said. "Did you ever have an idea then that Kerouac would become a writer, much less a *famous* writer?"

Duke appeared stymied. "A writer?" He articulated the words as if he had never heard them before. Then he said with finality, "No. Not a writer." But then he tried to retrieve some of it. "But that doesn't mean I am amazed by the idea that he *did* become a writer. I think I realize now what the hell was inside of him when I knew him as a kid from junior high on."

"What do you mean?"

"Well, it's kinda hard to pinpoint. He was always so quiet and yet I always had the feeling that he was simmering, no boiling really."

"Like a volcano?"

"Yeah, that's it."

"You say he was quiet as a kid. That's not the way he comes through in his novels about himself and Lowell."

Duke became a little uncomfortable; he fidgeted a bit. He scattered his gaze around the room and finally settled it on me. "This may surprise you," he said slowly, "but I've only read a couple of his books, the first one, what was it called?"

"The Town and the City."

"Yeah. And also *Maggie Cassidy*. Well, it's been a long time and I don't remember too much of them. They had quite a bit to do with his athlete days at Lowell High."

"But they weren't the ones that made him famous, Duke. *On The Road* did that. But anyway," I wanted to get him back on his perception of the young Kerouac, "I'm a bit startled when you tell me that Kerouac was quiet when he was a kid."

"Oh he was quiet all right. At Bartlett Junior High we were in the same classes, and I don't remember him saying one word in class in the three years that we went there."

"How about when the teacher would ask him a direct question?"

"Oh, he would answer, and he always had the right answer, but I never saw him volunteer anything."

"If he always had the right answer, then he must have been a good student."

"He was a very good student, especially in English, and he

never took a book home. I remember once he wrote a paper in Miss Mansfield's class (Miss Wakefield in *Maggie Cassidy*). It was about the Irish cop on the beat. I remember how excited she got over it, and how she read it to us in class."

"I don't suppose you'd recall any of the essay."

"No, I don't, but I recall Miss Mansfield showing it to the other teachers and they all agreed it was brilliant."

"Maybe that was the tipoff on Jack's future as a writer."

"If you knew Jack then, you wouldn't have the slightest idea as to what he would become. He was like a tomb—all closed in."

"That still sounds incredible to me, Duke. You should read *Maggie Cassidy* and *Dr. Sax* and you'll get a picture of a kid that you won't recognize."

"I don't care what those books say. I knew Jack as well as anybody, and he was anything but a free and easy going kid. But don't get me wrong; he could talk whenever he made up his mind to, and he could talk on almost anything; but that was a rare thing. Most of the time he was silent."

"You mean even when you were playing your kid games?"

"Well now, that was a bit different. He'd break out of his shell and he was a different kid. He'd get so wrapped up in a game that he'd forget to go home. He used to love to act out parts, you know like the old movie cowboys or Dracula or Frankenstein. But the next morning when I'd see him in school, he was back in his shell."

"I imagine that must have confused you," I suggested.

"It probably did although I don't remember exactly being confused. I guess I accepted him that way."

"How about in high school, Duke? Was he still moving around in his silent cloud?"

"Yes, I think he was. I remember we'd go to the Lowell High football practice and after banging heads for a couple of hours we'd walk back home; it was a couple of miles. There were times when he wouldn't say ten words. I can just see him; he'd have his head down as we walked along, and whenever he decided to speak he wouldn't even turn his face to look at you. I mean he'd be staring down at the ground, and he'd sort of mumble."

"Would you call him morose at times like these?"

41

"I suppose you would."

"Didn't you think it was strange, Duke? You know, walking along with your buddy after football practice. One would expect that you'd be chattering about what happened that day on the field."

"Well, as I said before, I had come to accept Jack and his ways." Duke stopped and I could see that he was reaching for something. "I could be wrong," he came back on, "but there were times when I always felt he was mad about something."

"You mean angry, hostile?"

"Yeah, that's it. Hostile. As I said, he was quiet most of the time, but it wasn't only that he was quiet, he seemed to be harboring some kind of anger, as if somebody had done something to him."

"That's very interesting, Duke," I said and at *this* point in our dialogue, *I* recalled something Kerouac had said to me. In the middle of one of his "speeches" one night, he said, "The biggest mistake *I* ever made in my life was allowing myself to be born." I'm still not sure at this writing if this thought has any relevance to what Duke Chiungos said about Kerouac's constant subterranean hostility. If it *were* hostility, what was Kerouac mad at? *Visions of Gerard* came at me: Gerard died, Jack survived; the wrong one died; Gerard was the saint, Jack wasn't even a faded carbon copy of him. Was it an agonizing guilt that continually tore at Jack's young mind? A guilt whose wells he couldn't discover but whose devastation he felt?

"Was this hostility, if that's what it was," I resumed my questioning, " was it ever directed at you, Duke? I mean did you ever get into a fight with Jack?"

Duke shook his head vigorously in disagreement. "No, no, no. It wasn't that kind of thing. I mean I never saw him speak crossly to anybody. As a matter of fact, he never complained about anything. When we first went out for the Lowell High football team, I found myself being moved up to the varsity very quickly. Jack stayed with the jayvees for his sophomore year and much of his junior year. But he should have been with me on the varsity from the very beginning — because he was really good. And I mean that sincerely. He was the hardest runner on our team, and the toughest, most durable kid I've ever met."

"If he were that good as a sophomore, Duke," I interposed, "why wasn't he moved up? In his book, *Vanity of Duluoz*, Kerouac gushes with bitterness at the cruel, vicious ignoring of his football talents. He portrays his father especially as a man who walked around in a monumental wrath because the coaching staff was playing favorites, and his son was being denied the chance to show the great ability he had. How valid is all this Duke?"

He did not hesitate. "I'd say that part of this was true."

"Part of it?"

"Well, first of all, Jack wasn't moved up to the varsity early because he was a backfield candidate. I was a lineman so there were more positions to fight for. But the backfield had room for only four guys and our coach was the sort of man who, once he started the season with a certain lineup, that was *it*. It was frozen like that for the rest of the season. Besides, we had plenty of good runners which made it even tougher to break in the lineup. But let me say again that nobody could run as hard and as strong on a straight line as Jack Kerouac. But, as I said before, he never complained about not being in the starting lineup much sooner than his senior year. At least *I* never heard him."

"What about Jack's father, Duke? Do you remember much of him?"

"I remember that he was a fireplug, short, stocky. But I never saw much of him."

"What you saw of him — was he the intensive, loud personality that Jack portrays him to be?"

"I honestly cannot say, Chuck. He came to the games and all that, but that's all I remember of him."

"What about girls, Duke? How was he in high school? You know, for a long time there has been a dispute here in Lowell — at least among Lowellians who are interested in Kerouac — there's been a dispute as to who Maggie Cassidy was. It's become some kind of game, but after all the guesses, two candidates are sifted through. Do *you* have any idea?"

"I've heard about Maggie Cassidy all right, but I can't say for sure who he had in mind. But I know this: he was really bugeyed over Margaret Coffey. She was a slim, nice looking kid and she used to love to sing. And Jack was really after her for awhile."

"Did he actually date her?"

"Well, I think he did. I'd see him talking to her in high school and I assume he went out with her. He used to talk to me about her and it was one of the few times where you could actually say he would show some feelings, some emotion."

"Well, the initials are the same, Duke. M.C. — Maggie Cassidy, Margaret Coffey. If you look in *Vanity of Duluoz*, you will see that he uses another name, with the same initials, who could be Margaret Coffey."

There is a passage in *Vanity of Duluoz* where Kerouac speaks of a Moe Cole: "I spend most of my Friday nights (Summer of 1941) singing every show tune in the books under an apple tree in Centreville (Centralville, really), Lowell, with Moe Cole: and boy could we sing: and later she sang with Benny Goodman's band awhile. She once came to see me in broad afternoon summer wearing a tightfitting fire engine red dress and high heels, whee." [15]

In *Maggie Cassidy*, there is another girl besides Maggie that surfaces occasionally. She is Pauline Cole; she is also called Moe Cole, and Jack Duluoz speaks of her future as a singer for Artie Shaw's band. In fact, in this book, Kerouac plays with the initials M.C. Maggie Cassidy becomes M.C. Number One and Moe Cole becomes M.C. Number Two.

The names, Moe Cole or Pauline Cole, didn't mean anything to Duke Chiungos when I offered them to him. "But it certainly sounds like the same person," he added. "I don't know whether Margaret Coffey ever sang with Benny Goodman or Artie Shaw but I do know that Kerouac really would get excited over her."

"You can see that the initials are still the same, Duke. M.C. Moe Cole. Maggie Cassidy. As a matter of fact, I, myself, remember Margaret Coffey. I was a year behind you in high school, but I recall this girl who was tallish and slender. I'm almost sure she was in a couple of my classes, but my remembrance of her is that of a reserved almost shy individual. Then again, it could be that she really blossomed into a personality in her senior year and Kerouac discovered her. And from the way Jack describes her in *Vanity of Duluoz*, she had become a very

44

attractive young lady. Of course, here he writes about her after they had both graduated from high school. As for her singing, I do remember that she had a tryout with a big band. At any rate, Duke, this is the girl you say that Jack was interested in in high school."

"This is the girl that Jack ever talked to me about, the one that I ever saw him really go for."

"Then I guess the debate about who Maggie Cassidy was is still unresolved."

Duke smiled. "I thought that you had just about decided it was Margaret Coffey."

"No, I couldn't decide that," I said. Then I smiled back at him. "I couldn't decide that because there is more evidence to indicate that Maggie Cassidy was in reality Mary Carney. You can see how the initials also match out here, M.C."

"I've heard of Mary Carney," Duke said, "but very vaguely. But I can tell you this. In our high school days, Jack never mentioned her to me. It was Margaret Coffey that he always raved about."

"Now that's what makes it so puzzling, and that's why the argument is not really settled," I said. "I've talked to others about Maggie Cassidy, people like Albert Blazon who was another boyhood friend of Kerouac's. He, too, did not recall Mary Carney."

"Well, as I told you, Jack was a mysterious, silent sort of kid. It wouldn't surprise me if Mary Carney was a secret love of his."

I caught the word, secret. "It's strange, Duke, that you should say that. Sometime ago, I went down to the Lowell City Library and began reading through copies of the Lowell newspapers of the late 1930's. I concentrated especially on 1938-39, Jack's last year at Lowell High. In the book, *Maggie Cassidy*, Jack devotes a lot of pages to Duluoz's birthday party. Maggie is there as are many friends. Newspaper photographers are there. Maggie appears in one of the pictures. Now what I'm getting at is this: I went to the Lowell City Library hoping to find a picture of this party in the papers. You may remember that Lowell had three newspapers then. I checked them all, especially the editions that came after March 12, Jack's birthday. Now here's the weird part: there were no pictures of the party in two of the papers; but in the third paper in the social pages, there is a picture that is *cut out*! Somebody came to the library and snipped it. That could be *the picture* — either of Mary Carney or Margaret Coffey. It's unfortunate that this newspaper has been defunct for years. I've been unable to trace the picture elsewhere."

"Have you tried to find Mary Carney or Margaret Coffey?" Duke suddenly asked.

"I understand that Margaret Coffey is no longer in the area. As for Mary Carney, she's still around, married and all, but she prefers to remain invisible, especially as regards any relationship she might have had with Jack."

I no sooner had finished this remark than I was fascinated by the concept that Maggie Cassidy might have been the idealized woman that men live with in the realm of their beautiful dreams. Maggie Cassidy — Mary Carney — Margaret Coffey: they were the marble from which Jack Kerouac sculptured the serene goddess that dwelt only on Mt. Olympos. Lord Byron, Edgar Allan Poe — Jack Kerouac: they all had their Maggie Cassidys. The controversy then as to who Maggie Cassidy really was becomes an intellectual exercise. Maggie Cassidy is everybody's first love.

I once asked Kerouac, himself, about Maggie Cassidy. He gave me a sly, but really innocent, look. "She was a joy," he said "she was a joy." When I threw the names of Mary Carney and Margaret Coffey at him, he repeated his words. I have found other friends of Kerouac who confirm that he knew both girls. Let it go at that.

I got back to Duke Chiungos. "Duke, how about that downtown cocktail lounge where you saw Jack and had trouble recognizing him. You said you hadn't seen Jack in twenty years or so. Did he recognize you? Did you talk to him?"

"Yes, I talked to him — for a few minutes. When they told me it was Jack Kerouac, I went over to him, that is after I got over the shock of seeing him so destroyed, and I greeted him. I didn't tell him my name. I didn't have to. He looked at me, stared actually, and suddenly became very quiet. 'Duke,' he said. 'Duke Chiungos.' How are you, Jack, I said. Then I sat down

46

with him and as I said before, I had trouble convincing myself that I was looking at Jack Kerouac."

"What did you talk about, Duke?"

"Not much really. About all that I can remember is that he kept telling the guys that were with him that I was the greatest Greek that ever lived."

"Greek athlete?"

"No, although he did say a little about our football days."

"But you didn't say much to him."

"I didn't get a chance. He just kept talking."

"That sounds familiar."

"But there was one other thing about this meeting with Jack. My mind kept playing tricks on me. The young Jack Kerouac would flash in front of me once in a while, the one that I had last seen at the old Plaza Lunch at the Square."

"This was that meeting you mentioned — at two o'clock in the morning — during the war."

"Yeah. And I felt real freaky seeing him now — shouting, all liquored up, and his face all chewed up."

"You said you had a long talk with him at the Plaza Lunch. I know it's been quite a few years, but do you remember any of the conversation?"

Duke crinkled his eyes; he was trying. "He had been in the Merchant Marine, and he talked about that. At one point, he got angry when he talked about his wife."

"That must have been his first wife," I urged him on.

"I don't know," Duke admitted. "How many times was he married?"

"The records show three times," I answered.

"Well all I remember is that he was really upset when he talked about her. The thing that has stuck with me all these years is this: 'She has more money than brains.' That was it. That's what he told me and I think he was looking for a way out'."

"Obviously, he found it," I said, "because he married a couple of more times. Did he mention anything at that time about doing any writing?"

"I don't remember anything like that," Duke came back quickly.

47

"What about future plans?" I persisted. "Did he say anything about that?"

"I think he did say something about college. I remember that he went into a long explanation about why he left Columbia, but the details escape me. I think it all came down to the idea that he got fed up with it, that he got tired, exhausted."

"But do you think he was interested in returning to Columbia, or to another college?"

"Well, as I say, he talked about it."

I decided to change direction. "Did Jack seem much different to you then than he did when you were kids and high school buddies?"

"He hadn't changed much physically. He was still strong looking. He still looked like he could run in the backfield."

"You said he did a lot of talking," I went on. "That doesn't sound like the silent kid you described earlier."

"That's right. And he wasn't. He had really opened up. His whole personality seemed to have changed. I was really surprised."

"Anything else you remember about that conversation, Duke?" I gave it one last shot.

He hesitated. "Not at the moment," he said finally. "But I'll tell you this," he continued. "When I saw him again at that cocktail lounge twenty years later, I decided that I would avoid any future meetings with Jack."

Duke's words somehow sounded offensive to me; there was a kind of cruelty echoing around them and I was on the verge of challenging them when he added: "Don't get me wrong. I still consider Jack one of my most cherished friends. But I wouldn't enjoy his company the way he had become in the last years. It was bad enough that he was always boozed up and loud; I guess I could get used to that. But it was the way he looked. I couldn't get over it. As I said before, it was heart-breaking."

"Then you didn't see Kerouac any more when he finally came back to Lowell to stay."

"I just saw him one more time, at another cocktail lounge, and it was the same old thing over again. He was drunk, he was all over me, it was just a bad scene."

48

Our Kerouac dialogue had apparently run out. I got up to leave. Duke Chiungos remained in his seat. I sensed a reluctance in him, a reluctance to end our conversation. There was something in his eyes that made him want to linger. "He was really something though," I heard him mutter. The tone and cadence of his words made them sound like the end of a thought whose beginning had been silently created. The words that I heard seemed the trailer to the unspoken beginning. What followed next was obviously Duke Chiungo's eulogy to his ever-youthful, ever-strong, ever-valiant friend, Jack Kerouac. "I never saw Jack Kerouac do a dishonest thing. I never heard him squawk about anything. What a football player, what a runner."

CHAPTER 5 - SAMPATIS GEORGE SAMPATACACUS

"I made up my mind to become a writer when Sebastian Sampas befriended me," Kerouac said to me one day. In its simplicity and directness this brief assertion seems to neatly solve the matter of Jack Kerouac's beginnings as a writer. It's true that before Sebastian Sampas influenced him, he had written some things: little home newspapers, short stories, child diaries, etc. But it remained apparently for Sebastian Sampas to focus *the writer* for Jack Kerouac — or so Kerouac wants us to believe. In truth, however, it is impossible to determine the extent to which Kerouac felt the literary urgings of his young friend.

That he would have become a writer had not Sampas ever existed is an easily defended concept. Still, the figure of Sebastian Sampas can never be minimized as a force in the life of Jack Kerouac. It is there, glowing, singing, talking, imbedding itself deep into the psyche of Kerouac; it is there, in Kerouac's first book, *The Town and the City,* and in his last book, *Vanity of Duluoz;* it is there in books that came in between these two, books such as *Dr. Sax, Book of Dreams, Visions of Gerard, Big Sur.* In all of these works, Sebastian Sampas is painted as a youth who is madly devouring all the poetic thoughts of man, and in turn, is madly spewing them on Kerouac. He flashes through in great bursts of passionate oratory and inevitably ends with great rolling sadness for his fellowman and for the mutability of all that's beautiful in the world. He is a starry-eyed youth who goes on long walks with Kerouac and he acts out many a scene, with his friend as the audience.

When one considers that Kerouac and Sebastian Sampas became close friends during their high school years, and then saw each other only a few times after that (Sampas died of wounds in World War II), one can easily conclude that the brevity of their meetings is in direct contrast to the intensity of their relationship. Sebastian Sampas etched himself deeply into the memory of Jack Kerouac; and this becomes all the more remarkable when the setting of their high school friendship is sharply focused.

Jack Kerouac was a year ahead of Sampas in high school; he was a splendid athlete, ferocious in his competitive spirit; he was French-Canadian, and in ethnic-oriented Lowell of the 1930's and 1940's, it meant that most likely his steady friends would be of a similar ethnic background.

Sebastian Sampas was no athlete; in fact, he wasn't even a sports fan. At a time when Yankee baseball greats like Lou Gehrig, Bill Dickey, Lefty Gomez and Red Ruffing were triggering great fantasies of imitation in the minds of most high school kids, Sampas was fantasizing great Byronic flights of artistic ecstasy. Sampas came from a Greek home, a cultural milieu divergent (in a kind of oblique way) from Kerouac's French-Canadian world. Probably the most significant impediment to any friendship between these two young men might have been their personalities: Kerouac, traveling in a massive inward universe, collosal fires of vision burning and lighting future horizons of promise and fulfillment; Sampas, reflecting vividly every light and shadow of his soul on the mirror of his face, speaking every thought that was born in his brain, afraid that his friend might miss or misunderstand some nuance, some vaguely uttered syllable. Yet these two youths met—discovered each other—and enrichment flowed from each of them, one to the other.

I knew Sebastian Sampas long before Jack Kerouac met him. He was Sampatis George Sampatacacus then; we called him Sampati. We met in the first grade of the Greek Parochial School in Lowell and we were in the same class for the first five years of our elementary schooling. Our junior high school years separated us academically, though I would see him sporadically in the swirl of Lowell's Greek community. Then our educational pursuits brought us together again, at Lowell High School, and we shared a number of classes and teachers. We graduated from the Class of 1940 and thereafter, Sampatis George Sampatacacus became a memory for me. Like millions of others, we were swept up by World War II.

During the war, I remember coming home on furlough and hearing that he was killed. He had been in the Medical Corps, and anyone who really knew Sebastian Sampas would understand why he chose this life-giving duty. Sampatis' death saddened me, of course, but it wasn't until years later that I recalled

52

something else that was said about him on the occasion of his death: he had been writing poetry and some of it had appeared in service newspapers. In 1950, when Kerouac's first book, *The Town and the City* was published, Sampati was resurrected as Alexander Panos and in subsequent Kerouac books he would appear as Sabbas Savakis, Savas Savakis, Sylvanus Santos, Sylvester Santos. In all of them, he was inevitably the poet, the idealist, the seeker of truth and beauty.

As a pupil in the Greek Parochial School, I remember my classmate Sampati moving about quietly. Black-haired, (his hair so curly it was almost in ringlets) olive, chubby, cherubic — he stared at the world through child, sad eyes. The super structured, Old World discipline of the Greek Parochial School had to grate painfully on the sensitive little soul of Sampati Sampatacacus. The teachers from Greece who taught the Greek language subjects were militant, sharp-voiced, and brooked no indulgence of emotion from anyone in the classroom. And emotion was what Sampati was all about.

The first recollection I have of a pupil crying in the classroom was soon after I had begun my education. We were first graders and we were trying to learn the Greek alphabet. Our male teacher from Greece loomed over us like King Kong. When I was called upon to recite the alphabet, I ran through it with a skill that could only have had its roots in the desperate circumstance of self-preservation. A few minutes later, Sampati was commanded to recite. Even now, so many years after it has happened, I see Sampati standing beside his desk; he began slowly: "alpha, beta, gamma, delta, epsilon, zeta, eta . . ." He stopped. "Eta, eta," he resumed, repeated.

"Eta, theta," prompted King Kong.

"Eta, theta, kappa," Sampati lurched ahead.

"Ochi, ochi (no, no)" reprimanded King Kong.

"Eta, theta, lambda, kappa," Sampati stumbled on.

"Ochi, ochi," snapped King Kong, his voicing rising and he moving closer to Sampati. "Eta, theta, iota, kappa," he threw his words out hammer-like.

"Eta, theta, iota, kappa," Sampati seized on them. By now, his black curls leaped freely as his head bobbed with every letter he pronounced. "Iota, kappa . . . kappa." Sampati was now floundering badly. He was a couple of desks behind me and I had turned around and was watching him with a sense of innocent fascination. His full, pretty baby face had become two huge eyes out of which beamed bewilderment and a cry for someone in this horror world he found himself in to help him.

Sampati had now become imprisoned by the letter, kappa. "Kappa, kappa," he writhed, unable to free himself.

Finally, King Kong had had enough. He released a roar that rattled the windows of our classroom. "Kappa, kappa!" he mocked. "It is easy to see that you have not done your homework! What were you doing last night, picking your nose?!" King Kong was now roaring directly over Sampati's shattered little brain.

I can still hear that question: "What were you doing last night, picking your nose?!" And I can still see Sampati's stricken face, his huge wide eyes suddenly closing and then everything opening up and a woebegone cry flooding the room and letting everyone know that if there were an ounze of mercy left in the world, Sampati would reach for it like a drowning man reaches for a lifeline. Sampati crumbled in his seat and I somehow perceived a sense of satisfaction among the rest of us that *we* were stronger than that, that *we* were not the ones involved in such a shameful exhibition of weakness.

That first year saw an occasional recurrence of Sampati's crying scene — and not necessarily with the same teacher. It was inevitable that he be labeled a crybaby; and it was inevitable that he become the target of unconscionable child games. I, at the time, shared the cruel glee of the rest of my classmates whenever Sampati became the sacrificial lamb of the monstrous rituals of childish pranks. Yet I also remember reserving a residue of awe for Sampati as he bounced back from his latest disaster and resumed his relationships with his classmates. There was never any revenge that he sought from those who had mistreated him; in fact, he always seemed to go out of his way to show his tormentors that he wanted to live in kindness with them.

Lest anyone misunderstand, Sampati's willingness to forgive was not in any part motivated by a fear of a revisitation by a particular tormentor. No, his forgiving sprang from the well of pure delight in living in harmony with his fellowman. No, Sampati was not afraid, and I was convinced of this when I saw him engage in a fight with another pupil. It was the only time I ever witnessed Sampati in such a situation.

We were at recess in the schoolyard. In the pell mell movement of our play, two boys began wrestling. One of them was much the larger and it was he who had provoked his opponent: a classic bully scene. The rest of us became willingly enthusiastic spectators, and it wasn't long before we could see that the smaller lad was bravely but futilely battling for his survival.

Suddenly we were all stunned: Sampati comes flying through the crowd and intervenes in the fight. He pulls at the larger boy and tries to get him off his embattled victim. The larger boy is so amazed at Sampati's precipitate presence that he releases his hold. "Don't do that! Don't do that!" Sampati yells at him. "He's too small! He's too small!" (The truth was that Sampati was not much larger than the boy he was helping). Then the bully recovers himself and sails into Sampati. Sampati neither retreated nor cried. He fought bravely and was making it a fairly even contest when a teacher came up and ended the struggle

Sampati continued to sporadically break out in tears in class whenever a teacher would chastise him. But I (and I'm sure other of my classmates) had sculptured a new image of him. Oh sure, he was still the cry baby, but we were sure now that his crying did not stem from weakness but from a source we could not identify, a source that puzzled us immensely.

That Sampatis George Sampatacacus was different from most kids is true; that he developed into what most people would call a dreamer is also true; that he grew into a high school youth who would recite poetry anywhere, anytime, I (and others who went to school with him) can confirm.

After our Greek Parochial School years, Sampati faded somewhat in my consciousness until he strongly focused again in our high school period. We were in many classes together, and I would sometimes feel strange as I listened to him recite a passage or contribute a comment in a class discussion. Strange I say, because his image flickered; flickered between the now voluble young man and the curly haired, devastated little boy who first stammered his own mutated version of the Greek alphabet.

55

Oh yes, he was voluble now. But more than that, he had acquired a theatrical manner, one that brought forth his words as if they were divinely ordained. There was rarely a syllable that he uttered which was devoid of an emotional chord.

Chapter 6 - Sammy and Jack

I distinctly, vividly remember one Spring evening, 1939, in front of the Lowell City Library. This grey, stone, gothic-looming structure was a favorite rendezvous area for many high schoolers. There were about five or six of us including Sampati (all descended from Lowell Greek immigrants) milling, shifting about at the foot of the stone steps. Our dialogue ranged far: sports, girls, world news, teachers, school subjects. When the matter of school subjects came on, Sampati (whose name had evolved into Sammy) launched a long commentary on Lord Byron, "the greatest poet and the greatest patriot that ever lived." The rest of us listened, though we were not exactly enthralled by his topic. We loved Sammy, but we could not always take him. Occasionally, we would rebel at his incessantly emotional approach to life.

On this evening, in front of the library, one of us decided to rebel. In the middle of Sammy's Byronic flight, this person tried to shoot him down. "Lord Byron was one of the biggest whoremasters around," he fired. "I read that he lived in Italy for a number of years and he had more 'gash' (women) there in one week than most guys have in a lifetime."

A bullet through his chest could not have had a more traumatic effect on Sammy. He seemed to stagger on the podium (actually, he stood a couple of steps above us) that he had climbed while delivering his Byronic eulogy. A tragic shadow darkened his face. "A whoremaster?!" he echoed the word painfully, as he tried to extricate it from his body like one does a bullet. "Lord Byron loved women as if they were goddesses!" he exclaimed. "Lord Byron never hurt a woman in his life. He worshipped them, and they in turn worshipped him!"

"Boy, he must have had something to get all that action," Byron's detractor (who was now doubling as Sammy's heckler) shot back.

I could see by now that we were enjoying this baiting of Sammy. We were standing around watching with amusement and a touch of sadism as Sammy was stoking up his emotional fires.

"Lord Byron made any woman he loved the happiest woman

in the world!" Sammy spoke these words like a passage from Scripture.

"Then he must have had a wang as big as a buffalo's!" his opponent fairly shouted. The rest of us roared.

Sammy did not retreat. "Why can't you see it?" he bore on. "Byron was a poet, a creative artist. He felt so much more than other people did!"

No sooner had he finished this comment than I sensed a twinge of compassion for Sammy. I still remember the pathos with which he uttered the word, felt; and I still remember how the rest of us exchanged glances in anticipation of what his adversary would do with this word.

"I should *say* he *felt* much more than other people did!" his tormentor seized his advantage. "Like just about every woman he could get his hands on!" We roared again. Sammy almost toppled from his perch. He regained his balance and moved his right arm in a grand gesture.

"I would expect something better from you — a descendant from the Greeks," he began evenly. "Lord Byron gave his life to Greece. If it weren't for Lord Byron, your parents and mine would have been born in Turkish slavery. *You* (he made a spear of his right arm) might have been born a Turkish slave!" Sammy was cranking up for a strong finish. "How can you speak so crudely of a man who spoke so beautifully of Greece," he continued, his voice sliding, almost imperceptibly, into a rhythmic pattern of lament. Then he began:

> "The isles of Greece, the isles of Greece!
> Where burning Sappho loved and sung,
> Where grew the arts of war and peace,
> Where Delos rose, and Phoebus sprung!
> Eternal summer gilds them yet,
> But all, except their sun, is set.
>
> The mountains look on Marathon
> And Marathon looks on the sea;
> And musing there an hour alone,
> I dreamed that Greece might still be free;
> For standing on the Persians' grave,
> I could not deem myself a slave."

For only five or six people who were clapping their hands, our applause sounded more like five or six hundred pair of hands beating together. Add to this our shouts of approval, and I have no doubt that we were heard in the grating, clanking traffic beat of Kearney Square (Lowell's focal point) a half-mile away. And the one who cheered the loudest was Sammy's debating mate. Sammy smiled at him and then at the rest of us. "And this was the little kid in Greek school," I thought, "who would fall apart at the idea of getting up in class and reciting." Still smiling, Sammy stepped down from his podium.

Our group continued to stand in front of the library and other topics occupied us. Sammy, possibly feeling that he had made his contribution for the night, now became a listener. A few minutes went by and then, almost unnoticed, a handsome young man came out of the library, skipping lightly down the stone steps. He nodded to us as he went by and then Sammy said crisply, "I'll see you later fellers," and joined him.

"Who's that?" somebody asked.

"That's Sammy's literary soulmate," came the answer.

"Literary soulmate?"

"Yeah. He and Sammy take long walks and discuss literature, music — all that stuff."

"Bullshit." This was another voice. "That's Jack Kerouac, the football player at the high school. He was also on the track team. You mean to tell me that *he* talks about poetry with Sammy? He must be a strange athlete."

"That's for sure." This was still another voice. "I can't picture a 'Galli' (a slang Greek synonym for a dumb Frenchman) being interested in any of that stuff; or for that matter having anything in common with Sammy."

For some strange reason, I felt compelled to defend Jack Kerouac, or possibly to defend Sammy's relationship with him. "I don't know about the 'Galli' part of it," I began, "but Kerouac is no ordinary athlete . . . I mean he's a good athlete, but he seems to be different." The silence shouted at me for an elaboration. "I was talking with Johnny Koumantzelis a few weeks ago — you know that Johnny was on the track team with Kerouac — and we happened to talk about him. He said he never saw a runner get so worked up inside before a track meet."

"Inside?" someone challenged.

"Well yeah, that's what Johnny said. I mean he would go off in a corner by himself and practically freeze in a starting position. Then when he would rejoin the group, Johnny told me, he'd have a look on his face like he had just come back from the Second Battle of the Marne — those were Johnny's exact words. He'd look tired, exhausted. But once the starting gun went off, Kerouac would run like a cheetah. Johnny also told me that Kerouac was the leading scorer on the track team."

"I still don't know what the hell he's doing hanging round with Sammy," one of the skeptics persisted. "We've all known Sammy all our lives. Have you ever seen him play any sports — out on the Common (the North Common in the Acre Section of Lowell) or at the Lowell Boys Club, or the Y (the Y.M.C.A.)?"

"So what?" I came back at him. "That doesn't make him a sissy. And you certainly can't say that Kerouac is a sissy because he likes to hang around with Sammy."

"Maybe Kerouac likes to hear Sammy talk," somebody else suggested. "It's almost like looking at a movie or a stage show whenever you're in Sammy's company. And you can always count on him to give a great performance."

I couldn't resist. "Well I certainly think that he earned the Academy Award on his Byron performance tonight." Then impulsively I added, "All those in favor of giving Sammy — oh excuse me, I mean Sebastian; that's what he likes to be called now, isn't it? — all those in favor of giving Sebastian Sampatacacus the Academy Award say aye!" We all shouted acclamation, and on that note we dispersed.

It would be easy to surrender to the cliché thought that Sammy Sampas's (the last name also evolved from Sampatacacus to Sampas) friendship with Jack Kerouac was an example of opposite personalities attracting each other. I say easy because outwardly, they *were* in vast polarity. Sammy acted everything out; Sammy articulated every syllable that entered his brain. Jack moved about in silence; yet within him there thundered a world that stormed with a million ideas. Yes, opposite — but only on the surface.

In Sammy Sampas, Jack Kerouac found the temple he had been seeking as a child-youth in Lowell. His other Lowell buddies

60

— G. J. Rigopoulos, Scotty, Vinny, Lousy, Duke — were outside this temple; they were of a world that could never see Kerouac's flaming candle that burned with his ecstatic will to find, to enter the temple of the arts. In the riot of his French-Canadian, Lowell youth, Kerouac played hard with his boyhood gang, the gang he writes about in *Maggie Cassidy* and *Dr. Sax* and *Vanity of Duluoz*. But after a day of adventuring with them, Kerouac would walk home with a lingering melancholia as his companion. They were not enough, these neighborhood buddies; they only met Kerouac on the edge of the forest of his mind. They could not perceive Kerouac's deep journeys into that forest as he sought the temple of beauty and strived to hear the great organ chord of emotion and love that he knew was waiting for him.

Before he met Sammy Sampas, the only human being that had touched the depths of Jack Kerouac was his brother, Gerard. Though Gerard died when Kerouac was four, Gerard had never left him. In truth, Gerard's death kept him alive in Kerouac's mind as the horizon symbol of tragic beauty and compassionate love. Gerard was the one who wept for mankind.

Sammy Sampas also wept.

I believe it was in the third year of our Greek Parochial School days. One of our classmates, a little girl, died. On the day of the funeral, classes were suspended and the teachers and the student body attended the church services. The Greek Orthodox religion, monumentally traditional, has elaborate services for all occasions; a funeral especially mirrors its centuried doctrine.

The church was full and the priest and his chanter sang ancient hymns that spoke of death and Christ's victory over death. In front of the altar, the open casket held the body of the little girl. From where I sat, I could see the glow of the white dress that she wore. The hymnal flow was occasionally interrupted by someone coughing. I remember feeling strangely embarrassed by this; embarrassed, that is, for the person who was unable to control his coughing.

The chanting seemed to stop suddenly (though it was actually the end of the service) and then the priest spoke a brief eulogy. Then, row by row, we began to walk by the funeral bier for a final farewell to the dead girl. I could see my classmates ahead of me, each stopping briefly, bending down to kiss the small ikon that was propped by the little girl's side, and moving on. As I neared the bier, I remember having just about made up my mind to avoid looking at the child's face and to close my eyes while bending to kiss the ikon.

There must have been three or four pupils ahead of me when another thought came at me: I was momentarily fascinated by the realization that my classmates all around me looked so subdued, so somber, so different. I was working on this idea when I was shattered by a wail that came from someone in front of me. It fell like an avalanche in the hush quiet of the church. It wasn't until this person began to utter words that I realized it was Sammy Sampas.

"You will go to heaven, you will go to heaven!" he cried. He seemed to be hunched over the casket. "I know you will go to heaven!" he kept on. "But why did you leave us now? Why? Why?"

I do believe that I was on the verge of turning away and going back to my seat; I was frightened. But one of our teachers came up quickly and enfolded Sammy. He was still uttering teary words and just before he surrendered to the teacher, he reached down and kissed his dead classmate on the forehead.

In the classroom the next day, I caught myself a number of times staring at Sammy. He was, of course, in his usual state of acute sensitivity and treating everyone else as if they too caught the world around them with the same heartbeat. I stared at him with an ambivalent eye: a kind of revulsion that his lips had touched the waxen, lifeless face of our departed classmate — and an awesome respect for his free, unashamed spirit and its capacity to manifest love openly, sincerely.

Today, I can still see little Sampati sobbing helplessly, wailing the question why in rhythmic mourning, and being led away by our teacher. I can still see his quick gesture of kissing the little corpse. Today, there is no ambivalence in my thoughts of Sammy Sampas. There is the uncomplicated conviction that he was one of the most honest, loving creatures I've ever known. And yet I must confess that in all the years that I was with him, only a particle of this conviction was in my grasp. Conversely, in the few years that Jack Kerouac knew him, Kerouac focused the essence of this youth, the meaning of him, the beauty of him.

62

And we can begin to understand why Kerouac embraced Sammy Sampas with a wild sense of rediscovery and resurrection when he first saw him and heard him speak. We can begin to understand if we think on Kerouac's lost child-brother, Gerard.

In *Visions of Gerard,* Kerouac writes: "Without Gerard what would have happened to Ti Jean (Jack Kerouac) . . . It was only many years later when I met and understood Savas Savakis (Sammy Sampas) that I recalled the definite and immortal idealism which had been imparted me by my holy brother—And even later with the discovery . . . of Buddhism, Awakenedhood — Amazed recollection that from the very beginning I, whoever 'I' or whatever 'I' was, was destined, destined indeed, to meet, learn, understand Gerard and Savas and the Blessed Lord Buddha (and my Sweet Christ too through all his Paulian tangles and bloody crosses of heathen violence) — to awaken to pure faith in the bright one truth: All is Well, practice Kindness, Heaven is Nigh." [16]

Jack Kerouac took long walks with Sammy Sampas; by his own admission, he was nourished by this friend who was different from all the others; nourished in a way that caused him to write the above passage almost twenty years after Sammy's death.

"I . . . was destined, destined indeed, to meet, learn, understand Gerard and Savas . . ." he exulted. Gerard and Sammy — the idealists. Yet Gerard had never met Sammy; Gerard had died years before Sammy came into Kerouac's world. Even more interesting is the fact that Kerouac himself barely knew his brother. No matter; as stated earlier in this work, Kerouac "learned, understood" Gerard through his parents and even more significantly, through his deep longing to love someone purely, completely. Thus, one day, a person like Sammy Sampas comes along and begins talking of poetry and music; he begins talking in a way that ignites Kerouac's mind. Kerouac listens and as he does so, he creates with a sense of wonder and discovery the concept: this is how Gerard would have talked had he lived; this is how Gerard would have reached me, with lovely thoughts that would take away the ugly pain that keeps coming at me; this is how Gerard would have wept for all the dead and dying of the world; this is how Gerard would have walked with me, along the Merrimack River, and this is how he would have

63

taught me that the true splendor of life is in our hearts.

Gerard Kerouac came briefly into his brother's life, but his influence was anything but brief. Sammy Sampas, too, was only an interlude for Kerouac, but it was really a continuation of Kerouac's incessant search for the brother who had said to him: "All is Well, practice Kindness, Heaven is Nigh."

It is always fascinating to conjecture on someone who has been prematurely cut off — as Sammy Sampas was. When we were in high school together, I remember that he would occasionally show me something he had written. Some of it was in verse and some of it was in prose. Even now, that I think of it, it all seemed to come to the same theme: the tragedy of man. (Would he have become a writer?)

In a downtown cafeteria one day, he began reading one of his essays to me. Between huge hungry mouthfuls of an egg sandwich I was destroying, I tried to project the image of an interested listener. At first, Sammy read quietly, and there were just the two of us. But as he got in deeper, he gradually increased his volume. I began to glance around nervously. Sammy bore on and soon assumed what I then thought was a Churchillian (Churchill at that time having burst on us as a world figure) tone. It was probably not Churchillian at all; most likely it was Sammy Sampas emoting in his own pure way.

Sammy was about halfway into his essay, when I realized that what had begun as an audience of one (me) had multiplied quickly so that our area had expanded into a little amphitheater and Sammy was winging off into ancient Greek tragic heights. The faces of the people around me told me that they were caught between laughter and admiration. *I* was caught between trying to enjoy my sandwich and somehow letting Sammy know that I was feeling embarrassed.

Sammy flew on, steadily gaining oratorical altitude. Soon he had left us all behind, and I was stranded on the ground with the others with the squirming feeling that I had to explain to them what the hell was going on. This feeling was soon relieved by a voice, other than Sammy's, that came clattering through. "Why don't you hire a hall." Laughter echoed. I was certain that this would bring Sammy back to earth. I was even more disturbed when I saw that it seemed to stimulate him to higher soaring.

The laughter sputtering all around me finally pushed me to say, "It sounds great, Sammy. Why don't you read the rest of it to me when we get out of here. There are too many distractions."

It took him a few seconds to descend. He gave me a surprised look, one that seemed to mirror disbelief at the absurdity of my suggestion. "I'll be through in a few minutes," he said. And so he pressed on and finished his reading; and when a few applauded, he smiled. "I see we had an audience," he said and I was amazed and bewildered by my friend ,Sammy Sampas.

We headed out of the cafeteria and began walking slowly to the city library. Sammy wanted to talk about his essay. "I wrote it last night," he said. "I think it needs more polishing. What do you think?"

I didn't know what the hell to think — because I had actually heard so little of it. "Well, you can always improve something you've written," I said evasively. "Isn't that what English teachers tell us?"

"I suppose so," Sammy answered blandly. Then his voice took on a note that I rarely heard. It had its usual emotional quality but it was muted. "I'm going to read it to Jack tonight," he said. "No offense to you, Chuck, but Jack really knows, really hears with a beautiful ear."

"I suppose he reads some of *his* things to you," I said in mild derision.

"You know that's strange," responded Sammy, ignoring my needling. "I have to beg Jack to let me read some of his essays."

"Are they any good?"

"I think *some* of them are." Sammy looked at me earnestly. "There is so much feeling in Jack. You just don't know how deep he is. We're both reading Thomas Wolfe now and every time we get together we just can't get over how beautiful his writing is. A few days ago, he was reading to me from Wolfe. Jack reads beautifully. Anyway, as he was reading, he came to a passage that was just too much for both of us. Jack stopped reading. We looked at each other and do you know what happened? We both had tears in our eyes! I mean it! We were so overcome! We decided that Thomas Wolfe was the greatest writer that ever lived."

I confess I was intrigued by the scene of Sampas and Kerouac sitting there, staring at each other, and crying. "You mean a tough football player like Kerouac was bawling over something he was reading?" I threw the thought at Sammy.

"Tough?" Sammy threw it back. "Jack tough?" He looked at me as if I had uttered an obscenity. "Jack is the most gentle person I know."

"Gentle?" I challenged. "For Christ's sake, Sammy," I said, "haven't you ever seen a football game? They don't just sit around and smile at each other."

Sammy shook his head impatiently. "You don't have to believe this," he said, "but the only reason he plays football is because his father is driving him to it. That's right. Jack has told me this. He said his father told him that he couldn't afford to send him to college. So Jack struggled to get a football scholarship. But it's more than that even. Jack says that his father is pushing him to football because he's got this pride thing."

"Pride thing?"

"Yes. His father loves to go all over town and tell anybody who will listen to him what a great star his son is. I think it's terrible. Jack doesn't want any of that."

"What *does* he want?"

I remember Sammy pausing at this question and turning his eyes upward. "Jack wants to read all the beautiful literature of the world," he said quietly. "And he wants to feel all the deep things in the world. Nobody understands Jack except me. Not his mother, and certainly not his father."

"Then why don't you adopt him?" I tried to be flippant.

Sammy ignored my attempt. "We have adopted each other," he said. "We are really like brothers. Did you know that Jack had a brother who died years ago?"

"No, I didn't."

"Jack read me a beautiful thing he had written about his brother. I almost burst into tears while he was reading it." What I did not know then, of course, (and neither did Sammy) was that he was revealing the early period of gestation in Kerouac's mind of the book that was to be written some twenty years later. The book: *Visions of Gerard.*

In June of 1940, Sampatis George Sampatacacus (that's how

66

his name was listed on the commencement program) I, and about 1,000 other students graduated from Lowell High School. I saw Sampati, Sammy, Sebastian — sporadically after that. He went to Emerson College in Boston in pursuit of a career in the theatre arts, though I don't doubt that he was also intent on writing as an additional outlet for his creative urge. I don't doubt this because in one of our meetings, he spent about an hour showing, reading and explaining to me a poem he had recently written. I had gone this route before, of course: Sammy baring his artistic soul before me. I remember the poem as some kind of foreboding about the war which had already started in Europe; and I remember Sammy reading it like a member of a Shakespearean theatre group. (No doubt, his Emerson College training had started to assert itself). I praised his poem — somewhat charitably I thought.

We talked about our mutual friends who had scattered following our high school graduation. And we, or rather, Sammy, talked of Jack Kerouac. Kerouac had finished his first year at Columbia University.

"I feel terrible about Jack," he was saying. "He was telling me that he feels so lost. This Columbia University thing is really getting him down."

"I don't understand," I prodded.

"Well, it isn't what he wants to do. You know he's there on a football scholarship and half the time he spends practicing and playing in the games. It's just dreadful. He was telling me that he doesn't have time to do any of his homework or even any of the type of reading that we loved to do when he was in Lowell."

Years later in Lowell, Kerouac was to reminisce one day about his Columbia football days. Jim Curtis and I were stitting with him in my living room. "Why these college athletes have it easy today," he was protesting. "When I was at Columbia in my freshman year I ran my tail off. First of all, I had to wash dishes for my meals. Then I remember that one of the first reading assignments I got was to read *The Iliad* by Tuesday and *The Odyssey* by Friday. But in between, I had to go to my classes, then travel two hours from the Columbia campus to Baker Field, and practice for three hours. This was every day! Why, by Jesus, I never got to read *The Iliad* or *The Odyssey*! I remember I

67

opened up the first page of *The Iliad*, read the first line, 'Sing goddess the wrath of Achilles,' and fell off my chair and went to sleep on the floor of my room! Besides, what the hell did I want to read *The Iliad* for, with all its helmet crashing, brain smashing, body mangling, when I got the same thing everyday at Baker Field! Why, I was Achilles ranging the battlefield, looking for Trojans to devour. I was creating my *own* Iliad!"

While Kerouac was rampaging, I thought of Sammy Sampas' words years earlier. "You know, Jack," I said, "a long time ago, somebody else was talking to me about your Columbia adventure."

He frowned. "Who was that?" he demanded mockingly. "Was it Agamemnon? Why that sonumbitch should have had his balls snipped."

"No, it wasn't Agamemnon. It was another Greek, one that was generous, kind, and full of love."

"There's no such Greek," he said, and then he cackled.

"There was at least one," I pursued. "One that we both knew quite well." Kerouac waited. "Sampatis Sampatacacus, better known as Sebastian or Sammy Sampas," I announced.

Kerouac shook his head slowly, disbelievingly I thought. "Man," he said, "that goes back a millenium. Sebastian, yes. The Prince of Crete." He tipped his head and stared at me. "Sammy talked to you about my Columbia days?" he said.

"He sure did, Jack," I replied. "He was lamenting your unhappiness there."

"Oh sure. That was Sammy all right. He was always lamenting about something. But then, that's what made him such a beautiful kid."

"And I guess that's what made him such an interesting character for some of your books," I said.

"Well, everything I wrote about his character is true. It is all Sammy, the heart and soul of him."

"Did you ever think you'd marry his sister?" I suddenly asked.

"Marry his sister?" Kerouac echoed. He appeared to be thinking it over. "There was a time in my magnificent days of youth when I had made up my mind to be ever the world traveler, to be a first mate, or maybe even a captain of a great merchant ship that would touch all the mighty seaports of the world — from Hong Kong to Piraeus — and at each of them, I would have a beautiful courtesan at my fingertips. They would look like Marlene Dietrich or Hedy Lamar and *I* would look like Clark Gable or John Wayne or Larry 'Buster' Crabbe or Kane Richmond."

I think I blinked at the last two names; I think Curtis did, too. "I thought Crabbe was Tarzan," said Curtis.

"I said I wanted to *look* like him," retorted Kerouac.

"And who the Christ is Kane Richmond?" Curtis came on again.

I've been a movie buff all my life. "He and guys like Robert Lowery were considered kings of the B movies," I informed him somewhat arrogantly.

Kerouac threw me a frowning stare. "For a goddam professor," he said, "you sure know some weird things." Then he turned to Curtis. "But as a matter of fact, he's right. Guys like Kane Richmond and Robert Lowery were regarded as the poor man's Clark Gable. But as a kid, I used to love their movies. They were either on some ship in the Far East or on some Colorado mining camp. They were great."

"But did you ever think you would marry Sammy Sampas's sister?" I replayed my question.

Kerouac blew out some breath as I remember it and seemed uncomfortable with the question. But he didn't evade it. "When I was going out with Sammy," he began slowly, "I at first thought he was some kind of a strange kid. Certainly, he was nothing like my other friends. He was a big old kid who lumbered or shambled along; I guess today you would probably use the word, klutz. I was the big athlete and sometimes I wondered what the hell I was doing hanging around with this guy. As a matter of fact, my Phebe, Gershom, Sarah Avenue buddies wondered about it, too. 'Hey Zagg,' they'd say to me, 'what the hell do you see in that crazy Greek?' I'm doing an experimental study, I'd say."

"*Were* you Jack?" Curtis asked.

"Well yeah, you could say that, in a way. My whole life has been a kind of experimental study."

"You mean digging people?" I said.

"Yeah."

"And you dug Sammy," I encouraged.

He seemed to suddenly become impatient. "Sammy was a

starry-eyed kid who saw the world through the mists of a beautiful dawn or a twilight haze."

"Why Jack," I went at him, "that is so devastatingly poetic!" He drew himself up in a gesture of arrogance. "What would an English professor know about poetry?" he hit back.

"Nothing," I went along with him, "absolutely nothing."

"You bet your Greek bippie," he said.

"You were saying about Sammy Sampas?" I resumed.

I think he tried to sneer at me, but succeeded only in breaking out in a smile. "Sammy, Sebastian, Savas, Sabbas Alexander Panos — they were all that other part of me. I say they; of course, they were all one person. Sammy made it a joy for me to be alive. Oh, I'd get shit house at him once in awhile, because occasionally, he'd make me feel that everything else I was doing, like playing football, seeing my other friends, etc., was a waste of time. And in a way, he was right; because if there was any doubt as to what I should do with my life, that doubt disappeared after I met Sammy."

"You mean about deciding to become a writer," I interposed.

"I mean that I knew then that I wanted to be a scholar, a creative person."

"You probably were always that, Jack," I said. "Sammy helped you believe it."

He grinned. "I remember talking with Sammy's brother, Charlie." (Charles Sampas is the news editor of The Lowell Sun and has been associated with that newspaper for many years). "Charlie told me," Kerouac went on, "that if I wanted to become a writer, the first thing I must do is to get out of Lowell. I've never forgotten those words."

"You certainly took his advice, Jack," said Curtis.

"The more I think of it, Jack," I said, "the more I'm beginning to realize how much of an influence the Sampas family has had on your life." Kerouac seemed amused. I continued. "First, there was Sammy; then Charlie obviously impressed you with his advice; then you really became part of the Sampas clan by marrying Stella. I think you planned it that way all along," I added facetiously.

Kerouac did not smile. "It's a rusty cliché," he said evenly,

70

"but marrying Stella was the best thing that ever happened to me."

"Even if I wanted to — which I don't," I said, "I never could argue with you on that." There was a short lull; I broke it with, "You probably don't know this, but Stella was a good friend of my sister Pat when they were both young girls. They were members of the Holy Trinity Church choir here in Lowell." Jack's facial reaction prompted me to add, "You didn't know that your wife sang, did you?" He was obviously pleased. "And let me tell you something else you probably aren't aware of: your sweet little wife Stella was also a thespian." Kerouac raised his eyebrows and then stared at Curtis as if seeking confirmation that his ears had not deceived him. "That's right, Jack," I kept going. "Stella was in a play that a church group put on. My sister Pat was in it, too. I saw that play; I remember it very vividly. All the parts — men's and women's — were played by girls from the Greek community of Lowell."

"Sort of a reverse on acting during Shakespeare's day, right?" Kerouac offered. There were times when he loved to show that he was well read. I always felt that this intermittent pedantry had something to do with his failure to graduate from college; a compensatory motivation, you might say. His allusion to Shakespeare's day was concerned, of course, with the idea that young boys assumed the girls' parts in a play.

I nodded at Kerouac's Shakespeare information. "This play that Stella and Pat were in was a comedy, and the dialogue was in Greek, no less. The audience was made up of Greek immigrants and their offspring — like me and Curtis here."

"That's a hell of an audience my poor little wife had to face!" Kerouac said.

"Well, she faced it, Jack," I said, "and as I remember it, she did a great job." He looked pleased. "You're not the only one with artistic talent in the Kerouac family," I added.

There was a sudden sad light in Kerouac's eyes. "Stella's talent," he said quietly, "goes beyond anything that *I* could claim. Stella's talent is pure, unselfish love."

Jack's visit to my house that day ended on other topics, but his words on his wife, Stella, and her brother Sammy left me with a rather intriguing concept. Granted the husband-wife relationship

71

of Kerouac and Stella Sampas, Jack Kerouac loved Stella for another reason: she rekindled for Kerouac the virtues of his youthful companion, Sammy; Stella's innate sensitivity refocused her brother's character — and Jack Kerouac found inordinate comfort in this.

There were those who believed that when Kerouac married Stella Sampas, he merely did so to acquire a nurse for his invalid mother. Certainly, the life style they adopted following the marriage seems to strengthen this opinion. The newly married couple, together with Kerouac's mother, moved from Cape Cod to Lowell in 1966. Not long before this, Kerouac's mother had suffered a crippling stroke. When they settled in Lowell, a rather monotonous pattern evolved: when he wasn't writing, Kerouac wore a path between his house and Nicky's Cafe, a bar owned by a brother-in-law; Stella and her mother-in-law took up pretty much of a recluse existence; I rarely saw Kerouac's mother whenever I visited their home — she was usually out of sight in a back room, and Stella was usually with her.

Despite this arrangement during Kerouac's last years in Lowell, there are additional factors evident that seriously challenge, if not defeat, the concept that Kerouac married Stella Sampas "to take care of his mother." In 1962, in one of his infrequent visits to Lowell, Kerouac met with Stella Sampas a number of times. He had known her years before when Kerouac became a firm friend of her brother, Sammy. In his 1962 visit, Kerouac stayed a few days in Tony Sampas's house. (Tony is another of Stella's many brothers.) What appears to have happened during this period is that the Sampas family "adopted" Jack Kerouac; they took him into their family circle and Kerouac was more than appreciative. He had reason to be; because even though Kerouac was a Lowell native, had written novels about Lowell, knew many people in Lowell (among them his old boyhood chums), had relatives still living in Lowell — despite all this, Kerouac had no place to stay, unless he wanted to stay at a motel. There must be some paradox in there somewhere.

Sometime ago, I talked with Tony Sampas about Kerouac's stay in Lowell in 1962. According to him, Jack was delighted to be back in his hometown. "He even considered buying a house in Lowell at that time," Tony said to me. "There was something here that he had never let go."

"Maybe," I said, "he was trying to prove one of his literary idols, Thomas Wolfe, wrong. Maybe he was trying to tell him that you *can* go home again."

"I saw Jack every day that he was here," Tony revealed. "Stella saw him almost as much."

I reminded Tony that during that visit, my friend Jim Curtis and I had done a radio interview with Jack on a local station. "As a matter of fact, Tony," I said, "on that broadcast, Jack actually volunteered the comment that he wouldn't mind moving back to Lowell. At the time he said this, I thought he was just trying to be nice, just trying to make us believe that Lowell still held a great interest for him." As I talked to Tony, I also thought of something else. "I had almost forgotten," I went on. "Your sister, Stella, was in the studio with us on the day that we taped the broadcast. That's right; and Jack mentions her on the tape."

Tony smiled. "Well, as I said, Jack came to know Stella very well during this stay and — this may surprise you — he wanted to marry her *then*."

I *was* surprised. "But it didn't happen," I said.

"No it didn't. But after Jack left, he went back to Orlando, Florida where his mother lived. The following year, Jack and his mother moved to Northport, New York and Stella visited them up there."

"Their relationship then continued," I said.

"Yes. And the next three years, Jack and his mother moved back to Florida and then back up north to Hyannis at Cape Cod."

"And that's where he married Stella."

"Right. Jack had bought a house in Hyannis and Stella and others of us visited him there. We had some wonderful times there. And Jack's mother really liked it there. But it was strange, because Jack was the one who wanted to move back to Lowell. Stella didn't especially want to come back. Then just before they got ready to come to Lowell, his mother suffered this stroke. I remember her before that as a vigorous woman who talked freely. Jack was really disturbed when she got sick."

"So they came to Lowell," I said.

"That's right," Tony punctuated my remark.

"Thinking about this now, Tony," I volunteered, "it was very fortunate for Jack that Stella married him when she did — I mean with Jack's mother becoming sick so suddenly, so unexpectedly." Tony nodded in agreement.

I truly meant what I said, for in the last years of his life, Jack Kerouac needed someone like Stella Sampas. He needed somebody who could suffer the agonizing spectacle of his slow death by drinking and offer to him in return the saving grace of being truly loved by someone; he needed somebody who would accept with mercy the care of his mother — though I'm convinced that this was not overwhelmingly significant in Kerouac's proposal of marriage to Stella; he needed somebody to bring him a pure loving concern, especially during the long spells of loneliness in his few remaining years when his crown as King of the Beats had lost its glitter and his books had begun to molder, and the door of his home now opened to admit just a few friends who still remembered him.

Finally, Stella Sampas Kerouac brought to her husband strains of another era when he was a youth in Lowell walking along the Merrimack River, talking with her brother, Sammy, feeling the strength of his magnificent compassion. I believe that my own sister, Pat, who knew Stella well, put it best when she said to me: "I remember her best during our church choir days. She was somewhat shy but whenever she talked, there was this tone in her voice that made you feel she would never do or say anything that would hurt you." I think if Jack Kerouac were alive today, he would agree with my sister, Pat.

CHAPTER 7 - SYMPOSIUM — AND THEN SOME

Yet long before Jack Kerouac married Stella Sampas and came back to his native Lowell, he met other people in other places. Jack Kerouac graduated from Lowell High School in June, 1939. The five years that followed saw him go through a period of inconsistency in terms of his later emergence as a writer. He attended Horace Mann Prep School for a year, thence to Columbia University where he was being groomed as a football star. After his freshman year there, Kerouac went back anticipating this football stardom — it never materialized. He quit before the semester began.

He remembers it years later in *Vanity of Duluoz*: "Morning, breakfasts, saltpeter so we wouldn't get horny, showers, taping, aching muscles, hot September sun tacklings of silly dummies held by assistant coaches and idiots with cameras taking our pictures dodging this way and that . . . I began to see that good old Lu Libble (Lou Little) wasn't going to start me in the starting lineup but let me sit on the bench . . . He insulted me in front of everybody (again) by saying, 'You're not such a hot runner, you can't handle the KT-79 reverse deception' . . . I stared into the darkness of the bunkrooms thinking what to do."

Kerouac didn't stare too long; he packed up and went home. It was at this juncture of his life that a seldom to be broken skein of quarrels evolved between him and his father. This was the first deviation by Jack Kerouac; the first expression of his disenchantment with the American success. His father was bewildered.

After leaving Columbia, Kerouac worked at odd jobs for awhile. There were short stays in Connecticut and Washington, D.C. December 7, 1941 found him in Lowell, becalmed, drifting, wondering. It was soon after this that he got a job in the sports department of The Lowell Sun. "I could have been another Grantland Rice," he told me years later. "I wrote some immortal stuff for that one lung newspaper." This was his boasting but really self-satirizing tone.

An example of Kerouac's abbreviated sports-writing career

justifies his satirical tone. This article appeared in the February 19, 1942 edition of The Lowell Sun and Citizen-Leader (all one newspaper); his by-line was mispelled: Jack Korouac.

"Coming back for the second half of their game with the Lawrence high hoopsters in an aroused mood, Coach Jimmy Liston's Lowell high basketballers staged a brilliant reversal of first half form in the Memorial Auditorium last night and took control of the situation for the remainder of the game, winning 32-21 in a well-played and exciting engagement. The renewal of the hoop classic between the rival schools drew a large and enthusiastic gathering of fans.

"The Red and Gray got off to a slow start, trailing Lawrence 11-4 at the end of the first canto. A brief rally in the second period brought the locals within two points of the Blue and White, but the Devlin-coached downriver outfit seemed to have the edge in general team balance, and looked as though it was ready to keep it up for the remainder of the clash.

"However, the Kirk streeters poured out on the floor for the second half of the game with renewed gusto. Before a few seconds had elapsed, Tommy Petroules dropped in the tying basket. This was the precursor of a new and vigorous Lowell high attack. The Red and Gray five began to function beautifully, sporting an iron-clad defense, all the while passing and shooting with rare skill. Lawo, Ciszek, and Petroules were splitting the twine from all parts of the floor, while the Lawrence hoopsters were barely able to get near enough for scoring attempts. Captain Payton and Arvanitis were mainly responsible for Lawrence's difficulties, while the two Lowell lads were also extremely effective leading the Lowell plays.

"The score at the end of the third period was 26-16 in favor of Lowell, and the locals had no difficulty maintaining their superiority right up to the end of the clash. The final score read Lowell 32, Lawrence 21, and a grateful ovation was tendered the lads by the victory-minded spectators. Petroules led Lowell in scoring with 11 tallies. Gartside of Lawrence duplicated the feat for the losers, with second honors going to Vose, the Lawrence captain, who bagged five markers. The game was the first of an annual series between the Merrimack valley high school rivals . . ."

Grantland Rice can rest easy in his grave.

I reminded Kerouac that besides his sports prose, he was writing something else at the time. (In *Vanity of Duluoz*, he claims that he was working on a Joycean novel in which he first used the term, Vanity of Duluoz.) His face brightened. "That was — and is — a great novel!" he exclaimed.

My eyes shadowed with doubt. "Then why don't you publish it, Jack," I said.

He acted out a sly movement. "Because the world is not ready for it," he said.

"So you really did the Joyce bit," I said. "Stream of consciousness and all."

"Well, yeah," he said. "But I was still all hung up on Thomas Wolfe and even way back then, I think I knew that if I was ever going to get around to writing a serious novel, it would have a Thomas Wolfe scenario."

"Voila," I said. *"The Town and the City."*

Kerouac looked sad. "Man, that book seems like a million years ago."

Following his short career as a sports writer early in 1942, Kerouac went to Washington, D.C. and worked for awhile in a government construction job. One of his closest boyhood chums was working there in a government office at the time: George Apostolos, better known in Kerouac's literary planet as G. J. Rigopoulos. Kerouac got together with him for a few months.

I've known George Apostolos for many years. In a recent talk with him about Kerouac, he reconstructed this Washington episode in Kerouac's life. "When I left Lowell to go to work in Washington," he told me, "I thought it would be quite a while before I'd see Zagg again — what with the war and all.

I interposed. "Jack uses the name Zagg in some of his books. I had wondered whether it was fictitious. Now I know that it isn't."

"It's a real name," Apostolos assured me. "We called him Zagg, Zaggo, because he was always doing things quick-like, shifting. He called me Fouche."

"So you met him in Washington," I prompted.

"Right. But the *way* I met him is what really shook me up."

I settled back in my chair expectantly. We were sitting in

77

George Apostolos's real estate office in downtown Lowell. He is a tall man with ample graying hair; his voice and manner project him somewhat younger than his fifty-one years.

"I was living in a pretty decent place in Washington," Apostolos continued. "I was rooming with another guy, and we were sharing expenses. One night, as I was sleeping, dead to the world, I'm rudely awakened by somebody holding a spotlight in my face. I heard this voice: 'All right, you lousy songbird, you sang to the cops and now you're gonna get it.' The next thing I realize is that there's a gun stuck right in my face! I'm terrified as you can well imagine. I'm trying to get some words out but I can't get my vocal chords to function! I'm trying to say, 'You've got the wrong guy,' but I can't say it. Remember now, I can't see anything but that gun, because the room was in total darkness except for the spotlight in my face. I was sure that the guy behind that gun had been hired to rub me out, as we used to say in those days. I remember thinking how stupid it would be if I died in this way — a case of mistaken identity, and also how much trouble it would cause my family to transport my body back to Lowell."

Apostolos stopped his narrative and was amused by my laughter. I managed to say, "The whole thing sounds like a George Raft movie."

"You bet it does; only it didn't seem like a movie to me then. I think I finally managed to say something like, 'I didn't do anything.' Then the voice behind the gun comes on again. 'You did it, you dirty little squealer.' Those words were like music to my ears because the way they were said, I knew then who was behind that gun. Only one guy in the world could have spoken them that way — and that was Zagg."

"I suppose," I said, "that after you stopped trembling, you started to laugh."

Apostolos shook his head in disagreement. "Like hell I did. I reached out for him and we tussled a bit. Now don't get me wrong, I was really glad to see him, but I wanted a little revenge after the way he had scared the hell out of me."

"Was that a real gun he had?" I asked.

"It sure was. I forget where he had gotten it from. Anyway Jack was glad to see me." At this point, Apostolos slowed up and looked a bit pensive. "You know, Jack stayed in Washington a few weeks and I saw a great deal of him. As I remember, he worked at a couple of jobs. But it's a funny thing; it seemed to me that he had changed somehow."

"In what way do you mean?" I urged.

Apostolos was striving for clarity. "Well, I'm not quite sure, but his personality was sort of different."

"How long had it been since you had seen him?"

"As I recall, it was quite awhile. After he had gone to Columbia, I didn't see him too much, though I did visit him there once. Then when he came back to Lowell after leaving Columbia, I saw him occasionally. Then I left for Washington, D.C. But really, it's hard to pinpoint. All I know is that from the minute that Zagg caught up with me in Washington, holding that gun in my face in the dark, I sensed a change in him. He was not the careful kid that I had known all my life. He had become loose somehow; that is, he had kind of broken away from his Lowell personality."

"And how would you describe his Lowell personality?" I asked.

My question stopped him for awhile. Then he started again, quickly. "Well, it certainly wouldn't give me a picture of a guy with a gun in his hand."

"But that was just a big joke," I challenged.

"Yeah, I know. But a gun and Jack Kerouac didn't go together. I mean, the last thing Zagg would ever think of was to carry a gun." Apostolos then began shaking his head as he struggled to focus his thoughts. "Another change I noticed," he picked up, "was drinking. I had never seen Zagg drink — until Washington. He hadn't yet become an alcoholic, but I was surprised that he had started to drink. I was really amazed, because he was always a great one for physical conditioning."

When I left George Apostolos, I found that his remark about Kerouac's drinking kept coming at me. Yes, Kerouac's drinking, among things, was a startling departure from his "Lowell personality." But ironically, when Kerouac came back to live in Lowell, the major facet of him that flashed through in the minds of many of his fellow townsmen was that he had always been a boozer.

I think it proper at this juncture of this work to insert an account of an episode that affords deeper penetration into the image of Jack Kerouac. On April 5, 1973, a "Jack Kerouac Symposium" was held at Salem State College in Salem, Massachusetts. The organizer and moderator of this symposium was Assistant Professor of English John W. P. McHale; the panel consisted of Gregory Corso, Allen Ginsberg, John Clellon Holmes, Aaron Latham, Stanley Twardowicz, and myself. The discussion consumed nearly three hours, and an analytical x-ray was mercilessly (though not intentionally vicious) trained on Jack Kerouac. In the constantly shifting play of the discussion, an unscheduled participant would surface. This was Peter Orlovsky, occasional poet and Allen Ginsberg's "wife." It was uncanny (and somewhat comical) the way he would ease into the flow of the dialogue; but it was even more uncanny the way he would inevitably make the thrust of his remarks sound like a hortatory evangelistic tirade against the evils of drinking. He was really a grand cliche of the reformed drunk.

Jack Kerouac was Orlovsky's supreme example of the "wages of drink." He would go on interminably and even though he protested his love and admiration for Kerouac as a literary artist, his conclusion would frame him in a silhouette of the hapless victim of his own spineless character. It was pretty weird, because, as I said, Orlovsky was not a scheduled member of the panel; furthermore, his contributions were pretty much unrelated to the symposium's chief purpose of examining Jack Kerouac, the writer.

Most of the audience appeared amused by Orlovsky's preaching; a few seemed ambivalent. However, one (by his own admission) was incensed by Orlovsky and some of the panel members who tacitly agreed with his observations. This man was Henry Beaulieu. He had been sitting in the audience for a couple of hours and from the tenor of the comment that he made, he had become unhappy and frustrated by the dissipated, degenerate Jack Kerouac image that had been focused before him.

Henry Beaulieu stood up, presumably to ask a question. It was definitely not what he had in mind. He first identified himself as one of Kerouac's closest boyhood friends (though he did not give his name) and then went on to create a brief character sketch of Kerouac — B.B., Before Beat. Beaulieu praised Kerouac as "a wonderful young boy who was interested in sports and lived a good life." Although he spoke briefly, he communicated two distinct thoughts: one, that Kerouac grew up as a normal, healthy American boy; the other thought, though unspoken, came through much louder, much stronger. Henry Beaulieu ended his remark on the move, literally. He began to walk off and as he did so, he said in essence, "Jack Kerouac when I knew him, was a clean cut kid. But when he left Lowell and took up with you guys (Ginsberg, Corso, Orlovsky, et al.), you screwed him all up with booze, drugs and all that Beat Bullshit."

Jack Kerouac romanticizes his boyhood gang: G. J., Vinny, Lousy, and Scotty. They ramble through Kerouac's world, at times shining forth as fantasy figures, as figures in a Charlie Chaplin movie with all the tragicomic essence they so brilliantly portrayed. They're still around, these figures — that is, all but Kerouac. They still live in the Lowell area and the memory of their famous buddy has grown wondrous with the passing years.

However, in recent years, this memory, this remembrance of Kerouac has been threatened, if not supplanted by another image. Dorian Gray and Jack Kerouac may have had some things in common, but unlike Gray, Kerouac had no picture hidden away; his dissipation was constantly on display, and this incessant exhibit has caused most people to forget the beautiful youth that once was. Henry Beaulieu (who was "Scotty" in Kerouac's books) has come forth as a spokesman for "the gang"; he wants to finish the incomplete portrait of Jack Kerouac.

A few days following Beaulieu's comments at the Jack Kerouac Symposium, he wrote a letter to Mary Sampas, feature columnist for The Lowell Sun; she covered the Symposium. (Mary Sampas, by the way, is married to Charles Sampas, Jack Kerouac's brother-in-law). Beaulieu's letter appeared in Mrs. Sampas's column, and it more than adequately states the sensitivities of Kerouac's old buddies. Here it is in part:

"... I was one of Jack's boyhood pals, chumming around with him for over 12 years. I am 51 years old, one month older than Jack. What I did (i.e. coming to Kerouac's defense at the Symposium) was because after Jack's death if you read about him and did not

81

know him as we do, you would picture him as a drunken bum who had a way with words and could write books. I talked with a few of Jack's close friends and we all agreed this was so. Therefore, if you have read any of Jack's books, you know that Scotty fights for his rights and therefore we want people to know that for half of his life Kerouac was a kind, hard working, good-natured friend.

"We, his close friends, are proud to have known him. I speak of G. J., Vinny Bergerac, Maggie Cassidy, Salvey, Kid St. Louis, Red McNulty, Bob Rondeau, Bob McArthur and others . . . I am not much of a book reader but I've read four of Jack's books. Of course, I am in them, but *Maggie Cassidy* is my speed, which is told just as it happened."

Yes, "just as it happened." But a lot of other things happened to Jack Kerouac after he left his old gang, and these other things were to be the backdrop that catapulted him to fame as the King of the Beats. One can not fault Henry Beaulieu for trying to balance the picture as it were, but the tempting thought persists that if Kerouac had remained in Lowell, had he remained the "kind, hard working, good natured friend," his Beat novels would never have been written — and literature would have been poorer for it.

So Kerouac had to leave Lowell, had to confront new people, new situations, new forces — be they good or bad. But after his brief Washington, D.C. stay with George Apostolos in the Spring of 1942, Kerouac came back to Lowell, still in the throes of a young man who felt deeply his need to search, but did not know where to begin. He moved impulsively: he joined the U.S. Marine Corps; that is, he was sworn in and waited to be called. Still impulsively, he ignored this commitment and got on a merchant marine ship, the S.S. Dorchester of "four chaplains fame," and found himself sailing in the North Atlantic heading for Murmansk, Russia.

It was a Melvillian action: young man, writer to be, sails the seas to enrich his soul. What was *not* Melvillian was his account of his last night in Boston before sailing. It's an incredible comment that has to startle and disgust the reader. It appears in

Vanity of Duluoz: "Before we sailed, that morning, as I said in *On The Road* book I actually got so drunk I wrapped myself around the toilet bowl of the Scollay Square Cafe and got pissed and puked on all night long by a thousand sailors and seamen and when I woke up in the morning and found myself all covered and caked and unspeakably dirty I just like a good old Boston man walked down to the Atlantic Avenue docks and jumped into the sea, washed myself, grabbed a raft, came up, and walked to my ship fairly clean." [17]

Ah, but that is fiction you say. Nothing that Jack Kerouac ever wrote was fiction, was ever contrived. One of his favorite sayings about his works was, "It is all true stories." As for the above quoted passage, we know that a thousand sailors were not involved; we can even challenge the all night toilet bowl scene; but what we can not dispute is Kerouac's monumental, destructive drunkenness that night. The clean cut Lowell kid, "Scotty" Beaulieu's boyhood pal, was on his way.

Yet the scene seems to say even more than the beginning of another dimension for Jack Kerouac. The physical horror involved: "got pissed and puked on," he writes, The unutterable indignity is worthy of a biblical martyr. The narrator suffers this indignity, cleanses himself, and walks up to his ship a new man. It sounds like a passion play, resurrection and all.

Kerouac wrote this account during his last years in Lowell. When the book was published in 1967, he was still living in Lowell. I talked with him about it one night. "It's a bit like your first book, Jack, *The Town and the City*," I said, "Only in this one you are speaking 'ex cathedra'; you are the old philosopher."

"I ain't no philosopher, Jarvis," he quickly checked me. "A philosopher is a guy who sits on his ass all day and watches people go by. And when he gets a bit bored, he jots down a few notes — or plays with himself."

"You never played with yourself?" I tried to provoke him.

He frowned. "I stopped when I was sixteen," he said. "When are *you* going to stop?"

I laughed. "When *you* do," I answered. I didn't allow him to react to this; I followed quickly with, "No, Jack. I mean this book, *Vanity of Duluoz,* goes over a lot of ground that you covered in *The Town and the City.*"

"You mean to say that I'm repeating myself?" he mocked a sense of outrage. "How dare you insult me this way!"

As always, I was amused by his antics. But I wanted to go on. "I mean that in *Vanity,* you appear to tell it like it was, whereas in your first book, you're the romantic kid who always seems to hear moonlight music in the background."

He threw a half stare at me. This was a favorite gesture of his; I always interpreted it to say: "Hey, that's not bad, but I think I can do better." There was nothing malicious about it, because Kerouac liked people too much for that; it was merely a touch of ego — which he had certainly earned.

"Moonlight music in the background," he responded to my comment. "Ah yess," He was W. C. Fields now. This was a choice portrayal with him. He suddenly dropped it. "If you're implying that *The Town and the City* had some fakery in it, then you'd better give up your title of English Professor at Lowell Tech. There isn't a word of fakery in anything I've ever written."

"Simmer down, Jack," I said. He wasn't really getting angry; I think *I* was getting annoyed. "I'm only saying that in *Vanity,* you're looking back after twenty-five years or so, and you see some things differently."

"Well, of course I do. Doesn't everybody? But there are some things in both books that I've never changed my mind about."

"Such as?"

"Such as the fact I had to fight against favoritism, coaching stupidity and every other kind of human horseshit (yes that's the term he used) you can think of, to emerge as the star of the Lowell High football team."

"What else?"

"My friendship with Sammy Sampas, who, if he hadn't been killed in the war, would today be my favorite brother-in-law. I've never changed my mind about him and what he meant to me." I saw Kerouac's eyes get filmy; I had seen him get this way before — when he talked about his brother, Gerard.

I tried to divert him. "*Vanity of Duluoz* is more confessional, Jack," I said. "After all, you *are* addressing it to Stella, your sweet little wife."

"And I couldn't think of a better father confessor," he said.

I nodded. "It's kind of interesting, Jack" I asserted, "that you wrote *Vanity* in a conventional prose style; I mean that you abandoned your driving, Beat classical attack on ideas. From that aspect, it's similar to your very first book, *The Town and the City*."

"Anything wrong with that?" he demanded. "I had to catch the attention of today's reader who's all fucked up living in a T.V. kindergarten world."

"You say as much, Jack, in your very first paragraph when you use the term illiterate generation."

"That wasn't very nice," he said. "But I meant it."

"Also, there's a hell of a lot of bitterness in this book, Jack. You seem to be remembering things with a kind of anger, a kind of regret."

"Regret? Me?" He gave a short laugh, as if he were satisfied about something. "That's how much you professors know," he continued. "My only regret is that I didn't tell off more of the fuckheads that I met on the way. My father was great for that. That's what made him so great. But if I have another regret, it's that I didn't meet a thousand other guys who knew more about writing and love and beauty than *I'll* ever know."

It was the term "a thousand other guys" that pinged in my mind. I had heard Kerouac use it before. As he looked at me, waiting for a response to his words, it came to me: it was in our radio broadcast of a few years before when Jim Curtis and I had interviewed him on WCAP, Lowell. Kerouac had been talking about his hometown when he suddenly injected the thought: "There are a thousand guys out there who know more about heaven than I do."

I reminded Kerouac of this quote; he lapsed into flippancy: "Now that you've learned to quote Kerouac, you've arrived, you dingbat professor."

"Then I'll give you another quote," I followed seeing an opening. It was an opening I had been seeking regarding the "thousand sailors and seamen" passage in *Vanity of Duluoz*. "You talk about wrapping yourself around a toilet bowl and having a thousand sailors pissing and puking on you," I said. "Seems to me that there's always been a thousand guys in your life either doing something better than you can do it, or stomping all over you or being better than you are. What's all this self-abasement, Jack?"

I was sure that he wasn't going to be flippant this time. He drank from his ever present bottle. "Self-abasement?" he began. "I have never practiced self-abasement. From the time I was a little kid, I wanted to excel — and I did. My mother and father taught me a sense of pride that left no room for a morbid self-pity. I mean, it wasn't the kind of pride that made you feel you were better than anybody else; it was the sort of thing that gave you confidence and made you put everything you had into going after something." I had noticed that as he was expressing these words, his gaze was increasingly diverted away from me. "Self-abasement?" he repeated, and with this, his gaze came back and fixed on me; it gave off a nuance of having eliminated a problem.

But the problem wasn't eliminated. "I can understand your kind of pride, Jack," I said. "But your intermittent reference to these one thousand guys—"

"What one thousand guys?" he cut in. "Who are these fucken one thousand guys?"

I knew immediately that I had touched a nerve. I also knew that I had to make a split decision on whether to pursue or drop the subject. I certainly didn't want to quarrel with him. I realized that he was more in pain than in anger. "I guess I'm being over interpretive, Jack," I said. "That's the way professors are, always looking for obscure symbols; and most of the time, the symbols aren't even there."

I could see that Kerouac appreciated my breaking away. He smiled. "Now if you want to know something about my sailing days," he said, "why then frame your question. Or better still, I'll save you the trouble." He cleared his throat accompanied by another draught from his bottle. I remember that this gesture reminded me of Joseph Conrad's story, "Youth," in which Marlow sits around a table with his friends, passing the bottle around, and exchanging stories about their earlier sea adventures. Kerouac and I were not passing the bottle back and forth; Conrad's story faded quickly from my mind.

"I sailed the North Atlantic just like Bogey did with Raymond Massey in that movie, remember?" Kerouac went on. "But I was better than them, because I caught the whole thing in my mind. James Joyce went up to Cornwall to catch the sounds of the Atlantic, but he died before he could do it. Well, I'm doing it for him. And before I'm through, I'm going to catch the sounds of all the oceans of the world — from the Indian Ocean all the way up to the Bering Straits."

"That sounds great, Jack," I said, "but right now I'm interested in your voyage on the S.S. Dorchester."

"It's all down there in *Vanity of Duluoz*," he protested mildly. "Or haven't you learned how to read yet?"

"Maybe that's my problem," I went along. "That's why I want you to tell me about it."

Kerouac had this short laugh which gave off an attitude of coyness and amusement. He responded now with this laugh. "If your mind is as dirty as I *think* it is," he said, "then I'll tell you right now that, yes, there *was* buggery on the S.S. Dorchester." I confess I was surprised at the sudden introduction of this subject; it didn't matter, really, but I rather expected some observations on the sea. I said nothing, but waited. "There was always some hairy guy," he continued, "who lusted after some fair skinned lad like me. But I was too fast for them and they couldn't corner me! But there were some fair lads who weren't as fast as I was — and they were buggered but good! I remember one kid who came to me all shook up and crying that his insides had been destroyed and that he was going to die. We must have been in the middle of the North Atlantic by then and I recall how stupid his words about dying sounded to me; because I knew that at any time we could have been torpedoed into eternity and that we'd never get a chance to die of a nice longlasting disease like tuberculosis or cancer. Anyway, this kid tells me that a black, mustachioed Bulgarian stuck it to him the night before and he was sure that he was dying of some horrible thing!"

"You're a long way from your prose-poetry sounds of the sea, Jack," I said.

"That only shows how little you know about the sea!" he raised his voice. "Are you sure you're Greek?" he added. "What do you think that Greek fleet that headed for Troy was doing? They were sailing on the beautiful Aegean Sea and they must have been thinking about possibly dying on the plains of Troy. They'd look up at the stars at night and wonder if they'd ever get a piece of ass again. So what could be more natural than to pick out a nice tender little cabin boy and reach the heights of ecstasy one more time!"

"There were no cabins on Greek ships in those days," I needled.

"Maybe not," he came right back, "but they sure had some boys!"

"So what did you tell that nice lad who thought he was going to die from the disease of the Bulgarian bugger?" I could see he was tickled by my term, Bulgarian bugger.

"I told him that he was not going to die and that all he had to do was to take some castor oil and all would be well."

"By the way, Jack," I said, having now completely accepted my role of straight man in this phase of our dialogue, "you didn't tell me whether this kid had actually been raped or had been a willing lover in this affair."

He released his short laugh again. "Nobody has ever been raped on the high seas — and that's a fact."

Then I decided to become more bold. "Are you sure that you, being a devastatingly handsome lad, did not succumb at least once to such attentions and to what *you* have told me are the charms of the sea?"

"I ain't no Greek."

"But this guy was a Bulgarian."

Kerouac stared at me. "What are you — a fucken lawyer? Don't you know that sodomy is a sin. You'll never get to heaven *that* way."

"Do you really want to get to heaven, Jack?"

"Do I want to get to *heaven?*" he threw it back at me, seemingly shocked at the crassness of my question. "Why, that's all I'm working for down here — to get up there."

I was about to respond with the idea of self-abnegation and his thoughts about "a thousand guys knowing more about heaven than he did" and "a thousand sailors pissing and puking on him all night" — thoughts that show the lowly place Kerouac assigned himself on the human scale. I say I was about to respond in this way — but I didn't; it would have served no purpose. If

I had suggested to Kerouac that he was constantly wallowing in a swampy bog of guilt and that the above references were screaming, hysterical proof of it, he would have responded with an anger reflecting the absurdity of such an idea or an uncomprehending stare. Yes, an uncomprehending stare; because Kerouac never did know why he battered himself,why he was the incessant, medieval flagellant. Therefore, the last thing I would have done in this particular dialogue (or any dialogue) with Kerouac was to raise the specter of his long dead brother, Gerard, whose place Kerouac always felt he had usurped, or to advance the evidence that his Catholic child years had strapped on him an horrendous moral straightjacket against which he continually struggled and exhausted himself, but from which he never escaped.

No. I said none of these things when Kerouac expressed to me his desire to ascend to heaven and stated, "Why, that's all I'm working for down here — to get up there."

I said, "If anybody has a chance of making it, Jack, it's you."

He was pleased, of course. "That's because I'm a holy bum!" he exclaimed. "There aren't many of us left, you know."

A few weeks after this conversation, the matter of "sodomy on the high seas" came up again — but in a somewhat different way. My attorney friend, Jim Curtis, had acquired a client from England. This client was a young man who had moved to Lowell and was starting a business venture in the area. In one of their meetings, it somehow came out that this young man was an avid reader of Kerouac. He became very excited when Curtis informed him of his close friendship with Kerouac; the young Englishman, of course, wanted to meet the celebrated writer.

It was soon all arranged. Curtis and I picked up Kerouac at his house and drove to the Englishman's home. A lovely young lady (the Englishman's wife) met us at the door. As we walked in, another lovely lady (the Englishman's mother-in-law visiting from England) greeted us. Finally, the young Englishman confronted us and his native accent was spilling all over the place as he verbally embraced Kerouac. So the six of us sat down and began rapping.

In the beginning, Kerouac did not say much; he seemed satisfied to listen to his English admirers. Oh yes, they (all three) had read many of his books; they found them a thrilling reading experience; many of their friends in merry old England are great Kerouac fans; they are looking forward to reading his latest book, *Vanity of Duluoz;* and on and on.

Curtis and I were somewhere in the middle of this "one way conversation." Our principal function was an occasional informative remark about Kerouac which made us feel awkward, really, because Kerouac, himself, could have supplied this information — and with more skill, more authority. But Kerouac sat there, mostly listening — and drinking. When we had picked him up at his house, he was well on his way to his alcoholic ambience. Now he was well into it.

I don't recall exactly what remark released Kerouac from his initial reserve, but I'm sure it was something about Shakespeare. "Now Shakespeare,"he responded, "was a man after my own heart. He checked everybody out and there wasn't a single person who could pull the wool over *his* eyes. He knew where everybody was at in this world."

"Just like *you're* trying to do, Jack, right?" I said, hoping to encourage him to go on. I didn't have to encourage him; he was off and running.

As he bore on, his English audience became absorbed. The two ladies especially reacted rapturously to almost every syllable that Kerouac uttered. Curtis and I sat back and enjoyed the scene. "All this talk," Kerouac was sailing along, "about Shakespeare's plays having been written by Marlowe or Bacon or somebody else is ridiculous. Bacon by the way was also known as Lord Verulam." As he threw this last line in, he glanced over at me. Though I could have been wrong, I interpreted this gesture to say: "you may be an English professor, Jarvis, but I know something about literature, too."

"Now as I said," he continued, "Shakespeare is a man after my own heart because he was the first great exponent of natural prose. He never changed a single word after he wrote it down. I don't think Shakespeare spent more than a couple of days and nights on each of the plays he wrote."

"Does that make you a literary descendant of Shakespeare, Jack?" I interrupted. He drew back in an exaggerated pose of self-importance; and it was here that the "fun" (depending on your sense of propriety) began. "You, Jack," I added, "are the modern exponent of spontaneous prose. You are carrying on in the tradition of the Bard."

I just knew from the pose that Kerouac had assumed that there would be a sudden change in the tone of our visit to this Englishman's home. Up to the point that Kerouac had been talking about Shakespeare, he was the professional writer expounding professional opinions about authors and writing. If my remark about his literary descent from Shakespeare was begun in seriousness, I knew before I finished it — from the look on Jack's face — that it served the purpose of releasing him from the writer's image and allowing him to function in his natural, uninhibited form.

"The Bard, ah yes, the Bard," Kerouac echoed my term. "Do you know that Shakespeare began in the theater as a young kid? I mean he began by holding the horses of actors, outside the theater. I can just see him now, a child, standing outside and yearning to be a part of the world of drama. Reminds me of myself when I was a kid walking the streets of Lowell dreaming of far off lands and great adventures."

"Well you certainly have traveled, Mr. Kerouac," said the mother-in-law in elegant British tones. "Your books are marvelous testimonials of that."

Kerouac, ever ready to assume a role, bowed his head slightly, "Yes, Madame," he said striving to sound British, "I have gone hither and yon, I have sailed the bounding main."

What followed was not entirely unexpected by me; what surprised me was the timing; I thought he would sustain his role a little longer; but he didn't. "I got buggered once when I was a handsome lad sailing as a scullion on the high seas," he blurted. Now, this was Kerouac; Kerouac abandoning a pose, dropping a pretense, crapping on intellectualism, laughing at pretenders.

Kerouac's English audience was frozen momentarily by his remark. I looked at Curtis and I think we began with a snicker and eventually blew up with laughter, a kind of nervous laughter I might say. Kerouac looked at us as if annoyed; he wasn't. "Yeah, that's right," he resumed, returning to the English lady. "I was corn holed by a nasty, lecherous fatso cook who deflowered

91

me." Now the young Englishman joined Curtis and me in pure laughter. I was glad that he did, because Kerouac's sodomean comment created this scene in my mind: the mother-in-law fainting with disgust, the daughter ready to faint in sympathy, and the Englishman ordering us out. The scene remained only a vision.

Though the two ladies did not laugh, they did not fall apart either. "Oh you poor boy, how dreadful," the mother-in-law responded. I almost applauded her magnificent show of classic British stolidity.

"Oh, it was dreadful all right," said Kerouac. "Yes, my dear, it was dreadful."

It was an evening that I have never forgotten. Following his explication on the perils of buggery, he seized the rest of the evening and literally entertained our hosts with raucous bursts of song, sudden outbreaks of crazy dances, long wild narratives of *On The Road* vintage, and any other activity that was born in his fertile brain.

It was one of the few times that I recall seeing him succumb to liquor. No, he didn't pass out and he didn't stagger. I don't think any volume of booze could do that to him. It was his speech that betrayed him. His natural, clear enunciation began to slip and names like Allen Ginsberg and Gregory Corso did not behave for him; Ginsberg became Gissberg and Gregory Corso's name became a grinding sound of r's.

Once the English ladies transcended Kerouac's initial free choice of subject matter and language, they enjoyed themselves. The young Englishman proved even more responsive. He got into some vast exchanges with Kerouac on a number of topics. Modern music (the Beatles, certainly) modern literature, morality, politics — all passed through them. Yet it must be pointed out that he was frustrated at times by Kerouac's capricious changes of direction: but then, that's how Kerouac was.

It took about five attempts to get Kerouac to go home that night. He insisted on a Romeo and Juliet farewell scene — with two Juliets: the mother and the daughter. As bombed as he was, he recited passages from Shakespeare faultlessly. On the way home, Kerouac kept soliciting from us praise for his impromptu performance of Romeo. He also expressed admiration for the two English ladies. "Now *that's* why there'll always be an England," he said. "Because it was women like that who produced men like Shakespeare, the Duke of Wellington, and Lord Nelson."

The last name brought me back to Kerouac's story of his sea experiences — and his recounting of them to the English ladies. It further focused for me the concept that I now had two version of his buggery episode. In the first version which he had related to me, Kerouac was only the narrator; in the second version which he had related to his English listeners, he was both narrator and participant. I could not resist pointing this difference out to Kerouac.

"Which version is the truth, Jack?" I asked — and I suddenly felt a little cruel.

Kerouac looked at me ,smiling. "I've told you before Jarvis," he said, "I ain't no Greek. I'm a writer." I let it go at that. But Kerouac's reference to himself as a writer recalled for me his oft-stated remark that "it's all true stories."

At Jack Kerouac Symposium - Salem State College - April 5, 1973
Left to right: Paul Jarvis, Gregory Corso, Dianne Hughes, Charles
E. Jarvis

At Jack Kerouac Symposium - Salem State College - April 5, 1973
Left to right: Allen Ginsberg, James T. Curtis, Charles E. Jarvis
Photos by Tommy Belkakis

Chapter 8 - Jack "Would Prefer Not To"

In the Fall of 1942, after his first stint in the Merchant Marine, Jack Kerouac decided to try Columbia one more time. This was the period when college football squads were being decimated by the military services, and the caliber of the game would soon descend to a level just short of the high school variety. (The only exceptions here were the two service academies that provided military exemptions and would soon hoard the best football talent in the land. The era of Doc Blanchard and Glen Davis was just around the corner).

To Lou Little, the Columbia University football coach, a player of Kerouac's reputation must have looked like a precious commodity in the fast shrinking supply of good athletes. To Jack Kerouac, the chance to play football once again must have rekindled his boyhood dreams of becoming a great athlete. Both were to see their hopes destroyed.

When the season began, Kerouac found himself riding the bench. He claimed it was like before: his talent was being ignored — or even suppressed; Lou Little was the same old villain who played favorites; even worse, Lou Little was a deceiver of men because he promised Jack's father a job and never came through with it.

After Kerouac became a famous writer, someone asked Lou Little about him. The widely respected coach did not seem to remember very much about Kerouac. When reminded that Kerouac had quit the squad, Little responded quite simply that Kerouac was tired. That was it; no more. If one takes into account the famed reputation of Lou Little as a gentlemen and a winning football coach, it becomes somewhat difficult to accept in toto Kerouac's dark memories of him. Kerouac's failure to become a star on the team — or even a starter — could be attributed simply to his waning talent. It's true, he was still in his prime, twenty; but he had been away from it for a year, a year spent moving about in odd jobs, none of which helped him retain his hard muscled physique. The answer to his failure may be merely a cliché: he was out of shape.

Or the answer may be something else: Kerouac had lost in-

95

terest — though he had never come to terms with this idea. In this second attempt at football glory, he was not a kid fresh out of prep school; he was a merchant seaman who had made the dangerous North Atlantic run, who had boozed and bunked and bantered with a spectrum collection of mates, who had stood by a ship's railing far out at sea and wondered what in the hell it was all about. No, this was no rah, rah kid that stepped out on the practice field at Columbia in the Autumn of 1942.

This he made clear years later when he wrote: "Out on the field, the boys in light blue, Columbia, are all standing around in an early afternoon and here I come jogging out of the club-house for the first time, tightly cleated and ready. I stare at the new boys. All the good old boys are gone into the service. This is a bunch of weak-kneed punks, tall and disjointed and sorta decadent." [18]

One then can begin to understand Kerouac's chaotic state of mind at this time. First, he could not admit to himself that maybe, just maybe, he had been drained out of the last ounze of football desire that at one time was at flood tide stage. Second, he could not co-exist with the idea of warming the bench while the "weak-kneed punks, tall and disjointed and sorta decadent" played most of the game. So here was Kerouac at the age of twenty sensing alarming flashes of being a football has-been. Certainly the thought of being any kind of a has-been at twenty is devastating enough. Yet Kerouac contained this thought in the realm of flashes. "It was just a great big bunch of horseshit where they don't let you prove yourself," he wrote in retrospect twenty-five years later.[19]

So, even twenty-five years later, Kerouac would not allow himself even a brief glimpse of the possibility that maybe he wasn't good enough or willing enough to be a star on the Columbia football team.

When Kerouac quit the Columbia team and Columbia University — simultaneously — he severed, at last, his connection with "straight society." His child dreams of being a campus hero, walking about in chinos and football sweater, attending weekend parties in formal dress at wealthy estates — all were burned in bitterness. It was also the end of his athletic endeavors. What began with great sandlot feats — scoring nine touchdowns

96

in one game as a member of the Dracut Tigers — track and field achievements as a high schóoler at famed Boston Garden, a thrilling climactic touchdown in his last game for Lowell High — all of it died one day in the gloomy dusk of Columbia's Baker Field at the end of a practice scrimmage. Jack Kerouac, the marvelous, promising athlete out of Lowell, Massachusetts died on that day.

But Jack Kerouac, the Beat Prophet never forgot him. In later years he would speak of him in the third person. "He was magnificent," he would say. "But he was fucked over by the jerks of this world. If these jerks had only sensed one-tenth of the flaming spirit that roared in the splendid body of this athlete, they would have blessed him and opened all the doors to him. But that's what's wrong with this world. The jerks have inherited the earth."

What followed after Kerouac's farewell gesture as an athlete was the final proof of his private rebellion, private war against most things that society had taken thousands of years to establish. He waited around Lowell for a few months after leaving Columbia, and then early in 1943, he was called up by the United States Navy. He went willingly — at least he thought he did. But within three months, he was discharged from a psychiatric ward as unsuitable for military service.

He went through the whole syndrome: doctors questioning him trying to determine if his illness was authentic or if he was just another faker trying to get out. In all my talks with Kerouac, I remember only one time that he ever referred to his "navy career" — his label. As I recall, what brought it on was my reminiscing about my World War II days. "I was being trained as a secret agent, Jack," I said. "This was at Camp Ritchie, Maryland. They sent me there because I told them I could speak, read, and write Greek. At first, I thought I was eventually going to be assigned to a nice desk job in Washington, D.C. translating Greek documents. But after I got to Camp Ritchie, it didn't take me long to realize that the bastards were training me to become a spy. They were fixing to push me out of a plane behind enemy lines in Northern Greece! Can you imagine that? And I'm the kind that gets dizzy wearing elevator shoes!"

I could see that Kerouac was enjoying my narrative. He had a way of expressing this emotion by cocking his head and barely tracing a smile on his face. I went on with my story. "I cursed myself for revealing my Greek background. I cursed myself for having been born Greek — something that I never thought I would live to curse. I began to think of the different ways that I could develop some horrible disease so I could get the hell out of there. But the only thing I developed was a classic case of hemorrhoids, and that came from all the tension that I built up worrying about landing on a Macedonian cabbage patch."

"I would have loved it," Kerouac said. "Imagine dropping out of the clouds onto the ancient land of Greece."

"Yeah," I responded. "Right in the middle of a German battalion! They'd have shot my ass off — hemorrhoids and all!"

"You're here now, aren't you? Nothing happened to you."

"No, nothing happened to me because I never got to Greece If you remember, in 1942 Eisenhower landed in North Africa and eventually we invaded Italy. But if we had gone into Greece, I probably wouldn't be here today telling you all about my distinguished military career."

I believe it was the term, distinguished military career, that prompted Kerouac to remark about his own brief encounter with military service. "My military career was not distinguished," he started. "It was, rather, misconceived. Now that I look back on it, I can see myself something like Bartleby, old Melville's tragic little man. You've heard about Bartleby, haven't you?"

"Of course," I said. "He's the guy who kept saying, 'I would prefer not to' everytime his boss asked him to do something."

"Well that's pretty much what *I* kept telling those shrinks everytime they came in to chat with me. 'I would prefer not to'. But it wasn't easy getting through to them because they thought I was telling them that I would prefer not to go to war, that I was scared, that I was trying to bullshit them into thinking that I was some kind of a nut. But man, that wasn't it, that wasn't it at all. What I was really saying to them was that I would prefer not to suffer the indignity of having some little monster with a couple of bars on his shoulders clog up my beautiful brain with sawdust from his ugly brain. That's what I was trying to tell them, but they wouldn't listen. They kept trying to catch me off guard to prove to themselves that I was a slacker. But Jarvis, I was no slacker. My combat record as a merchant mariner is as good as

98

any American soldier's in World War II."

There was something pathetic in Kerouac's tone as he strived to convince me of his loyal service to his country; his earnestness seemed to turn back on him and then turn around and wink at me. I don't think Kerouac ever laid to rest his unhappy encounter with military life. I don't think he ever did this because this unhappy encounter was a mockingly sour note in the grand literary symphony he had composed of his beloved America. Few men loved America as Jack Kerouac did; and in this abiding love, there was no room for criticism—especially of its political institutions. Thus I am convinced that Kerouac regarded his aborted military service as an unforgivable betrayal of his country in its hour of need. And his dangerous merchant marine mission never quite relieved Kerouac of the nagging pain that he had let his beloved country down. Also, this pain must have intensified at times when thoughts of some of his early Lowell buddies came to him: Billy Chandler, killed early in the war on Bataan; John Koumantzelis, killed while training to become an Air Force pilot; Sammy Sampas, died from wounds received at Anzio beachhead. These buddies Kerouac constantly resurrected in his novels, and it's not unreasonable to presume the stabbing guilt that assailed him as he remembered the death of these men in the service of their country. There are some things that Kerouac never quite mastered; his distorted image of himself as a soldier was one of them.

In *Vanity of Duluoz*, Kerouac makes one last effort to place his military service in a more decent perspective. The following paragraph tries to sum up his feelings about the matter: "In the mess hall during the last few days at Bethesda (a naval hospital) I looked at all those guys eating that good food and yelling and talking and I felt I had betrayed not so much 'my country', which I haven't as you know; but this here United States Navy. If it hadn't been for that stupid dentist in Newport making me sick at the thought of being demeaned by a guy just because he has a higher rank. Isn't it true that the greatest admirals are the 'bulliest' and most intimate characters, 'one of the boys,' off their high horse?" [20]

I don't think that Kerouac expected anybody to believe that his betrayal was aimed at the United States Navy. The idea is, of course, absurd. Even more absurd is his insistence that a navy dentist bruised his sensitivities so horribly that he never quite recovered.

Yes, it was the dentist that was the cause of it all. No; of course it wasn't; it was Jack Kerouac. Yet if Kerouac didn't expect anybody to believe his story, what he *did* hope for was sympathy — and a little forgiveness. One can only hope to catch a glimpse of the massive sense of horror that must have engulfed the young Kerouac as he was dropped into a ward full of "loonies". The handsome young athlete, strong, clean cut, raised on the virtues of sportsmanship and fair play — the handsome young athlete was now in Hades, and tragic spirits wailed all around him. The nights must have been long and full of tears. Kerouac's pain might have been eased at that time if he had known that one of the great future friendships of his life would be with a man who would also be a patient in a psychiatric ward — Allen Ginsberg.

CHAPTER 9 - ALLEN AND JACK

When Jack Kerouac was discharged from the United States Navy in May, 1943, he went home — not to Lowell but to New York City; his parents had moved there earlier in the year. Also, in this year, his sister, Caroline, who was a couple of years older than Jack, joined the Women's Army Corps (WACS). Brother and sister passed by each other: one leaving the service, the other going in.

A number of people who knew Kerouac's mother have told me that she was especially pleased with the move to New York City. She had long been restless to get out of Lowell; she had her own dreams of new horizons; she could not see herself living out her years in milltown Lowell. (It's not unreasonable to assume that her son Jack had caught this restless spirit from her.)

It's true that her husband Leo did all the shouting and blustering about "Stinktown, U.S.A." But he could never persuade himself to leave its borders. He seemed to enjoy the private little war that he was conducting against Lowell; or, more accurately, he enjoyed the visibility of his identity there. When he moved to New York, he soon realized that he had become invisible; he was in the shadows, unheard, unseen.

Near the end of Kerouac's first book, *The Town and the City,* the old man (Jack's father) is dying. He says bitterly: "And do I hate this hell-hole New York! Joey, do *I hate* it! If God would only let me die in peace back in beautiful New England, that's all I ask. Men don't live the way God intended them to live in this place!" [21] Leo Kerouac did not die in "beautiful New England;" he died in New York. But he was buried in New England, in a family plot in Nashua, New Hampshire.

Soon after Kerouac joined his parents in New York, he shipped out on a merchant marine vessel that was heading for England. This was in June, 1943. This was a strange situation indeed: a young man is discharged from the United States Navy as unfit for service; a month later this young man gets on a ship that will travel the most dangerous sea lanes in the world. It

101

almost appears as if Kerouac were trying to prove something to himself. "I'll show those Navy bastards what I'm really made of; they and they're phony disciplines; and I'll show that Navy dentist that you don't judge a man by the metal that is on his shoulders or the stripes that are on his sleeve." These could have been the thoughts that motivated Kerouac.

The trip to England and back was uneventful — if one considers being attacked by submarines and sunk eventful. Yet for Kerouac there **was** one great event, one that had nothing to do with the dangerous crossing, the exploring of the mighty city of London, or the confrontation with the people of Great Britain. This great event burst upon him on a sunny morning when his ship found itself sailing between Ireland and Scotland. He caught the awesome miracle of these two coastlines and his eyes filled with tears. So here was young Kerouac, ever the poet, ever reaching for something beyond, something whose beauty could never be articulated.

When Kerouac returned from England in the Fall of 1943, he was becalmed. He was certain that he was not going to give college another try; he was also certain that he was going to devote the rest of his life to writing. Yet he remained becalmed and spent the next few months in New York moving about in various jobs. Though he didn't realize it at the time, he was on the threshold of a new direction in his life. Of the millions of people who lived with him in New York, there were about five who would change his life forever.

Edie (Frankie) Parker was one of them. She had met Kerouac a couple of years earlier on the Columbia College campus. Their friendship was an intermittent affair — until 1944 when they got married under rather bizarre circumstances. Kerouac was being held in jail under some vague charge of being an accessory to murder; the murder was charged to his friend Lucien Carr. In the middle of this sordid atmosphere, these two young lovers got married. Eventually, Kerouac was cleared and the newlyweds went to live at the home of the young bride in Michigan.

From the maelstrom existence of New York City, Kerouac suddenly found himself living with in-laws in a palatial home in exclusive Grosse Point, Michigan. The kid from ramshackle

"Little Canada" in milltown Lowell was now waking up in the morning to a world of opulence and elegant chimes. It was absurd. This was no way to become a writer — at least the kind of writer Jack Kerouac wanted to be. He writhed in this aristocratic straitjacket for a few months until he finally escaped — back to the Big City. Thus Kerouac's first marriage was no marriage at all. In the vast chronicle of his life, it emerges only as a footnote.

Yet if the marriage was meaningless, their relationship *preceding* the marriage was significant; because Edie Parker's New York apartment had become a gathering place for a small group of people. Among them were Allen Ginsberg, Lucien Carr, William Burroughs, *and* Jack Kerouac.

Next to possibly Neal Cassady, Allen Ginsberg became the most influential force in Kerouac's life in the fifteen years or so that followed. On the day in 1944 that Jack met Ginsberg, they were "a generation" apart; Kerouac was twenty-two, Ginsberg was eighteen; only four years difference; but at that period in their lives, the difference was more like twenty-four years. It took awhile to surmount this barrier.

"When I first met Allen," Jack told me years later, "I wanted to punch him in the mouth. I resented him immediately. And you want to know why? Because I thought he was a pushy little Kike who had no business hanging around us older guys."

"You mean you and Burroughs?" I asked.

"Well, yeah, and a few others."

"So why *didn't* you punch him in the mouth?"

"Because he kept on talking, and I kept on waiting for him to stop talking so I could get my shot in, but he just wouldn't stop."

"He must have stopped sometime, Jack," I said.

"Well, by the time he got around to stopping, I had changed my mind."

"So instead of punching him, you hugged him."

"You mean spiritually I hugged him."

This clarification of Kerouac's — that is, on how he hugged Ginsberg — I understood then to mean that Kerouac wanted me to make no mistake about his masculinity. The tone with which he uttered the remark and the gaze he leveled on me articulated eloquently the unspoken thought: "Yes — my friend Ginsberg is a homosexual, but *I* am *not*."

I did not want to get into *that* aspect of Ginsberg — at least not at that point in our conversation — so I responded to his "spiritual embracing" of Ginsberg by the quick acquiescence: "Of course, Jack. I meant that once you realized that Ginsberg's ceaseless chatter was revved up by his enthusiasm for everything around him, you began to dig him."

"Belay that Beat jargon, Jarvis," he said. "I did not begin to dig him; I began to *see* him."

We were in Jack's house on Sanders Avenue in Lowell; it was 1967. His wife Stella had gone out and his mother was, as usual, in another room, unseen, soundless. There was something else: Kerouac was sober — a rare interlude. It was evening, but the room we were in was dimly outlined. A floor lamp shedding a low light was off in a corner; Kerouac was in a rocking chair in the shadows in another corner; I was sitting on a couch — isolated. As I listened to Kerouac, I perceived something else: his sober voice was another instrument entirely. It performed on a slightly higher register and there was a quickness to his speech that was in ear-catching contrast to his normal booze propelled — but still clear — cadence. The whole room arrangement told me that Kerouac was avoiding even the tiniest stab of light, that if it somehow pricked him, he would be devastated by it.

"What's this 'belay' business, Jack," I responded. "You got a nerve checking me on Beat jargon when you talk as if you were Captain Ahab stomping around on the deck of the *Pequod*."

I thought I saw him nod his head slowly. "I've been walking the deck of the *Pequod* all my life," he said. "But I've seen no White Whale — just a few flounders."

"Then how come one of your legs isn't made out of flounder bone?" Kerouac laughed softly. "Are you against Beat language," I added, "when you invented part of it and recorded the whole thing in your books?"

"No, I'm not against it, but that was such a long time ago. And besides, Jarvis, you as an English Professor ought to know that there is no new language within a language. They're the same words but with a different intent."

"Can we get back to Ginsberg?" I said abruptly.

"What about Ginsberg?" He was playing with me.

"You said you wanted to punch him in the mouth, but changed your mind."

"Yeah, I changed my mind, but if you ask my wife Stella about him she'll tell you that *she* would love to punch him in the mouth."

"Stella could never punch anybody in the mouth. You know as well as I do that she is one of the most gentle people in the world. She is one of the lambs of this earth."

"Well this lamb you're talking about turned into a tiger — what was Blake's line about the tiger? Did he who made the lamb make thee? — this lamb turned into a tiger who went for Ginsberg's throat when he showed up here a few weeks ago."

"I heard about that."

"Well it's true. Stella wanted no part of him and told him to get lost."

"I haven't had a chance yet to talk to Stella about that incident. Maybe *you* can tell me why it happened — though I think I've got a pretty good idea already."

Kerouac leaned forward in his rocking chair so that momentarily his face emerged from his shadowy corner. He seemed to be mulling something over. "Bad company," he finally said. "That was it. Stella doesn't think that my old buddy Allen is a good influence on me."

"After all these years, Jack?"

"Well, my mother has been at this for a long time. These run-about friends of mine as she has called them, she has never approved of. My father felt the same way."

"And now so does Stella." Kerouac had retreated back into the darkness. "Seems to me Jack," I continued, "that the people who love you most don't think much of your literary buddies."

"Two different planets," is what I heard coming from Kerouac's corner. "Lowell is one planet and goofiness is another."

"So there's no room anymore for co-existence between Ginsberg's planet and the planet of Lowell," I said. "That's why Stella told him to take his bald head and his beard and fly away into some remote asteroid."

105

"What she told him was to get the hell out of here or she'd crease that bald head with a cast iron frying pan."

"How did *you* feel about that Jack? Your old buddy, your one-time Buddha soulmate who had come all the way to Lowell to see you — tossed out on his ear."

"I wasn't ecstatic over it, that's for sure. But I also felt that Allen and I have been through it all. I mean from alpha to omega."

"You mean alpha being Leon Levinsky of your first book and omega being all those other names you give him in your later books. Or maybe omega is still aborning; is Ginsberg in the book that you're working on now?" (Kerouac was writing *Vanity of Duluoz* at this time.)

"I don't see how I can leave him out," Kerouac replied. "Not that I'd want to, he's been such a fantastic light."

"Well if you begin with your initial portrayal of him in *The Town and the City,* he certainly started giving off sparks right away."

"Well that was Allen — trying to tell everybody that the world had gone mad and the only sane ones left in it were himself and the guy he happened to be talking to at that moment."

"I guess mad is the proper word, isn't it Jack?" I suggested. "Especially when you think of Ginsberg's most famous work, *Howl,* and that incredible first line: 'I saw the best minds of my generation destroyed by madness.' "

"I gave him the title for that poem, you know," Kerouac said evenly. There was no ego involved; his tone was that of a man who wants to keep the record straight.

"I think you gave him more than that, Jack," I said.

"Well, in those early New York-San Francisco years we gave of each other," Kerouac said crisply.

"No. I'm saying that, where the poem *Howl* is concerned, there is more that you contributed than just the title."

"*He* wrote the poem Jarvis, I didn't." Kerouac now sounded a bit annoyed. "I was too busy writing my own stuff."

"Well, that's what I mean: some of your early stuff crept into Ginsberg's *Howl.*"

"Writers influence each other. Don't you know that, Professor?"

"Of course I know it," I said, and now I was beginning to sense irritation. "But what I'm really getting at is that in your first novel where Ginsberg is introduced as Leon Levinsky, you've got him saying some things that sound like lines out of *Howl*."

Kerouac peeked out of his corner and threw a one-eyed stare at me. "You trying to say that my buddy Allen plagiarized from me?"

"No, not really. I think what I'm saying is that the sperm of *Howl* was ejaculated in your first book, *The Town and the City*."

Kerouac snickered, a reaction I fully expected. "Are you accusing me of jerking off?" he said. "I thought professors had exclusive rights to that."

"Maybe what I'm saying, Jack, is that *you* plagiarized — innocently, of course — from your friend Ginsberg when you inserted the character, Leon Levinsky, in your book."

"I created the character of Levinsky as I saw him, as he filtered through my brain. No writer can do anymore than that. So let's cut the bullshit about who plagiarized from whom."

"Okay, let's," I said quickly; I certainly didn't want to upset Jack — especially when I was engaged in a dialogue in which he was free of booze. "But you might do me a favor, Jack," I resumed somewhat cautiously. "The next time you get a chance, read again the pages on Levinsky in *The Town and the City* and then read some random lines from *Howl*. I think it's a rare and intriguing situation in literature: *your* characterization of Ginsberg in your first book and some of the thoughts you put in his mind anticipate by a few years Ginsberg's masterpiece. Will you do me that little favor?"

I was relieved to see Jack smile. "I haven't read either of those two things for years," he said. "Might be good to look at them again — on a rainy day."

"There's something else about that early portrayal of Ginsberg," I pushed on. "Our old friend Sammy (Alexander Panos in the book) is briefly compared to Allen. You write of both of them as young, super sensitive esthetes. But what is even more interesting is that you have Allen mildly objecting to the comparison; I guess on the grounds that Sammy is too much the dreamer while Allen fancies himself as really being in touch with reality."

While I was uttering this last thought, Kerouac had set his rocking chair in motion. When I finished my comment, he continued rocking, but said nothing. There was a short silence and I was trying to think of a follow-up remark, when he said: "As I said before, Jarvis, I'd have to look at all that again, it's been so long. But as I think about it *now,* I see Sammy as I've always seen him — a sweet babe. And so is Ginsberg a sweet babe; the difference is that he was given more years than Sammy to test his great big heart."

"So even though Ginsberg can't get into your house anymore," I said, "you still consider him one of the great companions of your life."

"Why not?" came the quick response. "He was one of the first to reach out to me in my early New York years and to really encourage me as a writer. Oh, he was a wild kid all right, and could throw out bullshit by the hour, but he was and *is* completely honest, completely pure."

The word, pure, sounded odd to me; not because it was necessarily imprecise, but because it seemed misplaced in the context of what Kerouac's wife and his mother thought of Ginsberg. To them, Ginsberg was anything but pure; to them, Ginsberg was a sex deviate, something that their Lowell culture condemned as evil; to them, Ginsberg was a devil who for years had sought to possess the soul of their beloved Jack.

I knew that my next utterance would be risky, but I chanced it on the strength and confidence of my friendship with Kerouac — and his wife, Stella. "I respect your feelings about Ginsberg, Jack," I began, "but the two women in your house see him as a shameless homosexual, and despite this era of liberal movements we are living in — including the Gay Liberation movement — despite all of this, your two women are positive that Ginsberg will go to a blazing, eternal Hell and that he's trying to take you with him."

"There ain't nobody that's going to go to Hell," said Kerouac, his voice rising slightly. "We're all going to Heaven

108

because that's where we all belong. You, me, Allen, Stella, Memere (Jack's mother) — we're all going to meet up there."

"You'd have a tough time convincing Memere and Stella of that. If they thought that Ginsberg would be up there, they'd vacate the premises."

"We're all up there now, Jarvis," Kerouac said quietly. "It's just that we're sleeping through it, but we'll wake up one day and realize it."

I wanted to get back to Ginsberg. "Have you ever been disturbed, Jack, by the fact that your great friend Ginsberg is a homosexual?" My question accelerated my apprehension about discussing this topic with Kerouac. In our countless previous hours together in which we had capriciously touched on a variety of ideas, I had always felt free and easy with Jack. True, he was always "glommed" and his satirical manner crushed any qualms or limitations I might have entertained about the kind of subject that could be considered fair game for dialogue. But on this day, in his house, Kerouac was acutely sober. My question about his friend Ginsberg's "gayness" could fall on him like a ten-story building. I felt stupid that I had picked this day — a rare sober one for Jack — to bedevil him with it; there were so many other "booze days" in which I might have formed the question.

Kerouac did not appear to hear my question. Oh, he *heard* it, all right, but he looked away from me as if pretending that the question was never asked. In these seconds, I remember experiencing a sense of alarm that maybe Kerouac had perceived my question as much too personal, or even worse, as a probing into his own psycho-sexual image.

Though I didn't repeat it, my question seemed to echo and ricochet around the room: "Have you ever been disturbed, Jack, by the fact that your great friend Ginsberg is a homosexual?"

"I never thought about it that much," the answer finally came.

"Well certainly Ginsberg hasn't let people forget about it," I said. "He seems to go out of his way to remind them of it."

"Man, that's his bag," said Kerouac. 'And that's got nothing to do with me. I've known Allen half my life and the one thing I'm sure of about him is that his range of feeling, emotion, spirit

109

— call it what you will — is incredible. Homosexual you say? That's just one aspect."

"And yet it's an aspect, Jack, that hardly appeared in your characterizations of Ginsberg in your books. From Levinsky in *The Town and the City* to Carlo Marx in *On The Road* to Alvah Goldbook in *The Dharma Bums* to the Irwin Gardens that appeared in some of your other books — only one of them comes on as being queer: the Irwin Garden of *Desolation Angels*.

"Would you go out of your way to insult a friend of yours?" he said with a touch of acrimony. "*I* wouldn't," he added. He then shook his head vigorously. "Besides, I don't think any of that is important. Allen has been a great inspiration. Let's let it go at that."

And we did. For the rest of the evening, Kerouac made sure that this edict—for that's the way he intended it—was enforced.

JACK KEROUAC

Cookout at a neighbor's house on Sanders Ave. where Kerouac lived.
Left to right: Paul Jarvis, Tommy Belkakis, Charles Jarvis, Jack Kerouac.
Lowell, Mass. Labor Day 1968.

111

Jack Kerouac was born in this house, on the second floor.
9 Lupine Road, Lowell, Mass.

St. Jean Baptiste Church in Lowell, Mass. where Kerouac
served as an altar boy and where a Requiem Mass was
celebrated for his funeral, Oct. 24, 1969.

Jack Kerouac lived in this house (third floor) during the late 1930's. Formerly 736 Moody Street, now 116 Textile Ave., Lowell, Mass.

The Merrimack River — Lowell, Mass. "broken at the falls to make frothy havoc on the rocks."

Jack Kerouac talking to students at Harvard University. March, 1964.

Jack "digging" his brother-in-law, Charles G. Sampas. Lowell, Mass. 1962.

Jack Kerouac among friends and relatives at home of Mr. and Mrs. Charles G. Sampas. Lowell, Mass. 1962.

Jack Kerouac displaying affection. Flanked by Mary Sampas and her husband, Charles G. Sampas, Jack's brother-in-law. Lowell, Mass. 1962.

Grandmother Kerouac

Leo Kerouac, Jack's father

Gabrielle Kerouac, Jack's mother

Chapter 10 - Literary Soulmates

Allen Ginsberg and Jack Kerouac are generally considered to be the two giants in the Beat School of Literature. Kerouac was published first, in 1950. His book, *The Town and the City*, made few ripples; Kerouac remained anonymous. Ginsberg became an almost instant celebrity in 1956 with the publication of his poem, *Howl*. By 1956, these two young writers had known each other for more than ten years. They had traveled — mostly independently — the breadth of the United States and Mexico. They had congregated with friends at various times in places like New York City, Denver, San Francisco, Berkeley, and Mexico City. They had been writing creatively and seeking recognition. Now, in 1956, Ginsberg was famous. Kerouac was still waiting.

But he didn't have long to wait: he had written so much, and so much of it was prose-poetry, and its genesis was of the stuff that had given life to *Howl*. Let's go back to Jack's first book, *The Town and the City*. In his philosophical diatribes Levinsky (Ginsberg) says things like:

> "Right across the street from here there's an amusement center — see it there? It's called the Nickel-O, see the big sign? — and there you have, at around four in the morning, the final scenes of disintegrative decay; old drunks, whores, queers, all kinds of characters, hoods, junkies, all the castoffs of bourgeois society milling in there . . . and when you go in there among all the children of the sad American paradise, you can only stare at them, in a Benzedrine depression . . . everyone looks like a Zombie . . . the disease of the age . . . Everyone feels like a Zombie, and somewhere at the ends of the night, the great magician, the great Dracula — figure of modern disintegration and madness, the wise genius behind it all, the Devil if you will, is running the whole thing with his string of oaths and his hexes . . .
>
> "You'll see great tycoons of industry suddenly falling

117

apart and going mad, you'll see preachers at the pulpit suddenly exploding — there'll be marijuana fumes seeping out of the Stock Exchange. College professors will suddenly go cross-eyed and start showing their behinds to one another . . . You'll see how everyone has become essentially mad — the whole insane world."

Now let's look at a few passages from *Howl:*

"I saw the best minds of my generation destroyed by madness, starving hysterical naked.
dragging themselves through the negro streets at dawn looking for an angry fix,
Angelheaded hipsters burning for the ancient heavenly connection to the starry dynamo in the machinery of night,
who poverty and tatters and hollow-eyed and high sat up smoking in the supernatural darkness of cold-water flats floating across the tops of cities contemplating jazz . . . .
who passed through universities with radiant cool eyes hallucinating Arkansas and Blake-light tragedy among the scholars of war, . . .
who got busted in their pubic beards returning through Laredo with a belt of marijuana for New York,
who ate fire in paint hotels or drank turpentine in Paradise Alley, death, or purgatoried their torsos night after night . . .
who chained themselves to subways for the endless ride from Battery to holy Bronx on benzedrine until the noise of wheels and children brought them down shuddering mouth-wracked and battered bleak of brain all drained of brilliance in the drear light of Zoo, . . .
Visions! omens! hallucinations! miracles! ecstasies! gone down the American river!"

There are differences, of course. In Kerouac's book, which preceded *Howl* by about five years, Levinsky speaks in a familiar, almost banal, language. There are few, if any, startling bursts of fresh imagery or poetic flight. Though Levinsky tries to

118

assume the role of the sage, the prophet, there is a hint of narcissism; he is listening to himself and his words fall on his ears with a sense of wonder.

In *Howl*, the narrator (Ginsberg) has invented a new language, a new sound; and this new language, this new sound communicate seldom heard chords of feeling and emotion; Ginsberg touches strings of the human experience that the reader never knew existed. And his tone: Ginsberg blends the voices of the innocent and the guilty, the weak and the strong, the evangelist and the confessor. Above all, Ginsberg has freed himself. He is the first human being to have achieved a panoramic view of the planet earth without benefit of a space capsule.

Yes, there are differences between Kerouac's Levinsky and Ginsberg's narrator. But there is a common background theme to their presentations that is dramatic in its recurrence. *It is the theme of madness.* Both voices howl, wail, scream the horror of the human condition; both voices are devastated by the spectacle of man masquerading as a rational animal when all they can perceive is a blind object taunted and shattered by the whimsy of an unknown force. Madness then is what creates the kinship between these two men; they're both awed by it and the only relief they get is to try to find the words that will give it some shape so they will at least know it is among them.

It is obvious that Kerouac's Levinsky came out of his early relationship with Ginsberg — or came out of Ginsberg's mouth. Kerouac had heard Ginsberg articulate many of the thoughts that Levinsky speaks. Yet it was Kerouac who wrote them down — not Ginsberg. Ginsberg read *The Town and the City*, read Levinsky's ravings. Five years or so later, he wrote *Howl*. Is it not possible that he borrowed some things from Levinsky, from himself, actually?

Probably what I'm saying is that few writers have influenced each other's work as much as the Beat writers have. Words, phrases, titles, scenes have been borrowed and exchanged in their works; some of it consciously, some of it unconsciously. A case for the latter can be made out in the name of Sal Paradise (Kerouac), the narrator in *On The Road*. In her biography, *Kerouac*, Ann Charters reveals an interesting thought regarding this name. She quotes an early Ginsberg poem (1947)

119

and focuses briefly on the passage, "Sad Paradise it is I imitate." The poem was given to Jack Kerouac soon after it was written. Mrs. Charters writes: "In Allen's tight handwriting scrawl, the words 'Sad paradise' looked like 'Sal paradise', and it became the name Kerouac gave himself almost four years later in *On The Road.*"

Yet, if the reader will look back at the Levinsky quotes I used from *The Town and the City,* he will see that another variation of this term is there. "And when you go in there among all the children of the *sad American paradise,* you can only stare at them, in a Benzedrine depression." Kerouac worked on this book from 1946 to 1949; Ginsberg gave his poem to Kerouac in 1947. It would appear that Kerouac took not only the distortion Sal Paradise from Ginsberg but also the correct version, sad (American) paradise. Yes, the Beat writers borrowed from each other — but never in a vicious way.

I cannot resist the temptation to include in this juncture of my account another curious example of interdependence among these young writers — these young writers who shook up the literature of the 1950's. John Clellon Holmes is another of the group who became a friend of Kerouac in the early New York City years. Holmes is generally credited with writing the first Beat novel: *Go.* The book is now out of print, a fate that I sincerely believe is unwarranted. It is a marvelous example of natural talent breaking loose and finding its true, high level. It is truly the precursor to Kerouac's imminent explosion as a Beat writer.

It is impossible not to feel that Kerouac and Holmes influenced each other — and were influenced by mutual friends. In the late 1940's and early 1950's, Kerouac and Holmes were in a milieu that saw people like Ginsberg, Neal Cassady and William Burroughs — all part of the Beat syndrome — recurring in their lives. Something different was happening. But no one was sure what it was. These people would meet and talk, and talk, and talk. Their subject matter was far ranging, but inevitably it always seemed to focus the concept that some sort of change was taking place in America, some sort of rebellion was being whipped up. But by whom?

Though they didn't know it then, *they* were whipping up this rebellion; they, and the millions of others of their generation who were merely waiting for someone to show them the direction this storm should follow. Holmes, Ginsberg, Kerouac, Burroughs, Neal Cassady (as a catalyst) — these men who sat around and tried to swamp each other with their festering psyches were the ones who were about to step up to the podium and proclaim "a new ballgame."

Jack Kerouac took the first shot in 1950 in the latter pages of *The Town and the City*. But it was a groping, unsure effort. Of the characters that appear in it, Ginsberg, Burroughs, Kerouac himself, only Ginsberg gives any hint that America is about to be rocked by a mighty new dynamism. A couple of years after Kerouac's book was published, John Holmes came on with *his* book: *Go*. It was a remarkable effort. This could have been the book that would launch the era of the Beat Generation. It caught these spawning rebels in sharp, vivid lines. The dialogues of search and frustration are there; the feeling that a national fever was about to reach a crisis is there. The early stirrings of Kerouac's first book seemed to have been caught by Holmes and moved to full blown action.

Kerouac's description of Ginsberg (Levinsky) in *The Town and the City* and Holmes' later etching of him (Holmes uses the name David Stofsky) in *Go* are incredibly synonymous — both in word choice and spiritual dimension.

The two characterizations, written about a couple of years apart (Kerouac's came first) are a stunning example of two minds being grooved on an almost identical sound wave. There is no question of plagiarism here; Holmes is too much the creative artist for that. What these two startingly similar descriptions reveal really is the raw, wild power of Ginsberg, a power that had begun to make itself felt and would eventually smash its way into the consciousness of millions of young Americans. Kerouac sensed this power — and so did Holmes. Thus, after Kerouac caught some of it in his first book, Holmes tried to flesh out this early etching in *his* first book. And he went further. Character delineations of William Burroughs and Neal Cassady flash through. And even more significant, a sharply focused picture of the young Jack Kerouac is developed. Jack is there, physically impressive, a surface calm belying the seething spirit beneath.

Yes, it was all there. Holmes had skillfully handcrafted a tapestry of the early Beat scene. *Go* then, was truly the first Beat novel. It was published in 1952 — five years before *On The Road*. It was favorably reviewed; everything pointed toward a wide reading audience and national acclaim for its author — but nothing happened. I'm sure that to this day (1973) Holmes must still be wondering why *Go* did not go. So am I, but I can offer an observation or two.

The tapestry structure of *Go* might have been too much for the reader, or more accurately, the reader of the early 1950's. He was expected to catch the galvanic episodes that erupted all around him and create from them a sense of relatedness, a sense of evolution. Or I suspect that the novel fell on the reader's eye and mind like a series of flash cards — and the reader was unable or not ready to interpret them into a meaningful whole. It is possible that the reader needed a commentator standing by the flash card projector who would provide transitional comments. And this is probably why Kerouac's *On The Road* succeeded. It provided this commentator in the person of Sal Paradise and indirectly in the voice of Dean Moriarty (Neal Cassady). There was no Dean Moriarty in *Go* to distill the Beat psyche; to seize the reader (and to not let go) and take him on the breathless roller coaster of the mid-twentieth century truth search.

So in 1952, *Go* did not make it; maybe someday it will. Or maybe Holmes should have listened longer and more closely to Neal Cassady's torrential monologues and trapped the "beat" and cadence of his American, parabolic spendings.

CHAPTER 11 - "IN SPITE OF OUR DIFFERENCE IN CHARACTER"

Neal Cassady came on the scene in 1946. He came to New York City from the West. A man named Hal Chase introduced Cassady to Jack Kerouac, and there's no doubt that none of the three realized at the moment of introduction the future significance of this meeting. Can one think of *On The Road* without Neal Cassady? One might as well try to conceive of Plato's *Apology* without Socrates or *Don Quixote* without Don Quixote. Jack Kerouac would have become a writer without Neal Cassady, but so have thousands of others — whose books have become food for worms.

One could advance an argument against the worm food opinion by pointing to Kerouac's books about his Lowell years. There is no Neal Cassady there; and they are beautifully written, sensitive, poetic, spiritual — especially *Visions of Gerard*. There is about them a Mark Twain mystique because they take the reader on a one-time journey where innocence becomes the key to wisdom, a journey that the reader thrills to because he has taken it himself. But, as I said, Mark Twain had already done that: would there be room for Kerouac's books? I guess the question becomes an academic exercise and only the future can render it legitimate.

However, we do not have to wait for the future to tell us that *On The Road* released Kerouac, freed his fantastic spirit, helped him to realize his powers, focused his magnificent vision. *And,* it brought him not only to the American reader but to the rest of the world. I do not think he could have done this without Neal Cassady.

In essence, *On The Road* is a biographical slice of Cassady's life and the orchestration and the libretto created by Kerouac are akin to the creative effort involved in a work like *West Side Story*. Cassady was the voice, the setting, the culture.

From his earliest childhood perception, Jack Kerouac needed and sought after someone he could admire and believe in. He succeeded in his very first effort when he discovered that this wondrous person was present in his own family: his brother, Gerard. The facts of Gerard's early death when Jack was only four

123

and Kerouac's idealization of him later on, have already been discussed in this work. The facts of Sammy Sampas, Jack's high school friend, emerging in his mind as a disciple of Gerard and the influence that Sampas had on him, have also been considered.

Both Gerard Kerouac and Sammy Sampas died much too prematurely — leaving Jack Kerouac with the painful, lonely task of finding someone to take their place; or more accurately someone to assure Kerouac that their spirit was still walking on this earth.

"Yes, and it wasn't only because I was a writer and needed new experiences that I wanted to know Dean more, and because my life hanging around the campus had reached the completion of its cycle and was stultified, but because, somehow, in spite of our difference in character, he reminded me of some long-lost brother; the sight of his suffering bony face . . ." This passage appears in the first chapter of *On The Road* and it speaks of Dean Moriarty (Neal Cassady) and Sal's (Kerouac's) attempt to justify or explain or even to understand the deep, melancholy feeling that flashed through him in his early meetings with Moriarty. The "long-lost brother" could only refer to Gerard because that was the only brother Kerouac ever had. It's true that one can create and envision a non-existent long-lost brother, a brother that would be given the pure, saintly kind of love that no one else in this world is worthy of receiving and a brother who would return *that* kind of love;the kind that one incessantly yearns for but never finds. Yes, one can imagine, conjure up that kind of brother; but Kerouac did not have to do that; that brother had actually existed in Gerard.

Then along came Sammy Sampas who was to become a spiritual transition between Gerard and Neal Cassady. But when Sampas died in World War II, Kerouac was alone again. That deep inner light within him whose flame had been fanned brightly, first by Gerard and then by Sammy, now had become a flicker. Kerouac looked about for someone to keep the flame from flickering out. Enter Neal Cassady.

But it wasn't that simple. Neal Cassady was no Gerard saint, no Sammy starry-eyed poet. He was no boyhood image floating in a Lowell twilight horizon, steeped in a Lowell morality. Neal Cassady was a hurricane of human activity, the spectrum of joy and sadness. His vast length and breadth of vision and movement must have hit Kerouac with the force of a typhoon, and it was this kind of mighty wind that was needed to feed Kerouac's inner light and make it burn brighter than ever.

But I'm certain that first, Kerouac had to work some things out in his precious relationship with Cassady. "In spite of our difference in character," he writes in the passage quoted above. What difference? Start with their childhood. Kerouac came from a super structured Catholic home where sin was the ever-present threat, where eternal damnation was the fate of anyone succumbing·to sin. And what was this sin? It was an horrendous code that had as its purpose the crushing of normal childhood desires: innocent sex play, innocent lying, innocent pranks. A few months ago, one of Kerouac's boyhood chums told me that "Jack squirmed through his childhood". I can easily believe this, and I can see the boy, Jack, writhing in the moral rack they had strapped him on.

What of Neal Cassady's early years? One doesn't have to look very far because these years are graphically spelled out in the book, *The First Third*. This book is a curious, uneven gathering of some of Cassady's literary production. The first hundred pages or so are purely autobiographical and they are written in a deliberate, pretentious style that seems to mock the liberating, flowing language that Cassady employs in his letters, which round off the last fifty pages of the volume. The letters are written to Jack Kerouac save for the last one which is addressed to Ken Kesey. (Kerouac freely admitted that Cassady's letter writing style was the open sesame to the discovery and evolution of his (Kerouac's) cataract, Beat novel prose).

But again, what of Neal Cassady's early years? A broken home, a drunken father, an unbelievably raunchy existence in Denver's skid row, an early start in stealing cars and creating a fuzzy image of the law, an early adolescent talent for "digging chicks" — this incredible cosmos served as Neal Cassady's first awareness, first perception of life. Compare this cosmos with Kerouac's tight, rigid Lowell planet and you have a polarity of endless dimensions.

When he was fourteen, Neal Cassady performed his first car theft. At fourteen, Jack Kerouac was a "good boy". His parents

— especially his mother — were providing a daily incantation for him which went something like this: "Now Jackie, you must pay attention in school, respect your teachers, do your homework, be careful who you make friends with, respect the police officer, respect your priest, say your prayers every day because if you forget God he will forsake you and the Devil will possess you; now Jackie, we want you to grow up and go to college and become a doctor, a teacher, a lawyer — something professional like that; we want you to marry a nice girl and have a nice family . . ." The incantation sounded deep into Kerouac's guts; and its echoes never stopped. The last thing that Jack Kerouac would think of doing at the age of fourteen was to steal a car.

Yes, "in spite of our difference in character," writes Kerouac of his buddy, Neal Cassady; and if one goes beyond their childhood, he easily discovers that the difference becomes even greater. Kerouac went through high school with the sporadic zeal of a missionary; he topped this off by emerging as a football hero. Then came an Ivy League college and it appeared as if Kerouac was well on his way to filling the mold that his parents had constructed for him. Contrarily, by the time Neal Cassady had reached high school age, he was a well schooled veteran in the elementary yet monumental art of survival — or self-preservation, if you will. Court room judges, reform school officials, and a day-to-day struggle to cling to a scrap of dignity were Cassady's high school education. College and Neal Cassady? Absurd.

So, up to this point in their lives, Kerouac and Cassady were moving away from each other — in tremendous bursts of time and action. The chances of reversing this direction seemed impossible. Yet, when Kerouac left Columbia for good, and began moving about searching for IT, the reversal had begun. When they finally met in New York in 1946, there was this sense of discovery, this sense of asking themselves, "Man, where the hell has he been? How come it took so long to meet this guy?"

But there was still this "difference in character." They both knew it, though I believe that Kerouac was more sensitive to it, more awed by it. Further, Kerouac's perception of Cassady as "some long-lost brother" added to his feeling of wonder. How could Cassady remind him of Gerard, the only brother he ever had, the brother he lost long ago? How could Cassady, the "young jailkid," be put in the same galaxy with Gerard, the virgin saint whose few days of life were filled with bringing home broken-wing birds, with visions of heaven, with nuns surrounding him wanting to know what he had seen of heaven. Gerard's brief life was a refrain of beauty and love and it was heard in the simple world of Lowell's "Little Canada." But Neal Cassady? His world was a grinding, grating sound of a desperate reaching out to catch something worthwhile before it all gave out.

Neal and Gerard? Yes — according to Jack Kerouac. "He's a Jesuit by the way," said Kerouac of his buddy in an interview for The Paris Review. "He used to sing in the choir. He was a choir boy in the Catholic churches of Denver. And he taught me everything I now do believe about anything that there may be to be believed about divinity." [22]

A few years before Kerouac spoke those words, he had talked of his brother, Gerard, in a remarkably similar way. This was in our Lowell radio interview. Among other thoughts, Kerouac had expressed his child-faith belief that it was Gerard in Heaven who was guiding him; Gerard, the divine source was lighting his way.

Gerard and Cassady, both divine melodies heard by Jack Kerouac. And yet, there *was* a "difference in character" and Kerouac could never get around it. If Cassady were a "divine melody" he was also a balling, full-speed-ahead, smash-it-all-up, that's-all-there-is human asteroid who was tortured by the specter of death but tortured even more by the howling, unceasing cry in his ears of a desire for death, a death wish. And Kerouac was fascinated, entranced by Cassady's pyrotechnics. Occasionally, he joined him, but mostly he watched. He watched because Gerard would not have approved of Cassady's blasting lifestyle. Balling women, making the drug scene, laughing at the law — what did all this have to do with Gerard Kerouac, he of the sweet face looking out of a window at a grey November; he of the rheumatic pain-wracked child body; he of the martyr-suffering existence?

So Jack Kerouac was the spectator who watched Cassady perform a great big tragedy, a tragedy which, though never quite reaching Sophoclean heights, brought to Kerouac in a strange wondrous way, recurring visions of his brother, Gerard.

In *The Paris Review* interview, Kerouac quotes thoughts of his "long-lost brother", Neal Cassady. "We know God, don't we Jack? I said, Yessir boy. He said, Don't we know that nothing's going to happen wrong? Yessir. And we're going to go on and on . . . and hmmmmm ja-bmmmmmmm . . . He was perfect. And he's always perfect . . ." [23]

In *Visions of Gerard,* Kerouac writes of his other long-lost brothers. "It was only many years later when I met and understood Savas Savakis (Sammy Sampas) that I recalled the definite and immortal idealism which had been imparted me by my holy brother (Gerard) . . . I was destined, destine indeed, to meet, learn, understand Gerard and Savas and the Blessed Lord Buddha and my Sweet Christ . . . To awaken to pure faith in the bright one truth: All is well, practice Kindness, Heaven is Nigh." [24]

See now the startling parallels: the immortal idealism of Gerard becomes the perfection of Neal Cassady; the understanding of the Blessed Lord Buddha and Sweet Christ becomes Cassady's exhortation, "We know God, don't we Jack"; the acceptance of Gerard's faith that "All is Well" become Cassady's, "Don't we know that nothing's going to happen"; and finally, the realization that "Heaven is Nigh" becomes the expression of Cassady's belief in the immortality of the soul: "And we're going to go on and on."

So there was this "vision" that Kerouac had of Cassady; a vision that would flash back on a line—to Sammy Sampas and to its original source, Gerard Kerouac. Little wonder that the word visions, besides its appearance in the title *Visions of Gerard,* appears in only one other of Kerouac's many books: *Visions of Cody* (Cody being Neal Cassady). Even more fascinating is the fact that *Visions of Cody* was written almost five years before *Visions of Gerard;* yet Gerard came long before Cody in Kerouac's life. It appears that Jack Kerouac saw the wonder of his apotheosized Gerard through the revelations of Cody, another holy brother.

Neal Cassady died in 1968, just short of his forty-fourth birthday. He was found beside some railroad tracks in Mexico, a victim of booze and drugs; at least *that* is the general verdict. Most likely, Neal Cassady decided it was time to come to terms with his death wish. No, it was not the kind of suicide where a man puts a gun to his head; it was more like the person who plays the game of leaning out of a window that is twenty floors up; he does this over a period of time and with each succeeding effort, he leans out more and more; everytime he looks down from his height, he senses a thrill of chilling desire; the further he emerges from the window, the greater becomes his exhilaration—until one day he leans way out and decides there is nothing to come back in for.

Jack Kerouac was living in Lowell at the time of Neal Cassady's death. A few days after I had heard of Cassady's passing, I went to Jack's house. We began talking about Cassady — but *not* in the past tense. "Whoever made up that story of old Neal's cashing in, oughta be tarred and feathered," Kerouac was saying. "Guys like Neal just don't do things like that."

"You mean like dying?" I said.

"That's right. I mean, not at this point. Neal is in his prime. If I know that devil, he probably gave out the story of his death just to see me cry my eyes out. Well I ain't gonna do it — because any day now, I'll get a letter from Neal wanting to know if I'm wearing a black band around my arm!"

I don't believe that I had ever heard Kerouac's voice sound quite like that before. The tone and timbre of it was new to me. The familiar stop and go, half-satirical, booze-freed ring was missing. As he talked of Cassady's "death", there came across to me a subtle haunting of fear, a hint of hysteria, a pleading with me to respond to him reassuringly — so that he could believe his own words.

"If Neal Cassady isn't dead, Jack," I responded, "then I can't resist thinking of Mark Twain's remark that reports of his death were slightly exaggerated."

"Yeah, that's it." Kerouac seized on this. "Slightly exaggerated. Wait 'till I see that old sonumbitch."

Kerouac's words had barely trailed off, when my mind focused on a scene from one of Edgar Allan Poe's short stories, *The Cask of Amontillado:* Fortunato, the drunken victim is being walled up in a tomb by Montresor; Fortunato at first does not realize what is happening to him; then as the wall around him looms higher and higher, Fortunato begins to perceive Montresor's design; then just before the last stone is put into place, Fortunato speaks. "Ha! ha! ha! he! he! he!—a very good joke indeed—an excellent jest. We will have many a rich laugh about it at the palazzo — he! he! he! — over our wine — he! he! he!"

Yes, that's the way Kerouac came through to me. He was Fortunato, refusing to believe the fact of death, unwilling to accept reality.

"An excellent jest. We will have many a rich laugh about it at the palazzo," said Fortunato.

"Slightly exaggerated. Wait 'til I see that sonumbitch," said Kerouac.

"That sonumbitch" was never to be seen again by Kerouac. And Kerouac knew it, though that night he was determined to put it aside. "Do you correspond much with Cassady?" I asked, being careful to stay in the present tense.

"Well I used to," came the reply. "But the past few years, I haven't. Neal's not an easy guy to keep up with, you know."

A few months later we talked again about Neal Cassady. Cassady had been out of Kerouac's life for some years. While Kerouac had lived mostly on the East Coast, Cassady persisted on the West Coast. They had remained buddies but during this period a new phase in Cassady's life surfaced that could not have escaped Kerouac's attention. The hero of *On The Road* had gone beyond the pages of Kerouac's epic and had emerged under his real name in another book: Tom Wolfe's *The Electric Kool-Aid Acid Test*. This was a non-fiction novel, a documentary really, on Ken Kesey, young author of the best seller, *One Flew Over the Cuckoo's Nest*. Kesey had become the leader of the LSD-Hippie Syndrome (until he dropped out later after a few legal adventures) and his story was chronicled by Wolfe in a massive volume written in a careening style which at times shouted echoes of Kerouac's *On The Road*. Certainly Dean Moriarty-Neal Cassady lived on as the inimitable con man-philosopher-individualist; the only difference now was that Ken Kesey had replaced Jack Kerouac as *the* focal point of reference for Neal Cassady.

As I said, a few months after Cassady's death, his name came up again. I wondered if Kerouac had finally accepted the fact of his demise. "I won't believe it," he said, "until I see Neal packed

130

away neatly like a new suit of clothes."

"I don't want to get morbid about this, Jack," I said, "but I understand that Cassady's body was cremated."

"Now that's a crock of shit," he almost shouted. "First of all, Neal has always been a good Catholic, like me. *He* wouldn't allow anything like that. Secondly, the story of his cremation sounds like one of Cassady's jokes." I had made up my mind that Kerouac was mad, psychotic if you will, on the matter of Cassady's death. I left this subject as hopeless.

"What about Tom Wolfe's portrayal of Cassady, Jack?" I injected suddenly. "Some of those passages seem to have come right out of *On The Road*."

"I'm flattered," he said impishly. "Tom Wolfe is no Thomas Wolfe — my first writer-saint by the way — but if he saw fit to echo some of my visions of Neal, then I'm flattered." He gave me a fish-eye. "And if you're going to start talking about plagiarism — and it seems to me that that's all you professors are ever interested in, playing cops and robbers with the students — if you're going to start in on plagiarism, then I give you the back of me arse."

I laughed. Kerouac had made a hip movement with those last words. "You injure my sensibilities, Mr. Kerouac," I said, trying to perpetuate his "me arse" intonation. "Far be it from me to suggest plagiarism. Tom Wolfe is such a skillful writer and such a skillful reporter. And after all, his book on Kesey and Cassady is a monumental documentary; it is a tribute, among other things, to his research talents."

"And a toodle-de doo to you, too," came Kerouac's response.

"No really, Jack," I went on. "What I'm asking you is: did you notice any difference in *your* Dean Moriarty and Wolfe's Neal Cassady."

"How in the fuck can I answer that," he said, half-smiling, "when I haven't even read Wolfe's book."

It hadn't occurred to me; that is, that Kerouac might not have read *The Electric Kool-Aid Acid Test*. "Well, then you ought to read it," I tried to recover.

"Man, I ain't got the time," he said. "I'm too busy reading other things, like Plato and Aristotle, Mutt and Jeff, The Bible

— and the greatest newspaper east of the Mississippi: The Lowell Sun."

"Then shame on you," I took another tack. "Your friend Neal would feel hurt if he found out you weren't interested in reading about him."

"My friend Neal could never feel hurt from anything I ever did that concerned him." I noticed immediately that Kerouac's voice had dropped in volume. He seemed to have uttered this remark to himself. "Everything I've written about Neal has been written out of love, the kind of love that one can feel only about his brother."

"Do you miss Neal, Jack?"

"Of course I do." He answered in a way that rendered my question an accusation. "Wouldn't *you* miss somebody who gave you so much? I mean, I'm not afraid to admit that Neal made me a better writer. His letters, his philosophy, his whole existence were a treasure to me."

"You're not implying that Cassady's name should also have been under the title of your books?" I wondered if I had pushed too much. Kerouac threw a stare at me — and I was relieved. I had learned to interpret his stares; he had about twenty of them. This one said: "Jarvis, you are trying to mindfuck me."

"My name is where it should be: under *my* book titles." He was admonishing me. "But I'll tell you one thing. Neal Cassady was the greatest writer of the bunch. Better than Ginsberg, Holmes, Corso —"

"Kerouac?"

"Ah yes, Kerouac." He didn't miss a stride. "Well, we will never know that because Neal was too busy to sit on his ass like the rest of us and scribble. But he did write some things and someday these will all be collected and Neal will emerge as the father of us all."

"But in the meantime," I said, "he keeps turning up as a character in your books and now, lately, as a character in Tom Wolfe's book. Do you feel any resentment against Tom Wolfe, or even Ken Kesey who obviously became Neal Cassady's buddy?"

Kerouac threw me the accusatory mindfucking stare again. "I'm too old to resent anybody — you diabolical professor, you." He smiled faintly. "But even if I weren't too old, and even if this were a few years back, I could bear no grudge against any man."

"Especially Neal — and the rest of your Beat brothers."

"Right you are."

"Do you miss them, Jack? I mean, besides Neal. Do you miss Burroughs, Ginsberg, Corso, Ferlinghetti?"

Kerouac's face flashed sadness. Then he spoke slowly, quietly. "No, not really. I still love them all but each time frame in life is different. Back in the late forties and in the fifties, I used to see one or two or three of them and we'd get together and we'd try to decide what the hell this cockeyed world was all about. When I went out West a few times, I'd stay with Neal sometimes and it was always a great thing. And in San Francisco we all had the great times."

"And you don't miss that now?" I interrupted.

He seemed to hesitate. "Naw. Once was enough. Besides, I always kept the door open."

"A door for what?"

"A door which would lead me back."

"Back to Lowell?" I suggested.

"Well you might put it that way, although that door was also a path to my own private little monastery where I would communicate with the angels."

"The angels," I echoed.

"That's right . . . Gerard, Sammy Sampas, John Koumantzelis, Billy Chandler . . . Memere." All the names Kerouac uttered were of dead people — except the last one, his mother. The first, of course was his brother; the second was his teenage Lowell poetic young friend; the third was a high school fellow athlete; the fourth was a childhood chum. Except for Gerard, the others had died in the war.

"Did you use that door often, Jack?"

"Man, I practically existed on the threshold of that door. I think I had one big toe in the room and the rest of me was up in a tall mountain walking through a little garden and talking with those angels."

"Sounds to me like you never really had your heart in it . . . I mean the Beat Brotherhood. By your admission, you had more than just one foot out the door." Kerouac did not respond to this. A short impasse settled between us. Then I thought of something else to say. "You know, Jack, this open door business you mention reminds me of one of Aesop's fables — something about a couple of foxes or bears breaking into a farmer's food cellar and one of them gorging himself, while the other one ate a little at a time and kept going in and out of the opening to the farmer's cellar to make sure he didn't bloat himself too much and not be able to squeeze himself out of the place. I guess the other bear or fox ate himself into a balloon and got trapped in there."

When I stopped, Kerouac affected an expression of mock surprise. "So I'm the fox," he said. Then he looked down at his distended middle. "Or maybe I should say the bear." He patted his belly, and then focused on me again. "But you're not implying, Jarvis, that I was some kind of thief, a man who only took and gave nothing in return."

"No, not exactly," I said somewhat hurriedly. "I'm saying that this going in and out the door was a manifestation of your desire to remain free, to leave your options open, so to speak."

"Beat Brotherhood," he said. Kerouac had a way of suddenly changing direction. "I think I like that term. Did you think that up all by yourself — or did you *plagiarize* it somewhere?"

I feigned being offended. "I assure you, *Mr. Kerouac,* that I did not steal it. Seems to me that all we've been talking about the last couple of minutes is thievery — on both sides."

"Beat Brotherhood," Kerouac repeated. "Yeah, I guess you could say that. We were all brothers; but we were all on the road, each unto himself."

"Except when you traveled with Neal Cassady."

"Well yes. That was something else. Neal was the man there." There was a quiet moment. "Now he's with the angels," Kerouac added.

I knew then that Jack Kerouac had at last accepted the fact of his friend's death; or passing on really, on to join the other angels of his life: Gerard, Sammy Sampas . . .

134

CHAPTER 12 - THE DULUOZ LEGEND

Jack Kerouac met Neal Cassady in New York City in 1946 and for the next fifteen years or so they would be in and out of each other's lives; Kerouac pursuing flashes of truth and a writing career; Cassady feeling that he had the truth in his pocket and that all he had to do was to take it out once in awhile and apply it to life — like a cool sip of wine on a twilight veranda.

One of the early results of this relationship was Kerouac's first "on the road" adventure. Not long after he had first met Kerouac, Neal Cassady left New York City and returned to Denver. Yet something of him remained behind with Kerouac: Cassady's intriguing narrative monologues of the Great West. The combination was irresistible: Cassady's presence exploding revelations and the open prairies reaching out to far, mighty mountains. Kerouac had to experience them both. In the Summer of 1947, Jack Kerouac began his first romance with the open road, the open American road. What he left behind was his mother, an unfinished manuscript (later to be published as his first book, *The Town and the City*), and a sense of lostness and frustration.

This first trip became the bone and marrow of the opening act of *On The Road*. The comical fits and starts of Sal Paradise's (Kerouac's) hitchhiking efforts; the brilliant portrayal of American characters he encountered once he finally got underway; the meeting with Dean Moriarty and Carlo Marx (Allen Ginsberg) and others in Denver; the beginning of Dean Moriarty's emergence as the "new American saint."

Though Jack Kerouac didn't know it at the time, the next ten years would see him travel a road that, if traced on a map, would resemble the impulsive pencil markings of a small child. New York, Denver, San Francisco, Mexico City, North Carolina, Florida, Lowell — these were the recurrent stops. There was no home base in terms of geography; home base was Memere, Kerouac's widowed mother. During this period, Mrs. Kerouac could be found in one of two places: New York where she worked in a factory and lived in a small apartment or North Carolina where she made long visits to her only other child, her married daughter, Caroline.

Kerouac's first trip to the West was very brief. After Denver, he managed to reach California where he spent a few days in San Francisco. When nothing sensational happened to him there, he started back for New York in a mood of disenchantment. (And disenchantment would become a constant companion in the next few years in his nagging quest for recognition as a writer.) Yet, as previously noted, this first short road adventure became the fount out of which later gushed the fantastic world of the Beat culture. Some of the most memorable passages in *On The Road* erupt from this initial experience.

At the time this was happening, Kerouac didn't know that he had imbibed from this luscious fount; because upon his return to New York — and Memere — he resumed work on the novel he had started a year earlier, *The Town and the City*. There is a curious bit of irony here; Kerouac was pursuing his conventional novel concurrent with the discovery of the new world that Neal Cassady had brought before him. While working on this novel, Kerouac corresponded with Cassady and their relationship deepened.

There followed months of frustration for Kerouac resulting from the rejection of his novel by a couple of publishing houses. Then late in 1948, Kerouac found himself on the road once more. He was driving westward with Neal Cassady who had come east to "rescue him." They wound up in California and, though their relationship hit a few bumps, the experience enriched Kerouac: he was gaining more material for his future Beat novels.

In the Spring of 1949, Kerouac was back with Memere, in New York. And then it happened. His novel, *The Town and the City*, was accepted for publication. The ecstasy of it was almost too much for Kerouac. Now, he was no longer a make-believe author. He was a writer, a professional writer whose creative thoughts, spiritual musings, grand concepts would touch thousands, nay millions, of readers.

Kerouac did not wait around for the book to be published. He moved with the pure faith and fervor of a new religious convert. He would dedicate himself completely to his art. Secure

136

in the thought that his novel would soon grace the bookstalls, he left Memere in New York and went to Denver. In Kerouac's newly discovered spirit and hope as a creative writer, Denver was the loft, the garret in which he would isolate himself and worship at the altar of artistic faith. One can already see the embryonic workings of Kerouac's next novel, *On The Road.* Though Kerouac could not envision it then, what was happening was that the book was gestating in his creative subconscious. Neal Cassady was the source, the fount; Neal Cassady was the protagonist who motivated the action; and Denver was the setting of this drama. So Kerouac ran off to the scene of the action; he would be inspired by the environment — where it actually happened.

But nothing happened. According to Ann Charters' biography of Kerouac, Jack struggled to give shape to his new book, but it resisted him. It was like a man wanting to write a book about the Acropolis and going up there to live in order to write it. He would discover that the ancient stones have nothing to say. Denver had nothing to say to Kerouac. Thus after a few weeks there, he went on to California, met up with Cassady who was living there at the time, and resumed his relationship.

It is extraordinary, really. Kerouac was literally chasing the source of his next novel — though he undoubtedly was unaware of this. And he caught up with it in San Francisco. What followed was a long wild trek back to New York: Neal and Jack on the road; Neal murdering every car he drove; a brush or two with police; exultation and exhaustion playing with them; Neal spewing tremendous thoughts and Kerouac gathering them in. When they reached New York they withdrew from each other for awhile.

But Kerouac had done something more — still unaware of it. He had written about one-half of *On The Road,* written it, that is, in his mind.

A few months later, in February, 1950, *The Town and the City* came out. It was not a success, though some reviewers praised it. Kerouac did not allow the book's failure to diminish his creative urge. He went back to Denver still apparently seeking some mystical wells for his next book. Eventually, Neal Cassady caught up with him and they went to William Burroughs in

Mexico City. It was not a happy interlude: Jack got sick, Cassady took off, pursuing some marital solutions. When, finally, Kerouac got back to Memere in New York, he spent the next few days trying to put himself together. If it seemed to him that he had arrived in New York emptyhanded, it was because his vision was still blurred. He could not yet focus the idea that the novel he had been struggling with had now been completed; and that all that remained was for him to find the right words to articulate it. This, he would do — later.

Probably the remotest thought in Jack's mind at this time was marriage. His first marriage had been preposterous. Yet in the Fall of 1950 he married Joan Haverty, a girl he had previously known. Memere was stunned, but it was probably Memere that he was trying to escape from. If this were the truth (though Kerouac could never himself believe this), it proved to be a short period of liberation. It was the last try by Kerouac — at the age of 28 — to break the bonds of being "Mama's boy."

By the spring of 1951, the marriage was over; it had lasted six months. It's not unfair to question whether this was ever really a marriage — except for the license. The newlyweds lived in New York and while the wife worked, the husband spent most of the time hammering out the final basic form of *On The Road*. Soon after the husband finished his project, he went home to his mother, mama, Memere. The wife was left in mid-flight, looking for some place to land.

In the last phase of his Lowell life (1966-1968) Jack Kerouac talked about many things — present and past. I was lucky to be in his company to hear and talk with him about much of this; and a quick retrospection by the reader of my book up to this point, will confirm my method of reaching into these dialogues as revelatory sources in the attempt to flesh out these "visions of Kerouac."

He talked about his second wife one afternoon at a cocktail lounge in the outskirts of Lowell. Jim Curtis and I had picked him up at his house and after a pleasant October drive, we stopped at this lounge for "a couple of drinks." (We knew, of course, that with Kerouac, there was no such concept as a couple of drinks.) Kerouac was bombing along in what I had long ago surmised were Cassady-scenarioed monologues. In the flow of his thoughts, he uttered the term, "women in my life."

"Jack, why don't you write a great love story?" I said.

He released a monstrous burp and looked at me with annoyance. "I thought you told me that you've read all my books. If you ain't lying to me, you better go back and read them again. You'll find out that *all* my books are great love stories."

"With you as the protagonist?" I said.

"Who else?" he said, and he let go with a cackling laugh. Then in a wavering crooner's voice, he sang a couple of lines from the song, "Boulevard of Broken Dreams."

"You loved 'em and left 'em. Is that it Jack?" Jim Curtis prompted him here.

"I never hurt no woman in my life," he said, trying to look wounded. "What did Zorba say about them? 'They are such weak creatures, and they give you all they've got'." (Kerouac definitely had *not* mastered a good imitation of Anthony Quinn.)

"And did *you* give them all you had, Jack?" Curtis needled.

"What do you mean *had*? I got enough left to fill up the harem of Suleiman the Magnificent. But I didn't give them any babies, which is no fault of mine."

"You mean nobody told you about the birds and the bees, Jack?" I said.

"Sterility, Sir, sterility," he came back, ignoring my comment. "It has become clear to me that I am the last in the long illustrious line of the Kerouacs."

"Like Roderick Usher in 'The Fall of the House of Usher'," I suggested.

He gave me a John Barrymore stare of admonishment. "You dare compare me to that worm," he asserted in a mock Shakespearean delivery. Then, ham actor that Jack always was, he added in a vague Humphrey Bogart, "That Roderick Usher couldn't get it up; *that* was his problem. He played with himself, and got nowhere." Then, he got back to his Shakespearean pose. "Impotence, Sir, impotence. *That* was Roderick Usher's problem. But I assure you that *I* was never plagued by such an affliction. And if you desire proof, I can provide it for you presently."

Curtis and I spoke simultaneously. Our choice of words was not exactly the same, but the thought was identical: "Jack, don't you dare!" Kerouac laughed.

139

"It's a pity, Jack," I said. "You might have sired a great athlete or two." He enjoyed the thought.

"One Jack Kerouac is enough for this world," he said, "though I was designated as a sire by my sweet Joan." Curtis and I had heard of this matter from other sources. Joan Haverty had claimed — and probably still does — that she became pregnant while married to Kerouac and that the child that was born soon after the marriage broke up was Kerouac's. Jack never accepted this.

"You were not the father, Jack?" Curtis asked in a courtroom way, lawyer that he is.

"I would have no objection to being the father, if it were true," he said. "But there is no chromosome of mine there. The child has my name, but that's all it has."

"And all this was settled in court, Jack?" Curtis again.

"Well, yeah. I have no contact with Joan or the child, though it's no child now, all this happening years ago."

"How do you feel about Joan now?" I asked.

"I feel about her the way I feel about all the women in my life — splendid creatures."

"I remember your telling us, Jack, that you addressed *On The Road* to Joan," I said.

"When did I say this?"

"Well, as I recall, you told this to Jim and me one night when you visited Lowell a few years back. That is, before you returned to Lowell permanently."

Kerouac began nodding. "Well, it's true," he said. "I was writing it to Joan because she was the most receptive person I'd ever known. While I was working on it, I used to read long passages to her — and she was a great audience, digging everything that I would tell her."

"But you broke up," said Curtis abruptly.

He tried to lace what followed with anger, but he failed. "Nothing lasts forever, Curtis," he began. "Or wouldn't you lawyers know anything about that?" Then he said quietly, "Everything dies."

"Do you ever hear from Joan, Jack?" I asked.

"No. It's been years and a lot of things have happened in between."

140

"Yeah," I said. "Like Jack Kerouac becoming an internationally famous author."

"Cut the bullshit, Jarvis," he said. Then he got back to Joan. "As a matter of fact, quite sometime after we broke up, an article appeared in one of those confidential magazine things with Joan as the featured personality."

"What was it all about?" asked Curtis.

"Well it was one of those 'my life with Jack Kerouac' things," answered Jack.

"You mean something like one of Hemingway's wives writing about him?" I injected.

"Who's Hemingway?" said Jack. We laughed. "Anyway," he went on, "I didn't especially like that sort of thing and I even told Joan about it. 'What'd you do that for?' I asked."

Then Kerouac affected a comical female voice. " 'Well, this man came to me' she said, 'and told me he had a marvelous idea for an article; so I let him go ahead with it'." Kerouac chuckled. "I'm sure it was one of those barracudas who's always looking for fucked up elements in people's lives."

I remember that right after this comment, Jack became suddenly annoyed with the subject. "Ah, who the hell cares about any of this shit!" he exclaimed. The rest of our cocktail lounge meeting that day reverted to the usual capricious winds of Kerouac oratory; few topics lived longer than a minute on Kerouac's forum.

But his words, "fucked up elements in people's lives," rang loud. They were uttered in the context òf his second marriage, but they can be superimposed on Kerouac's relations with the rest of the women in his life. His first two marriages lasted a total time of less than a year. Measured in these terms, the concept of love becomes a mockery indeed. This is not to say that Jack Kerouac was incapable of loving another human being. The question really becomes: was there one sustaining love in Kerouac's life? Answer: yes — the ideal. A cliche, of course, but in Kerouac's case he pursued it with a tenacity that few people can claim. All his travels were frenzied quests for someone to tell him, "I love you." Kerouac never heard those words. They were spoken to him by some, but they were on another frequency, one that Kerouac never received.

141

George Apostolos, the G. J. Rigopoulos of Kerouac's Lowell novels remembers Kerouac's first dates. "He was shy. He used to get all tongue tied when we'd meet a couple of girls. It was strange, really, because Jack was the best talker in the gang — that is, whenever he decided to let go. But he'd never go after a girl himself. I remember when I worked as an usher after school at the old Rialto Theater on Central Street. I was around seventeen, eighteen, about Jack's age. Well, I'd meet a lot of girls there, and once in awhile I'd line up a couple for Jack and me. Now as you know, Jack was really a handsome kid, and I'm sure that every girl he'd meet could be nothing but pleased when they saw him. So we'd go out on a double date, and I'll be a son of a gun if Jack would lay a hand on them. Well no, he'd smooch; but here I was, a young kid trying to explore this thing called sex, and not really knowing what the next minute would bring, and here was Jack, also a young kid, and I'm sure, also going out of his cotton picking mind thinking about sex — and he would hold back.

"Yeah that's right. You know in those days nobody had a car, so if we wanted to do some smooching or even more than that, we'd wind up in some high grass field along the river, or some back alley after dark. Well, on a double date we'd separate for awhile — that is, Jack and his girl would be on one part of the high grass and I with my date would be in another part. Privacy. Well, after we did what we could, we'd meet and probably go for a soda downtown or whatever. *Then,* after we dropped off the girls, the big question would be asked."

I couldn't resist interjecting at this point. I knew the question George Apostolos was referring to, and it was a question I hadn't heard in that context for many years. " 'D'you get in?" I said. "That was it, wasn't it, George?"

"Right. That was the question. 'D'you get in?"

"If I'm not wrong," I followed, "the question they ask today is: 'D'you make it?' or 'D'you score?' "

George smiled. "Well everytime I'd ask Jack, 'D'you get in?' the answer was in the negative. But don't misunderstand. Jack was as normal as apple pie. I think he had this thing about sin."

"You mean that sex was something that was immoral," I said. "Unless you did it only with your wife."

142

"Yeah. I guess that was it. Don't forget that Jack came from a strict Catholic home. His mother especially was on top of him. She was a strong minded woman and I always had the feeling that she wanted Jack to hang around with more well-to-do kids; I mean kids that came from wealthy families. It wasn't that she didn't approve of me or Scotty or the rest of the gang. I think it was mostly her ambition for him."

"And how did Jack take all this?" I asked of George.

"Well, as far as the gang was concerned, he wouldn't trade us for anybody — not even a millionaire's son. But now that I'm thinking about all this, so many years later, I think it affected him in another way. He was so intent on doing no wrong. I mean I never saw anybody so obsessed with staying within the law. He wouldn't even steal an apple from an old farmer's tree in Dracut. He was always worrying about the rightness and wrongness of things."

"And do you think that this obsession spilled over in his early dates, the dates you've been talking about? You mentioned sin and how Jack seemed to be hung up on it."

"I think that was all part of it."

"So that this shyness you attribute to him was actually a monumental concern for staying within the moral boundaries set for him by his family — his mother mostly. Or, another way of putting it, Jack was bedeviled by a sense of guilt the first time he discovered he could masturbate." I remember George Apostolos laughing hugely at this.

"All I know," he said, "was that Zagg (Jack's nickname) was a great kid and a great buddy, and I never saw him harm anybody out of a sense of viciousness or hatred."

It's true that "Zagg was a great kid," but his contacts with women were anything but great. Once we get past his romantic high school image of *Maggie Cassidy* (discussed earlier in this work), we see that Kerouac never quite achieved a meaningful relationship with any woman. His first two marriages come across like a weekend at a mountain lodge. His third (and last) marriage emerges as a discovery by Kerouac that he had finally met a person who could truly care for him, but he never deluded himself that this was a marriage where flesh and spirit were ideally consummated. As a wife, Stella Sampas devoted herself

143

to Kerouac's welfare; and her devotion stretches even further when one considers that she calmly and willingly accepted the constant and demanding presence in the household of Kerouac's invalid mother. Thus where Kerouac's first two marriages, brief as they were, existed away from Memere, the last one gathered in both wife and mother, together; and through the fog of these last years, it is not improbable that, occasionally, Kerouac had difficulty distinguishing between the two.

"Jack was as normal as apple pie," said George Apostolos — but he was talking about his boyhood buddy. And this boyhood buddy went on to a Beat World populated by Allen Ginsberg, Neal Cassady, Gregory Corso, William Burroughs — definitely not "normal as apple pie."

"You know I made it with Kerouac quite often," said Allen Ginsberg in an interview in *The Real Paper* dated March 28, 1973.

"Now I'm not a queer," wrote Jack Kerouac in *Vanity of Duluoz,* a book he composed in 1967-68.

Until recently, the matter of Jack Kerouac's sexuality had never publicly come into question. Kerouac emerged on the pages of his books as a vibrant athlete, masculine, virile, or as a young man passing in and out of the lives of lovely, sometimes tragic young women. In his first book, *The Town and the City,* he's the high school football star; in *Maggie Cassidy,* he's the track star; in the last book published while he was alive, *Vanity of Duluoz,* he recounts his high school football days and goes on to his abbreviated college career.

As for his image as a "lover," it begins as a youthful idyll in *Maggie Cassidy,* then moves on to a brief, sad affair with Terry, the Mexican girl of migrant workers in *On The Road.* In *The Subterraneans,* the image takes on a new dimension as the black girl (Mardou Fox) comes into our hero's life. Then follows *Tristessa,* in which another Mexican girl provides the dynamics for our hero's erotic explorations. Finally, in *Big Sur,* our protagonist, Jack Duluoz, is nearly destroyed in a ghastly relationship with a young mother: she is in a cabin with her small child; Duluoz is there also; they want to make love but the child is in the way; the scene evolves into a Kafkaesque nightmare with Duluoz at last being shattered by an attack of

144

delirium tremens. In his account, Kerouac, the author, laces this Big Sur Scene with an apocalyptic element, a kind of religious redemptional force that hopefully will purify the hero.

The Duluoz Legend then, sculptures a figure that, in its agonizing search for meaning, is ever masculine, ever straight if you will. The only "deviations" that appear are deliberate observations (almost afterthoughts) on the unfortunate realities of abnormal eroticism. Here, he appears to advance a mild reproach towards those who pursue such fulfillment. Even more interesting is his attempt to eradicate any doubt that his magnificently vast relationship with Neal Cassady was anything but "agape" — a brotherly love.

In *Big Sur*, Cody Pomeray (Neal Cassady) is releasing a double clutching, screeching two-wheel sharp curve negotiating, barrel assing monologue. Cody is fixing up Jack Duluoz with one of his (Cody's) women, always feeling that it was right for them to share their women; sort of like two Indians cutting wrists and mixing their blood which would make them blood brothers.

Jack Duluoz is listening to Cody; he is wide-eyed, thrilled, ecstatic with disbelief that he is blessed with such a friend. As the narrator in the book, he expresses his joy that two men can love each other without homosexual overtones.

There is an attitude in his words; a wish, a hope that men can love each other in a clean, wholesome way without the threat of dirtying it up by erotic deviation. One can almost hear Kerouac thinking aloud: "I was taught that this kind of eroticism is evil — and I truly believe that it is. I want to be your true friend; give me a chance to be that; and if we become true friends, let's not spoil it, despoil it, by ranging off into dark alleys. Let's keep our friendship out in the open, under a pure sun where nature, always perfect, will nurture it in perfect symmetry."

Of the inner conflicts that attacked Jack Kerouac, the concept of sex gratification had to be one of the most intense. He was raised in an environment that not only considered sex a supremely private matter but also a sin oriented activity. The medieval doctrine that "Man is born in sin" was poured into his mind; thus his reluctance in his Lowell youth "to get in."

When he left Lowell, the medieval doctrine did not stay behind; and when he met Cassady, Ginsberg and the others, its somber awful voice would come at him and flagellate his spirit, and he would wriggle and writhe under a shadow of guilt. But these new friends were too attractive, too exciting, too overpowering to renounce. And large facets of their world became Kerouac's also, and he found himself strapped down on an ambivalent rack of erotic desire.

In the aforementioned Ginsberg interview in *The Real Paper*, the great Beat poet speaks willingly, openly — according to his lights — of his friend Kerouac's sexual azimuth: "Well, he was very mixed sexually. He had a lot of trouble with his mother, with attachment to his mother, and his mother's dependence on him. He was a football player, and he liked girls. He liked to eat girls, and you know, he was really hung up on girls. That's what really excited him: black panties! Black stockings! He also appreciated, he had a funny kind of interesting appreciation of beautiful boys, and an appreciation of older queens, like a really novelistic personal appreciation, which was like a sharing of common humanity, and a sharing of emotions, even a sharing of the erotic, except that he didn't feel it was right for him to participate in the erotic . . ." [25]

A remarkable passage indeed. Remarkable because it could easily suffice as the "sex biography" of Jack Kerouac — though there are people who were just as close, closer even, to Kerouac, that would look on this passage as the hallucinatory spendings of a madman. Certainly Jack's widow, Stella, would dismiss it, as would his mother; Jack's Lowell friends would also place it in the realm of fiction.

But the passage is there and it bears consideration. The reference to Kerouac's mother easily slides into a projection of Kerouac's unresolved feelings towards her. A number of times, Kerouac tried to snip the umbilical cord; his road adventures were part of that effort, and even more determination is exhibited in his first two marriages. But he failed, and his last marriage, which saw both wife and mother under the same roof, comes through like an aside in a play, an aside that speaks of a sad compromise. If there are Oedipal echoes in the aside, they are left to the indulgence of the audience.

Proceeding with Ginsberg's comment, we next confront the idea that Kerouac liked girls. Ah, that's more like it. But wait.

"He liked to eat girls . . ." adds Ginsberg. From heterosexuality to sodomy in one leap? (Those who are Kinsey-minded will challenge the term, sodomy, but I am bound to remind them that it is used in the context of Kerouac's indelible early morality.) From this stage, Ginsberg goes on to another level: "he had a funny kind of interesting appreciation of beautiful boys . . ." Homosexuality, certainly, but refined to an even more delicate image: pederasty. True, Ginsberg concedes it was "a funny kind" of pederasty, but that only deepens the deviation. From this point, Ginsberg (unknowingly?) seems to return to Oedipal regions. Kerouac had "an appreciation of older queens." The spectrum is complete. And what a spectrum!

And yet, how real is it? "He didn't feel it was right for him to participate in the erotic," Ginsberg adds further. This could explain Kerouac's incessant guilt syndrome, but it could also diminish the length of the erotic spectrum that Ginsberg delineates. If Kerouac didn't feel it was right to participate, then how much of this spectrum is reality — and how much the abstract gleanings, the interpretations of Ginsberg, himself?

In another part of the interview, Ginsberg says, "I blew him I guess. He once blew me, years later . . ." Certainly there are many people living today in Lowell and in other places, who sincerely wish that Ginsberg wouldn't *guess* about such things.

The face that Jack Kerouac saw in the mirror never reflected the attributes that Ginsberg sculptures into it. Jack never saw homosexuality, bisexuality, or whatever other devious dimensions the (monstrous) human brain can create. What he saw was a man whose depths of lust could be reached only by a woman; he could never admit that there was anything else but this man-woman relationship; everything in him fought against all other forces that might disturb, disrupt, destroy this perfect union.

In *The Subterraneans*, Kerouac refers briefly to his thrilling discovery of Wilhelm Reich's book, *The Function of the Orgasm*. He exults in the clarity of vision with which this author illuminates his mind. Yet the quintessence of the thesis focused by Reich is one that Kerouac credits to himself. "Something I'd always known and closely indeed connected to my 1948 sudden notion that the only thing that really mattered was love, the lovers going to and fro beneath the boughs in the Forest of Arden

147

of the World, here magnified and at the same time microcosmed and pointed in and maled into: orgasm — the reflexes of the orgasm — you can't be healthy without normal sex love and orgasm . . . (and even without the help of Reich who shows life is simply the man entering the woman and the rubbing of the two in soft — that essence, that ding dong essence . . ." [26]

It does not have to be an argument really — this matter of Jack Kerouac's sexual psyche. Ginsberg's portrait and Kerouac's self-portrait differ basically in the final touches. Kerouac paints "the andras" (the pure male) while Ginsberg paints the universal androgynous one, the one that also has the barely perceptible, but ever present brush strokes of the human personality. Who is he that can call himself the complete andras?

148

Chapter 13 - "Published In Heaven"

After Kerouac's second marriage ended in the Spring of 1951, he found himself back with his mother in New York City. Nothing had really changed. He had written two books (one already published), he had been married twice, he had traveled the United States and Mexico, he had met Neal Cassady who had now become his great hero, — and he was still helplessly dependent on his mother.

But in this year, Kerouac's mother decided to live with her only other child, her married daughter in North Carolina. The decision disturbed Kerouac; for awhile, he felt like a little boy lost in a carnival, parted from his mother. He looked around, bewildered. What to do? He was still the writer; he would always be that. But in the meantime, there was this task called living, the day-to-day confrontation with putting on one's clothes, going to a job, eating, digesting, worrying. Yes, what to do? He wound up in California living with Neal Cassady and his wife; this was after a crazy incredible chase pursuing a merchant seaman's job which began in New York and ended in California. The job (suggested by a friend) was on a ship that first docked in New York, refused Kerouac's application, continued on to California, found Kerouac waiting there insisting on a job, and moved on — without him.

It was prophetic, this desperate, unsuccessful pursuit of the seaman's job. In the six years that followed, Kerouac continued to write, chasing after another ship — the fulfillment of his art. But it, too, kept moving off from the pier — without him.

While living with the Cassadys, Kerouac began working on another book, *Visions of Cody*. It was really "visions of Neal Cassady," a voluminous series of characterizations, all distilled from the persona of his friend. This time, Kerouac did not have to follow his source on frenzied expeditions. Neal was right there, and Kerouac took "a thousand snapshots" which he developed rapidly, excitedly. Like all the other books that would gush from his mind in the next six years, *Visions of Cody* would remain unpublished, squeezed in with other manuscripts. A short version appeared in 1960, and the entire work was published post-humously in 1973.

"Published in heaven" is the way Allen Ginsberg characterized the early, anonymous years of his work and that of his Beat buddies. And for a long time, Jack Kerouac lived by this credo — though not necessarily by choice. It's true that he had published one book, *The Town and the City,* not in heaven but on earth; but it would be seven years before he would find another publisher in this world. In the meantime, he would conceive, his literary sperm flowing in a river of creativity that leaves one breathless. Something like fifteen works, poetry and full length novels, were born. And the scenes where conception took place were scattered everywhere: the West Coast, The East Coast, travels in between, Mexico — writing on the run, on the road.

And he was on the road again in the Spring of 1952. He left the Cassadys after staying with them a few months and headed for Mexico City to his friend, William Burroughs. His only luggage was a duffel bag holding his manuscripts. (If he happened to also have in it a copy of *The Town and the City,* he could claim that the duffel bag — at that time — contained the "complete works of Jack Kerouac.") Yet the works were not complete. *Visions of Cody* was still aborning; *On The Road* was still being worked over; and a new piece was taking shape: *Dr. Sax.*

Kerouac loved to say that he wrote most of *Dr. Sax* sitting on the toilet bowl in William Burroughs' Mexico City place. I suppose a psychologist could find passages in this book that would confirm the environment that the author claims for its conception. One could be the following:

> "When Joe lived on Bunker Hill Street and we were 8, 9, we explored first thing the banks of the Merrimac in that part along Lakeview Avenue then-Polish slums where the river swam dirtily, meekly without rock-roar along the huge red walls of Boott Mills—we'd on rainy Sunday afternoons in February run down there to kick at ice floes and rusty empty kerosene cans and tires and crap — One time we fell in to our hips, got wet — Big brother Henry shat against a tree, he actually did,

squatted and aimed an explosion on a lateral line, horrible." [27]

Yes, it was horrible — and Kerouac kept on writing.

William S. Burroughs was regarded by Jack Kerouac as a kind of wise man, a sage, a seer. Burroughs was a few years older than Jack and the latter admired Burroughs' incisive observations on the human condition. "He's the genius of the group," Kerouac said of Burroughs in our 1962 Lowell radio interview. What was also interesting about Burroughs was the family from which he came: it owned the great office machines firm, an economic empire. But Burroughs "dropped out" early and sought his own way of life; it led to friendships with Kerouac, Ginsberg, Cassady; it led to vast drug experimentations and drug addiction; and it led to social experimentations delineating a sliding scale between heterosexuality and homosexuality.

In Mexico City, at the time of Kerouac's visit, Burroughs was awaiting the publication of his first novel, *Junkie*. (This novel and a later one, *Naked Lunch*, would bring prominence to Burroughs as a serious writer.) Kerouac stayed with Burroughs a few months, writing *Dr. Sax*, ingesting the various drugs in Burroughs' collection, and drinking. Between the two, drugs and drinking, the latter was to become Kerouac's problem. Though he took drugs over the years, he never reached the level of addiction; his real addiction was drink — and it would eventually kill him. Of drugs, he wrote years later:

> "That long before I'll lose track of my beefs (complaints) I'll go cracked and even get to believe, like those LSD heads in newspaper photographs who sit in parks gazing rapturously at the sky to show how high they are when they're only victims momentarily of a contraction of the blood vessels and nerves in the brain that causes the illusion of a closure (a closing-up) of outside necessities . . ." [28]

Would that Kerouac had applied those words to *his* addiction.

When Kerouac left Mexico City, his duffel bag heavier by one more manuscript, he was on an aimless course again. In a situation like this, he did what he always did: back into the womb, back to his mother. Memere was staying with her daughter in Rocky Mount, North Carolina. They were, of course, glad to see him, but Jack knew that his visit would be a short one: Rocky Mount was no place for a writer aflame with creative desire and thirsting for experience. So in the Fall of 1952 it was back to California and the Neal Cassady scene. Jack worked as a brakeman on the railroad and out of this came *October in the Railroad Earth,* a vivid, sensitive, poetic-prose projection of his mind's eye as it caught the California landscape easing by, as it caught the railroad civilization of the men that created it and as it caught the twilight sadness of a train whistle hooting in the wind. There are great echoes of Thomas Wolfe here — but without the punctuation.

By late 1952, Kerouac was ready to move on again; the latest chapter of his California life had been completed; and he had had enough of Cassady for awhile. He was in New York in the Winter of 1952-53, and, of course, he was back in the womb, Memere. She had agreed to live with him again so they found a small place in Richmond Hill. They were still poor, mother and son, Jack being no nearer to writing success than the first day he had decided to make his living that way. Memere certainly was aware of all this — and yet she decided to go on with her son; she went back to the shoe factory to help out. Why? Gabrielle Kerouac liked New York; she had always wanted to leave Lowell and live in the big city. Gabrielle Kerouac wanted her son to succeed, not only artistically, but materially; when Jack was a boy in Lowell, she always urged him to seek playmates from well-to-do families. Finally Gabrielle Kerouac was a mother; she loved her son.

Thus the widow and her son took up their monastic existence again. I say monastic because Kerouac usually described this phase of his existence by saying, "I am the monk and she's the reverend mother." So Kerouac was again at his writing pad and his typewriter. And that's all that mattered, that's all that would ever matter. Some years later he wrote:

> "Nothing could stop me from writing big books of prose and poetry for nothing, that is, with no hope of ever having them published — I was simply writing

them because I was an 'Idealist' and I believe in 'Life'
and was going about justifying it with my earnest scrib-
blings — I wrote those manuscripts as I'm writing this
one in cheap nickel notebooks by candlelight in poverty
and fame — 'Fame' of self . . ." [29]

That winter of 1952-53, Kerouac began to see some of his
New York friends again. Ginsberg, Corso, Holmes — all were
glad to see him, but they also realized that Jack was still the
loner, the lonesome kid from Lowell who was still looking for a
simple, beautiful explanation of life. Also at this time, Holmes'
book, *Go* (discussed earlier in this work) had been published,
and one can only imagine the dismay and frustration that
Kerouac must have experienced. Both he and Holmes had
written about the new Beat civilization: Holmes had published
his one book while Kerouac had a number of books, still in
manuscript form, and reduced to performing only one function
— gathering dust.

But Kerouac bore on, writing with the passion and dedica-
tion of a martyr. He went back again to his Lowell years and the
result was *Maggie Cassidy*. It quickly joined the other manuscripts in the repository that at this time could only be mockingly known as "the complete works of Jack Kerouac." When
Jack finished the book, he was off again, leaving Memere deeper
in the well of wonderment about her son, "the writer". It was
California again and Cassady — and nothing. He was back in
New York, Summer of 1953, and, though he didn't know it,
was to find another diamond for his private collection of literary
diamonds. This would be known as *The Subterraneans*.

Some critics have called this book the "most beat" of
Kerouac's novels; for it attempts to portray the subculture of
poets, lovers, esthetes — artists all who lived outside of American society. The subterraneans according to these critics were
the beats, focused more intensively than in any other of Kerouac's books. The book, however, coagulates around a love affair
between Leo Percepied (Jack Kerouac) and Mardou Fox
(young black girl) which is complicated by a third party, Yuri
Gligoric (Gregory Corso).

I personally believe that the book is more of a confessional concerning Kerouac's feelings about propriety in the world. His remarks about the Reichian theory on orgasm are shouts of approval of normal relations between male and female. The affair between Leo (the white man) and Mardou (the black woman) actually points up the hopelessness of it: miscegenation becomes an unthinkable concept in Kerouac's mind. Leo Percepied's comments about his mother are nothing more than Kerouac's own unshakeable, if not tortured, emotions: a child is morally bound to love and take care of his mother.

I think the book is a monumental irony in that Jack Kerouac purports to explain "the subterraneans" (of whom he is presumably a part) to straight society when in reality he is explaining them to himself; thus the confessional essence of the book. But then I believe that Jack Kerouac's whole life was a massive irony: the King of the Beats was in essence the observer-biographer of the Beats.

Beyond its confessional aspects, *The Subterraneans* presents a characteriization of Gregory Corso; he completes the triangle in the love affair, though he is portrayed as the unwilling object of Mardou Fox's attentions.

I first met Corso at Jack's funeral, in October, 1969. He was subdued, saddened, a little confused. We didn't say much to each other and I was left with the impression (even allowing for the funeral atmosphere) that he was not particularly communicative — at least in conversation. Then I met him again almost four years later at the Jack Kerouac Symposium at Salem State College. What I saw was a compulsive talker who was surely breaking himself down with booze and drugs. His face was shattered and with his long hair straggling around him, all I could think of was an old hag.

We immediately hit it off very well. "You're that professor friend that Jack had in Lowell, right?" he said.

"Right," I said. "Actually, I'm also a native of Lowell — but I'm not a Canuck like our old buddy Jack."

Corso squinted; I was to discover that this is one of his favorite gestures. "You look like a Russian to me," he said. "You wouldn't be a Russian Jew, would you?"

"I'm a Hellene," I said deliberately, "otherwise known as a Greek to the barbarians."

It was then and there that our relationship solidified. Corso had visited Greece, had lived there, and from the remarks that followed, he obviously adored the country, its inhabitants, and their approach to life. He began to throw some Greek phrases at me and I responded in kind. My wife Rena who was sitting with us, began unraveling a long thought in faultless Greek. (She is also of Greek descent).

Corso was impressed. He turned to me. "Why didn't you tell me your big beautiful wife was from Greece?" he said in mock anger. "The minute I saw her, I just knew she was Greek. I just love the Greek women and their 'kolo' (Greek word for buttocks); it's so full and firm."

My wife and I laughed. It was easy to see that Corso enjoyed his on and off role as a comedian, a clown. In this respect, he reminded me, strangely, of Jack Kerouac. "Mr. Corso," I said, "I can fully understand your appreciation of the beauty of Greek women. However, just to keep the record straight, my wife is not from Greece. She was born in Lowell, like me and Kerouac. However, she *is* descended from the Hellenes, like me and unlike Kerouac. As for the Greek language, we both learned it from our parents."

"Makes no difference where a person is born," said Corso. "The blood is there. Your wife should be up in the Acropolis right now, walking around in a tunic and sandals."

We were having luncheon prior to beginning the symposium. My wife and I happened to be sitting next to Corso, and I was delighted with the opportunity to talk to him. But I didn't want to spend the time talking about my wife's Hellenic morphe. "Did you really take away that black girl from Jack?" I suddenly diverted the conversation. "The girl that Jack calls Mardou Fox in the *The Subterraneans?*"

Corso easily shifted with me. "I did no such thing," he said, effecting the tone of one unjustly accused. "That girl dug me, man, she dug me. I was just a younger buck, that's all."

"Did Jack really threaten you with violence?" I asked.

"Well, he never got around to that," Corso said, seeming to apologize for Kerouac. "I think he decided that nothing was worth violence — especially on a friend. Besides, old Jack never really dug that girl. It was all passing through the night. She was

155

just another character for his books. The last thing Jack would do was bring home a black girl to his mother. As a matter of fact, the last thing Jack would do was bring home any girl to his mother."

"He was married to a wonderful girl, Stella Sampas, and they all lived together," I said.

"Well then, in his old age Jack got lucky." Then Corso's normally loud voice suddenly subsided. "Except that he drank so much, and never got over that."

In the symposium, Corso became the crowd favorite with unexpected bursts of long oratory, not only on Kerouac, but also on a spectrum of other topics: from masturbation to death. It was easy to see that his buddy Ginsberg became annoyed at times when Corso would unceremoniously interrupt his (Ginsberg's) flowing commentary.

I remember Kerouac talking briefly to me about Corso. "He was a young kid with great talent, but he needed discipline," was the way he put it.

"You sound paternal, Jack," I had said.

"I ain't no pater," he had asserted. "You asked me about Corso, and I say to you that he is great — like the rest of us."

In his book, *Desolation Angels,* Kerouac provides more detail about how he experienced Corso:

> "Raphael Urso (Corso) I liked quite well, too, in spite or perhaps because of a previous New York hassle over a subterranean girl (Mardou Fox), as I say. He respected me tho he was always talking behind my back, in a way, tho he did that to everybody . . . But I loved him too because of his utterdust broodings, the way he stands on a street corner looking down, at night, hand to brow, wondering where to go in the world. He dramatized the way we all felt. And his poems did that best of all."

Desolation Angels was completed in 1961, almost ten years after *The Subterraneans.* Yet Kerouac still writes about "a previous New York hassle over a subterranean girl." It seems that the episode had left a rankling residue in Jack's mind.

156

In a fascinating taped dialogue (which I was privileged to hear) between Kerouac and Corso, a number of topics are "hassled over" by them. One of these topics is Kerouac's views on blacks. The tape is of middle 1960's vintage, recorded in the privacy of Jack's house; also it is evident that Jack is under his booze cloud while Corso is free of any stimulants, until the last twenty minutes or so. I say that the dialogue is fascinating because it quickly evolves into an effort by Corso to get at the truth of Jack's feelings. Corso does most of the talking, ending his long comments with pointed questions. And though Kerouac's answers are short, they are breathtakingly revealing.

In one of his Denver scenes in *On The Road* Kerouac writes:

"At lilac evening I walked with every muscle aching among the lights of 27th and Welton in the Denver colored section, wishing I were a Negro, feeling that the best the white world had offered was not enough ecstasy for me, not enough life, joy, kicks, darkness, music, not enough night . . . I was only myself, Sal Paradise, sad, strolling in this violent dark, this unbearably sweet night, wishing I could exchange worlds with the happy, true-hearted, ecstatic Negroes of America."

In the taped dialogue, Corso confronts Kerouac with this passage. "Did you really mean that, Jackie?" he asks. "Did you really wish that you were a Negro?"

"I meant every word," Kerouac replies.

"That's not the way you feel now."

"Nobody is going to tell me how to live, or come into my house, or insult my own people because they're not Negro."

"Ah, then that's where it's at, Jackie. How could you mean what you wrote when you feel that way."

"I felt that way *then, that night.*"

"But you weren't looking inside the Negro. You weren't seeing his misery, his isolation."

"I wanted to have a good time, the way the Negroes can."

"But they don't really feel that way, they don't want to be that way."

157

"I will never take back one poetic statement I've ever written."

The dialogue goes on to other matters and when at times it seems that Corso has driven Kerouac to the brink of anger, there is laughter from Corso, and Kerouac responds in kind. What appears to be happening here is a friendly kind of mindfucking (if one can ever be friendly about it) on the part of Corso. But near the end of the conversation, Corso wants to make sure that their friendship is still on firm ground. "We are the heralds of a new consciousness, Jackie," he says. "Jackie, you are the most wonderful person, the most wonderful soul."

That Jack Kerouac harbored prejudices is not startling, of course; the human race has been so afflicted since it first inhabited this planet. But the nature of his prejudices is what makes him one of the most startling contradictions in modern literature: the man who articulated the Beat Rebellion was in reality a small town conservative. "I believe in the mysticism of the Catholic religion," he asserted one night in a Lowell bar.

He might have put it another way: "I'm not really a 'beat,' but still a young boy who was raised in the "Little Canada" section of Lowell where fear of God, hard work, and material acquisitions were the only criteria for a proper life."

In Jim Curtis's law office one day, Kerouac added to his conservative, narrow dimensions. This was in 1967, about a year after he had re-settled in Lowell. I met Jack in Jim's office for a luncheon date. But there was an additional reason for Jack's presence; he wanted Jim to build up a case against the producers of the TV hit show, *Route 66*. Ever since the show had become popular some years earlier, Jack had festered in outrage. That day in the office, he told Jim and me what I'm sure he had told others many times.

"The thesis of that show was taken, lock, stock, balls and guts, from *On The Road!*" he shouted. "These two guys that go around experiencing life — hah! — are but mere appendages of Dean Moriarty and Sal Paradise — Neal Cassady and Jack Kerouac. Why even a lot of the background scenery that you see in this show is in the San Joaquin Valley — the very place that figures prominently in *On The Road*."

"We'll do all that we can Jack," Curtis tried to placate him.

"Well so far nobody's done a goddam thing and those fucken Jews are stealing my eyeballs." It had been awhile since I had seen Kerouac's eyes reflecting anger. They were doing so now. "The fucken Jews are stealing from me!" Kerouac smashed on. "They're presenting that show — *Route 66* — it should be called Route 69 — they're presenting it as an original creation. The only one that has any right to claim the thesis of that show as an original creation is Jean Louis Lebris de Kerouac — that's me. Now are you going to get after those bandits or do I get another lawyer?"

I remember pain on Curtis's face; and I knew the reason for it. The official name of his law firm was Goldman, Goldman, and Curtis. "Jack, take it easy," said Curtis. "Your emotions are getting the best of you."

"Emotions shit!" Kerouac bombed away. "What I'm telling you stems from pure, pristine reason!"

"Okay, okay," said Curtis. "I'll start working on it."

"Well, don't wait until we're all pinholes in the universe," Kerouac urged him on.

Nothing ever came of the *Route 66* issue, but Curtis had a chance to serve Kerouac in another way. In *Vanity of Duluoz* Kerouac writes: "The other night, now (1967), when my cat died, I saw his face in Heaven just like old Harry Carey saw the face of his loyal Negro porter in Heaven at the end of the picture *Trader Horn*. I don't care who the person is you love: you love the loyal, the helpless, the trusting." What he doesn't write here is the fact that he came storming up to Curtis's office demanding that a suit be brought against the veterinarian that attended his cat. Kerouac claimed that the vet gave his cat some medicine and soon after the animal died.

"I want that medicine chemically analyzed," Jack insisted. "That fucken quack killed my little sweetheart. He's a murderer of innocent beings!" (The reader may well realize that friendship with Jack Kerouac was not always an easy thing.)

Curtis was getting ready to do some homework on cases involving veterinarians. However, before he got into it very deeply, the report on the chemical contents of the cat medicine came to his office. There was nothing wrong with the medicine. The cat just died.

There's no doubt that Kerouac had a thing for cats. In *Big Sur*, years earlier, he writes tragically of another cat that died: Tyke. What is curious here is that he laments the cat's death in a manner that is reminiscent of his brother Gerard's passing. One explanation of this (if any explanation is possible) may be Kerouac's indelible image of Gerard in a St. Francis of Assisi setting: animals nuzzling him in a spirit of love and trust.

Chapter 14 - "Published On Earth"

Following the writing of *The Subterraneans* late in 1953, Jack Kerouac found himself standing "on a street corner looking down, at night, hand to brow, wondering where to go in the world." He wondered for a few months, living with Memere in New York. Then early in 1954, he crossed the country again and once more he was with Neal Cassady and his wife. For the time being, Cassady was no longer a chief source for a new book. *On The Road* and *Visions of Cody* had temporarily exhausted Cassady as literary material.

What happened during the few months that Kerouac stayed with the Cassadys was a venture into the study of Buddhism. Kerouac went into it with the thrill and wonder of a man who had discovered the secret of Life. But it was all a game; it could never be anything but a game. First of all, Kerouac at this time was seeking diversionary movement. He had become madly frustrated by the literary treadmill he was on. He had written six books since *The Town and the City*: all lay moldering in anonymity. To keep from rushing to the top of the Empire State Building and screaming to the world: "All you people out there — now hear this: I have written six magnificent novels — but you have not been allowed to read them, because those fink publishers won't let you — all they're interested in is counting their shekels — people of the world, rise up and stone these parasites to death!" Yes, to keep from doing this, Kerouac stormed into Buddhism.

But aside from the diversionary aspect of his new found religion, Kerouac could never be serious about it because he was a Lowell born, Lowell reared, French-Canuck Catholic. The only way he could free himself from this, was to break the mold — which would break *him*. But it was not a waste, this Buddhism phase; for a few years later he would write *The Scripture of the Golden Eternity* and *The Dharma Bums*, reminiscent musings and dialogues of his Buddhistic journey.

In the Spring of 1954, Kerouac was back in New York, with Memere. If there were nothing else to do, he could continue his writing. He put together a collection of impressionistic free verse which he entitled *San Francisco Blues* and he started scribbling dream thoughts which eventually would be published as *Book of Dreams*. Later that year, he decided to visit his hometown.

He hadn't been to Lowell for sometime; he felt the need for a return to innocence. The results of this visit are best reflected in a letter he wrote in 1958 to James Alexakos who produced the radio show that Jim Curtis and I had for a number of years on a Lowell radio station:

> "I'm very proud to hear about *Dialogues in Great Books* on WCAP, that Mr. Jarvis and Mr. Curits discussed my book . . . My best boyhood friend in Lowell was George J. Apostolos, I wonder if you know George. If you ever want 'reminiscences' of myself (like, if I died) just ask old G. J. Apostolos.
>
> "I do long to re-visit Lowell and will do in 1958 but also I'm a little bit scared too. Everytime I cross the Moody St. Bridge I feel a weight of guilt. But at the same time Lowell fills me with joy. As I told Charlie Sampas, I revisited in 1954 and hiked about 25 miles around town (much like Charlie does) and recognized all my old chums but they didn't see me. I was a 'Ghost.' Maybe that would be a good theme for our radio talk, a walk around Lowell, by a revisiting child of Lowell."

(Kerouac did not actually revisit Lowell until 1962.)

Later that same year (1958), in a letter written to me, he expressed in part:

> "I'm glad that you and James T. Curtis discussed Town & City — Soon I'll write another great big book about Lowell, to be titled MEMORY BABE, where I'll remember everything that happened in Pawtucketville and even Centerville (in my family circle, that is). The kids on Phebe Avenue called me memory babe when I was a boy because I could remember way back . . . even then . . ."

Yes. Kerouac's 1954 visit to his hometown was a return (just for a moment) to innocence. When he went back to New York, reality was there, waiting for him: those unpublished manuscripts mocked him. The next few months saw Jack and his mother transplant themselves from New York to Rocky Mount, North Carolina. They lived with Jack's sister. Jack was still pursuing his Buddhist discoveries, but more significant, he had declared a moratorium on writing about his beat world.

Jack stayed in Rocky Mount until mid-summer, 1955. By that time, he was ready to go again. But where? He had no money, he had no plans. Then it happened: *On The Road* was accepted by Viking Press, and a small advance followed. Kerouac didn't know it then, but it would be two years before the book would be published. Yet for the first time in years he felt redeemed. He threw off the burden of being looked upon — especially by his family — as a dreamer, a social mutation. He took off for Mexico City and he was back at the writing wheel. What resulted was *Mexico City Blues*, 242 choruses (poems) of cultural spectrum, a jagged line of thought from Lowell to San Francisco, from Zen to Christianity, from folly to wisdom, from life to death. (I have heard a tape of Kerouac reading from *Mexico City Blues*. What takes place is a kind of tragicomic performance. He begins reading with strength, but about a third of the way, his tongue begins to rebel. What was happening, concurrent with his reading, was a slow but steady consumption of booze. The clink of bottle against glass, and the flow of liquid from bottle to glass to mouth could be heard. He never got beyond the 150th chorus.)

Before leaving Mexico City that summer, he also wrote the heart of another book, *Tristessa*, a sad, drug-hazed relationship between Jack and a tiny, tragic, born-loser Mexican girl.

Kerouac headed for Berkeley, California to join Allen Ginsberg. His duffel bag of "the complete works of Jack Kerouac" was now bulging. What he found when he reached California was a cocoon of young poets who were about to burst from their prison. Though he spent quite a bit of time with Ginsberg, Ginsberg was involved in a project that left Kerouac outside looking in. The historic Six Gallery Reading was on the verge of realization. Ginsberg had gathered four young poets, Michael McClure, Gary Snyder, Philip Whalen, Philp Lamantia, and the venerable

163

San Francisco poet, Kenneth Rexroth, to participate with him in presenting a public reading of their work.

It was held on an October night in San Francisco and the ensuing years have etched the event in legendary proportions: the birth of the new American poetry. Kerouac was there that night, moving about, applauding, encouraging. Later, in *The Dharma Bums*, he writes, behind the face of the character Ray Smith, "And I was the one who got things jumping by going around collecting dimes and quarters from the rather stiff audience standing around in the gallery and coming back with three huge gallon jugs of California Burgundy and getting them all piffed . . ."

Is it unreasonable to deduce that Kerouac felt left out — when all the time he was burning with the conviction that he was the greatest writer present that night — waiting, still waiting in the wings?

The significance of Kerouac's visit to California that year was not his presence at the Six Gallery Reading or even his seeing his holy buddy Neal Cassady a few times; the significance was his meeting with Gary Snyder, poet and Buddhist scholar. Kerouac was still riding the wave of Buddhist discovery; thus when Snyder, a new person in his life, rose before him like a Buddhist temple of wisdom, he exulted in his good fortune. A fine friendship evolved rapidly and the climax was a brief mountain climbing sortie (High Sierras) that Jack was taken on by Snyder and John Montgomery. The importance of this was the adding of another dimension to Kerouac's drive for experience. This first brush with a mountain became a sizeable segment of *The Dharma Bums*. The concluding pages of this book recount his two-month hermitage the following year as a fire lookout on Desolation Peak in the Cascade Mountain Range of Washington State. In a subsequent book, *Desolation Angels,* Kerouac expands on this existence on a mountain top and reaches even more deeply into the depths of his isolation.

Thus the Buddhist found his retreat; Kerouac had to cut himself off, even for a moment of his life. It was the sort of thing that he felt was part of his integrity; something he would never forgive himself for if he had left it out of his life. And he properly thanked Gary Snyder for helping him fulfill this need.

164

There are two brief passages that in my opinion provide Kerouac's epilogue to his mountain life — if not all of his life. In *The Dharma Bums,* Ray Smith (Kerouac) has just come down from his mountain job. He looks up at the sky and says, "I have fallen in love with you God. Take care of us all, one way or the other." In *Desolation Angels* he writes of his time on the mountain: "In 63 days I left a column of feces about the height and size of a baby."

Near the end of the year 1955, Kerouac looked East again; he had been out of the womb long enough; he must return. Memere was in North Carolina — and that's where he went. His next novel was written here and the presence of his mother and his sister under the same roof with him must have helped. For it was here in the months that followed that he wrote *Visions of Gerard,* a prose-poetic hymn of his long dead brother and Jack's earliest recollections of the Kerouac family that lived on Lupine Road in the Centralville section of Lowell. Jack told me that this was his favorite work — and I believe it. "Of those millions of words that came exploding out of my brain," he said, "those that went into *Visions of Gerard* were the purest that came from heaven." (My various quotes from *Visions of Gerard* in the early portion of this work, I believe strengthen the truth of Kerouac's stated preference for his spiritual biography of his brother.)

Jack Kerouac left Rocky Mount in the Spring of 1956. He headed for California where now practically all of his closest friends were living: Ginsberg, Cassady, Corso, and the new friend, Gary Snyder. Before leaving Memere, he had received notice of an appointment as a fire lookout for the coming summer in the state of Washington. When he arrived in California, he settled down in a somewhat primitive one room dwelling (a shack, really) with Gary Snyder. (He was still pursuing his Buddhist dream.) The shack became his alone when Snyder left for Japan a few weeks later to study oriental culture.

While waiting to set out for his fire lookout job, Kerouac wrote. What came out was a collection of random thoughts entitled *The Scripture of the Golden Eternity.* Here Kerouac is the Buddha sage, yielding revelations in a Tibetan bell-tower mode; he is a bhikku who closes his eyes and sees the "mysterious

165

particle-swarming emptiness." The book is an uneven effort and its brevity probably reflects a paradox: Kerouac did not write his best whenever he tried to curb his naturally prolific creative urges.

Prior to his departure for Desolation Peak, Kerouac got together a number of times with his friends, Ginsberg, Cassady, etc. He soon discovered that the original Six Gallery Reading of the previous year (at which he was present) had blossomed into further readings. Ginsberg was acquiring limited fame, soon to become unlimited with the imminent publication of his *Howl And Other Poems* by Ferlinghetti's City Lights Bookshop. Kerouac had no choice but to wait his turn, and it's certain that he wondered if his turn would ever come.

In June of that year (1956), he turned his back on the San Francisco scene and headed north to keep his appointment with Desolation Peak. Kerouac's own account of the 63 days he spent alone on a mountain peak obviates any outside comment. I sincerely believe that it ranks with the more splendid aspects of Thoreau's Walden drama, the main difference being Kerouac's use of twentieth century liberated prose.

When Kerouac came down from the mountain, he could have done one of two things: perpetuate his mountain experience and devote the rest of his life to being a bhikku, a monk, a recluse holy man; or walk back, against the wind, into the storm of man and take his chances.

He took his chances. He rejoined his friends in San Francisco: Cassady, Ginsberg, Corso, others.

One would think that Kerouac would effect his re-entry into the societal atmosphere with some circumspection and a precious reluctance of surrendering too quickly his newly gained monastic aura; I say one would think this. But no. Kerouac plunged into the storm like a man who had a lot of lost time to make up. Girls, parties, long night drinking scenes — Kerouac ran through it all with a screaming sense of panic; Desolation Peak was already fogging up with mockery. Yet, I would not want to charge fakery here. What it proves to me is Kerouac's inordinate capacity to absorb experience and to recreate it magically on the written page. His Desolation life was sincere — while it was happening. This was true of just about everything that Kerouac ever did.

One day in September Kerouac woke up and decided to move on. There was no special reason. So he got on the road again — this time to Mexico City. He always liked Mexico City, calling it an ideal place for the struggling creative artist who needed to survive just short of starvation, until the world would wake up and embrace him. Kerouac was still a struggling creative artist.

What ensued at Mexico City after he got there was days and weeks of nothingness. He got together with an old friend, Bill Garver, whom Kerouac calls Bull Gaines in *Desolation Angels* and whom he characterizes as a junkie philosopher whose apparent mission in life was to turn on the world to drugs. Tristessa, his lover of earlier days, was still there; but the relationship was now but a pitiful memory. For Kerouac, at this time, Mexico City did not prove the ideal place for the artist—possibly because there is no such place. His writing did not stop, however. He put the finishing touches to *Tristessa,* the novel he had begun a year earlier in the same city he was in now, and he began a new book, *Desolation Angels*; this would not be completed until five years later.

What gloom had closed in on Kerouac as the days wore on, was somewhat dispelled by the arrival of Ginsberg, Corso and two friends, the Orlovsky brothers. A few weeks of the riotous life followed, until they all finally wound up in New York City. The year 1956 was running out and what Kerouac did not know then was that his years of anonymity were also running out. In *Desolation Angels,* Irwin Garden (Ginsberg) is urging Duluoz (Kerouac) to leave Mexico City and come with him to New York. "It's time for you to make it!" he yelled. Duluoz responded: "Make what?" Garden's answer: "Get published, meet everybody, make money, become a big international traveling author, sign autographs for old ladies from Ozone Park —."

And it would happen in just about that way — though Kerouac must have suspected Ginsberg's complete sanity as the latter unreeled his prophecy.

Kerouac did not stay long in New York. It was Christmas, 1956, and he spent that holiday with his mother, his sister and her family in North Carolina. It was nice being "home" for

Christmas; it was a lovely interlude and Kerouac was able to blur temporarily his years of "failure." Yet he must have sensed something stirring, something imminent. His manuscript, *On The Road*, was still in the hands of a publisher who had accepted it for publication. It had been there for more than a year and its birth was inevitable. But the waiting, the waiting.

In February of 1957, Kerouac left the family and embarked for Tangiers in Morocco. He stayed with William Burroughs who had a place there and would soon be joined by Ginsberg, Corso, and Peter Orlovsky. What happened to Kerouac in Tangiers constitutes one of the great ironies in literary annals: he abdicated the throne of the Beat Kingdom — a throne he had not yet possessed, a kingdom that had not yet been born. But it would all happen a few months later.

While waiting for his friends to arrive, Kerouac took a long look through the telescope of his life and it appeared to him as if he were looking through the wrong end: everything seemed so far away. There was an absurdity, a perverseness in what he saw, and a spiritual exhaustion came over him. His friends' arrival did not help; they brought with them their enthusiasm, their great expectations, their free souls. The din was too much for Kerouac; he had been this route too many times. What it came to finally was Kerouac saying to himself, "I want my Mama." And Mama is what he got.

He left the group and returned to the United States. He picked up his mother, bought two bus tickets to California, and soon the Widow Kerouac and her son were bouncing across the American highway in the wildest version yet of "on the road." Kerouac writes magnificently of this trip in *Desolation Angels*.

In an article for *The Atlantic Monthly*, (July, 1965) Dan Wakefield suggests: "If the Pulitzer Price in fiction were given for the book that is most representative of American life, I would nominate *Desolation Angels*." In his discussion of this book, Wakefield comments on this "cross-country pilgrimage." "Their bus trip from Florida to San Francisco is one of the most true, comic, and grizzly journeys in American literature." [30]

And so it was. Jack Kerouac, moving on — not with Neal Cassady and his thousand and one schemes, not with chance road

buddies who flashed on and off; Jack Kerouac, moving on —
with Memere! And, as the cliche goes, Memere was game.

They were going to California hoping to settle there permanently. But when they arrived in San Francisco, Jack almost
immediately realized that they had been chasing an evanescent
horizon. It was too late in life for Mrs. Kerouac to function
comfortably in a vibrant city like San Francisco; it somehow
frightened her. So back they went after a few weeks, to Orlando,
Florida, where Jack's sister was now living; they took an apartment near the sister — and waited. Or rather, Jack waited.

Before leaving San Francisco, Jack had received advance
copies of *On The Road*. It had finally found covers. This was
May, 1957. Now, Jack was in Florida, with Memere and Nin, his
sister. They were together at the moment when at last Jack would
be vindicated as a writer. The years of doubt, criticism, acrimony
would fall away. The timing was perfect.

In September of that year, *On The Road* hit the book stalls.
And it happened quickly. The book landed on the best seller list;
Jack Kerouac emerged from the shadows; and the Beat Generation had found its spokesman. The King of the Beats was now to
ascend to his throne. It (the throne) was waiting for him. But
he had renounced it (to himself) in Tangiers, a few months
earlier.

He decided to reconsider. The reading public demanded to
see, to hear, to learn about Jack Kerouac, new anti-hero of the
American Scene. So Jack went up to New York to lay himself
open. T.V., Radio, newspapers, magazines, cocktail parties —
all had their shot at him. And when it was all over, there was
something strange about it. Years later, Kerouac, himself, tried
to explain it to me. "I wrote about this somewhere," he said. "By
the time *On The Road* made me and my beat brothers famous,
I was beat — and I don't mean beatific, I mean *beat, pooped,
tired.* All that I had written about in this book had happened
years earlier. When it finally got to the reader, I was practically
in my middle age. These kids were thinking of a Kerouac who
was young, strong, full of piss and vinegar. And when they finally
saw him, they thought they were looking at Kerouac's father —
not Jack Kerouac, King of the Beats!"

"You mean it was all over before it got started, Jack?" I said.
"I mean, all over for you?"

"Well, my body said it was all over; and my mind, even. You
wouldn't expect me to keep running around with a rucksack on
my back — like a high school kid. Man, I was ready for my
slippers and my rocking chair."

But when *On The Road* lit up the sky, Jack was not allowed
to fall into his rocking chair and ease into his slippers. He was
set upon by the vast, tentacled monster of the public. They
ripped and tore at him and Jack was supposed to love it —
because it was all admiration and fame. Well, maybe he did love
it; but just to make sure that he wouldn't get hurt, he bombed
himself into a state of suspended animation: he drank more than
ever, so that more often than not, he appeared before the public
in a kind of novocaine stupor.

Some people feel that a natural shyness in Jack caused him
horrendous pain when the spotlight finally hit him. Bullshit. I
feel that there was this perverse thing in Jack (we are all perverse
in a Melvillian way) so that when fame came, he felt somewhat
like an impostor; he felt that his brother Gerard should be receiving all the adulation, or maybe Neal Cassady, or Sammy Sampas,
or George Apostolos, or all of them together, together with
every other character that appeared in his books. Guilt.

In the middle of this sudden fame, Jack wrote *The Dharma
Bums,* his Gary Snyder-Buddhist-mountain spiritual period. The
book was written in the Fall of 1957, and besides its artistic
worthiness, there is its added significance in point of time. It
marked the end of a seven-year period in which Kerouac
machine-gunned his way through twelve books; twelve books that
were written, not in the quiet of a private study or on the terrace
of an Italian villa overlooking the splendor of the Mediterranean,
but in places like the middle of a lonely Kansas road, in a dimly
lit kitchen in Rocky Mount, North Carolina, or on a toilet bowl
in William Burroughs' place in Mexico City. Besides the literary
achievement involved here, it was also a truly spectacular feat
of strength and endurance.

Jack Kerouac did not write another book for four years. He
didn't have to; he had a duffel bag bursting with "new books."
He could indulge in a rare luxury: producing new books without

170

lifting a finger. And the duffel bag gave up its treasure. *The Subterraneans* and *The Dharma Bums* were published immediately following the great success of *On The Road*. They seemed to be the likely successors to the beat bible, *On The Road*; they perpetuated the world of the beat, the holy rebel, the seeking dropout. It turned out they did not have the monumental thrust of the beat bible — at least with the reading public. They sold mildly and their main attraction was that they were written by the now generally acclaimed King of the Beats.

While this was going on (1958), the King of the Beats had taken up a quiet existence with his ever loving Memere. With more than ample money coming in now from his authorial success, Kerouac moved from Florida to Northport, New York, a tranquil town not too far from the Big City. It was not, however, a perfect transition because occasionally Jack chafed at the nearness of New York City where Ginsberg, Corso, Holmes and the rest of the old gang made the scene. Memere was aware of this "temptation," and it made her more determined to keep her son "down on the farm." Her efforts gained more credence when it was learned that Neal Cassady, one of Jack's few friends that she liked, was sentenced to five years in jail for possession of marijuana. Whatever arguments Jack had for wanting to go to his friends in New York City were temporarily wiped out. Memere was the boss. So Jack stayed home, drank some beer (he had abandoned booze for awhile) did some reading, and wrote an occasional magazine article.

It wasn't long, however, before Kerouac tired of the "good life." He began to break out (despite Memere's warnings) and get together with his soul mates in New York City. It was a replay of earlier times — bars, drinking, some women, dusk to dawn dialogues — but the joy was diluted; it wasn't the same. (Is it ever?) Jack would go home to Northport and face two things: Memere's scoldings and the nagging pain that this wasn't IT, the IT that Dean Moriarty talked about in *On The Road*; the IT that Sal Paradise asked about and Dean laughed and said, "Ah well, now you're asking me imponderables — ahem!"

So Jack lived at Northport and wondered why literary fame didn't taste as delicious as he thought it would. For years he had been the kid with face pressed against the store window; then

171

suddenly the goodies inside were his, but somehow the magic disappeared. And besides the magic, Kerouac's initial success was not sustained for very long.

The next two years, 1959-1960, saw a spate of Kerouac books published: *Dr. Sax, Maggie Cassidy, Mexico City Blues, Visions of Cody* (abridged version), *The Scripture of the Golden Eternity, Tristessa, Lonesome Traveler.* The duffel bag was practically emptied—and Kerouac wondered what the hell his struggles were all about. For these works were generally crushed by the critics. Some roasted Kerouac through a skewer of ridicule, and dismissed him as a fraud. Probably John Ciardi's discussion of *Maggie Cassidy* in the *Saturday Review* best reflects the critics' collective response. He writes in part:

> "My guess is that Avon (the publisher) is banking on whatever mileage may be left in the legend of the beat-jazz to sell a badly mothy bit of juvenilia . . . However, it is mistaken seriousness to treat this stuff as if it could be asked to respond to the criteria of serious writing. There is no interest here in the art of writing."

Kerouac read every line of criticism and each one cut deeply. It would have been easy for him to resort to bitterness, for he was seeing the best part of his literary life murdered. If he felt bitterness, it was short lived; he settled for an incessant pain, a pain rooted in the slow, steady rejection of him by the reading public. I doubt if he perceived this decline when, following *On The Road,* the rest of his books were published within a period of three years. It was too soon to hang crepe. But a few years later Jack told it to me this way: "They're putting us down now; they already have. But that's the way of it. We won't be the first nor the last to be rediscovered."

In the summer of 1960, still living at Northport with his mother, Kerouac must have experienced a crisis, a point of unbearable frustration. He had to change the scenery. What he did was to jump on a train heading for California. He had corresponded with Lawrence Ferlinghetti, poet-friend and owner of the now thriving City Lights Books publishing house in San Francisco. Kerouac had been trying to put together a new work,

172

Book of Dreams, the result of years of jottings capturing scenes from his apparently vast world of the subconscious; City Lights Books would publish it.

When Kerouac reached San Francisco, he tried living at a cabin that Ferlinghetti owned near Big Sur. Once more, Kerouac was seeking isolation, a catharsis of the spirit, IT. Absurd. Kerouac was beset with physical discomfits. His attempt at a Desolation Peak revival ended after a few days, and he was back in San Francisco hitting the bars and consuming alcohol with the frenzied desperation of a man who's about to lose his taste buds.

Kerouac learned that Neal Cassady had recently been paroled after serving two years of his jail sentence. Cassady had resumed his family life near San Jose. The two had not seen each other in more than three years — not since the publication of *On The Road,* the book that had made Neal Cassady (Dean Moriarty) one of the great anti-heroes of American literature. It is somewhat ironic that in the period of the book's greatest popularity, its protagonist was burning time in prison. Right to the last day of his life, Kerouac never quite focused Cassady's attitude concerning *On The Road.* Cassady seemed to be pleased; I say seemed, because Kerouac could never crush the notion that his buddy's expression of pleasure reflected a Mona Lisa light about it.

Jack and Neal got together and there were some good times. Yet, there was a beat missing (no pun intended) — there always is. The last big scene for Kerouac in California was at Big Sur (Bixby Canyon, actually). He ended up there with a young woman and her four-year-old son. The scene contains all the elements of a Kazantzakis novel: man's natural forces rushing against the spiritual tide, the result being a madness that seems to accurately reflect the human condition.

I could never get Jack to talk to me about this episode, though I tried a number of times. Yet if Kerouac's books are "all true stories" (as he always insisted) then we have the scene caught in his book, *Big Sur,* an account of this final farewell to California, to San Francisco, one of the meaningful settings in the tapestry of the Duluoz Legend. The episode moves horrendously: Jack in sexual struggle with the woman; the child there, in a wonder of innocence; Jack swept far out to a sea of delirium

173

tremens where he conjures a vision of the cross; then, peace. In *Dr. Sax*, Kerouac writes of childhood visions, in his room, in the dark: ". . . horrors of the Jesus Christ of passion plays in his shrouds and vestments of saddest doom mankind in the Cross Weep for thieves and Poverty."

Had the Kerouac psyche lived a thousand years —.

CHAPTER 15 - A BRIEF REIGN

Following his Big Sur experience (religious or otherwise) in the Summer of 1960, Jack Kerouac returned to Memere in Northport, New York. He "collapsed" there; not a breakdown, as it were, but rather like the feeling of a tire jack that's pumped up, almost reaches the pinnacle — and then slips. Kerouac spent the winter of 1960-61 trying to set up the jack again. It wasn't easy. His crown as King of the Beats, only recently gained and once sparkling, was beginning to totter and lose its lustre. It seemed like such a short reign. But Jack was not dead; he was still alive, breathing, feeling, thinking; he continued doing what he could do best — writing. *Book of Dreams* was published by his friend, Ferlinghetti; it was almost ignored. But he kept on; there was nothing else to do.

In the Summer of 1961, mother and son leave Northport and move south again, to Orlando, Florida, to be near Caroline again, the only other living member of the Kerouac family. Jack began to occupy his time by working on an unfinished manuscript he had begun a few years earlier. This was to become eventually *Desolation Angels*. In his pursuit of this book, he even took a short trip to Mexico City hoping that this old haunt would help him come on stronger. (One of the major settings of the book is this location.) But there was nobody there: Ginsberg, Cassady, Corso, Burroughs, Garver, Tristessa. But it made no difference really; Kerouac needed no props; he could write anywhere.

Back in Florida with Memere, he began another book: *Big Sur*; thus, he was working concurrently on two manuscripts. Yet this was nothing unusual for Kerouac; for years, his incredible creative energy had criss-crossed the boundaries of his inchoate manuscripts. There was still a substantial reserve left of this energy.

Jack and Memere stayed on in Florida until late in 1962, when they moved back to Northport. A few weeks before making this move, Jack visited Lowell. His arrival was almost simultaneous with the publication of *Big Sur*. The closeness of the two events was not planned.

175

As near as I've been able to find out, Kerouac had not been to his hometown for eight years prior to this visit. When his first book, *The Town and the City* was published in 1950 (the "town" being Lowell and the "city" being New York) his fellow townsmen took note, even though the general public was somewhat less responsive. The local newspaper, The Lowell Sun, did a feature on the book in its Sunday edition; but it all soon ended, and Kerouac submerged and did not surface again until 1957 when *On The Road* fell on the ears of Lowellians and the rest of the world with the force of a sonic boom. Fame followed, and even though this fame had diminished by the time he visited Lowell in 1962, the name Kerouac still created interest — in and out of his hometown.

I had not seen Jack since high school days, more than twenty years earlier; I didn't know him very well then. Now with this visit, I would become one of his close friends.

I found him at a local bar on Market Street. When I saw him, I was stunned. The once dark-maned, clear-eyed Endymion youth had become a soggy, booze-bloated hulk. He was bombed and he was noisy. He wore a pair of fatigue pants, a plaid shirt, three quarter shoes, and a hunter's cap which reminded me of the kind that Admiral "Bull" Halsey wore on the bridge of his ship. What I didn't know then was that all but four or five of my remaining contacts with Kerouac would be under these conditions: he in a state of alcoholic euphoria and I, sharply sober, gathering in every syllable that streamed from his brain. The booze never diminished his giant mind though, and his physical senses rivaled those of Roderick Usher.

In the bar, I was introduced to Kerouac as an English Professor. "I've long admired your work, Mr. Kerouac," I opened. He had been trying to sing with Andy Williams' version of "Moon River" sailing out of the jukebox, when he suddenly stopped.

"Do I remember you?" he asked.

"You might," I answered. "We were in high school together, though you were a year ahead of me."

"You mean I look as old as *you*? Impossible!" I laughed. "Are you really a professor?" he asked abruptly. I nodded. He bowed Arabic style, and when he came up he said, "Is it true that professors have the highest rate of masturbation in the professional ranks?"

I smiled, probably nervously, and said, "I don't know. Has such a survey been made yet?" He laughed. I sat down and for the next three hours managed to utter about forty words. Kerouac released about forty thousand of them. He sang, he made speeches, he roiled around the room. Occasionally, he would quote poetry, and then look mischievously over at me, presumably for approbation. I approved.

Before I left him that night I tried to solicit from him a promise to appear on our local radio show — *Dialogues in Great Books* — which I and Jim Curtis had been conducting for a number of years.

When I put the question to Kerouac, he looked at me suspiciously and I felt that he not only doubted the existence of the program but also my claim to being a professor. I added that we would tape the show but that we would have to go to the studio to do it.

"I'm leaving in a few days," he said. "Ain't got time for such pedantic displays."

"Tomorrow would be fine," I pursued. "Any hour of the day you prefer."

"You're not kidding me, are you?" he snapped. "You look like a member of the Mafia to me."

"Look, I'm not even Italian," I said. "My heritage is Greek. You grew up with some Greeks here in Lowell. That alone should reassure you."

He chuckled a Sodomean joke about Greeks and said, "Okay, you gray-haired lecher. I'll be up at your one lung radio station tomorrow at three."

And he was. My radio partner Curtis and I were disbelievingly overjoyed. He came up there with Stella Sampas, his wife to be, and we sat around a table and got ready to tape the program. The sound engineer was off to one side and just when we were ready to begin, Kerouac whipped out a pint of booze, took a quick gulp, placed the bottle before him, took a deep breath and said, "Okay, let's start throwing the crap around."

I have heard many literary interviews in my day and thus had assumed that ours would follow the general format of philosophical exchange. I began with an introductory comment intended to focus the idea of a milestone having been reached in our program. I never finished the comment for Kerouac seized on the word, milestone. "I am Louis Milestone," he announced. "Milestone, gallstone — death." I didn't know it then, but the pattern for our interview (which it really wasn't) had been set.

In the course of the next half hour Kerouac came at us like a thunderstorm, blowing and booming wild revelations. Yet, in between the gusts and whippings, he would enter periods of quietude, leaving us becalmed and awkwardly striving to keep the program going. He reached peaks of rapture and crashed to deep chasms of ecstatic melancholia. As I think on it now, it was a minuscule version of the human emotional scale. Curtis and I had difficulty focusing questions, so rapid and capricious was Kerouac's span of attention. I have heard the tape many times and I have come to the conclusion that, in that half hour, Kerouac was the epitome of Dean Moriarty with all the fits, starts, stops, and all the forces that impelled Moriarty to try to corner IT, to burn, burn, burn.

Yet despite the Kerouacian (he preferred Kerouquackian) storm that howled around us and his constant nipping at the bottle, we did manage to shout out a few questions — and get some answers.

He was indignant when he was asked about the extent to which he revises his work. "Once God moves that hand," he shouted, "and you go back and revise, it's a sin! Every time I turn on the faucet — in the toilet — no, wait a minute — and the water comes from the river — my thought doesn't have to be improved — because I got it from Heaven!"

As to his approach to writing, he said: "I write in vast 18,000 words a night bursts for about a week and the book is done. I use a sixteen-foot strip of teletype paper in the typewriter and blast away, single space, saying, 'I'm going to tell you what happened,' — because it's all true stories and all I do is change the names."

Kerouac likened his method to that of Honore de Balzac and his prose to Marcel Proust. "I've read Proust's *Remembrance of Things Past*," he said in a most serious tone, "and decided to do just like he did — but fast." To further punctuate his disdain of revision, he opined that Shakespeare wrote *Hamlet* in one night. Then, scooping up his bottle and belting one down, he muttered that Shakespeare died of drinking in Avon.

In the middle of a question that Curtis was framing concerning Kerouac's *Big Sur,* Kerouac boomed out that Proust and Joyce are the greatest writers of the twentieth century. He lamented that Joyce died before he was able to write down the sounds of the sea, but that he, Kerouac, would do it for him.

The chameleon mood of Kerouac came through vividly at this point. Following his near bombastic remark on Joyce, he announced that another of his manuscripts would be forthcoming soon. He didn't wait for a question but loudly proclaimed its title — *Visions of Gerard.*

"Who's Gerard?" Curtis asked. The question was devastating. A twilight haze veiled Kerouac's face, but through the veil we now could see a bewildered little boy striving to find his way out of the sudden darkness.

"Gerard is my brother," Kerouac said softly. "He died when he was nine. I was four at the time." I noted his use of the verb, is. There was silence as the tape kept spinning on, and Curtis and I looked at each other and I'm sure that we both felt that a wrong door had been opened.

We were relieved (but only for a moment) when Kerouac resumed. "When he was on his deathbed," he said in a halting, trembling voice, "nine nuns filed into his room and said, 'Gerard, repeat what you told us about Heaven'." Kerouac stopped; his jaw slackened and as he continued, "Gerard told them and . . ." a barely perceptible whimper escaped from his lips. Once more, silence fell on us and I thought I could hear the tape mutely turning.

I struggled for a transitional idea and said, "That's a very beautiful thought, Jack. Very beautiful."

He seemed to revive, though his voice remained subdued. "Before he died, Gerard told my Mother he was going to build her a beautiful white cottage in Heaven." The word, Heaven, trembled as it was uttered, and again Kerouac's eyes betrayed a questioning, a flash of pain. Suddenly, he bolted and regained his

179

windblown, capricious, impetuous voice. "*He's* the one that's doing all *this!*" he spurted. By *this*, Kerouac meant, of course, his books, written and to be written. Kerouac was Gerard, living on, writing, sucking up the wondrous wells of life. Gerard was not dead; he was alive; Kerouac was living proof of that.

We left Gerard and Kerouac's mystical reincarnation of him and plunged into a discussion of his Beat literary buddies: Ginsberg, Ferlinghetti, Corso. He praised them all and added the name of William S. Burroughs (he couldn't resist the term, "rotten boroughs") calling him a genius. He claimed credit for providing Burroughs with the title of his *Naked Lunch*. He didn't elaborate.

I brought up Ginsberg's *Howl*, framing a rather pretentious, grandiose question about the inspirational sources that motivated Ginsberg to write his best known poem. Kerouac chuckled and said, "Ashcans and unobtainable dollars! That's what inspired him, man!" I thumbed my nose at him, somewhat resentfully, and he thundered with laughter.

Before the program ended we steered Kerouac into the area of faith, God, belief. True, his words on Gerard had shed some light here. Yet now he became more flippant than ever, though I'm convinced his remarks were seriously intended. He was to repeat them a number of times as our friendship deepened. "I see God," he said, "in a deistic way, in an agnostic way, in a jesuitical way. I'm a Jesuit." Then his flippancy was jettisoned and he said, "I live in a house with my Mother. It's a monastery, and I'm a monk and she's a reverend mother."

Kerouac left Lowell a few days later and the ensuing years saw correspondence between us. For the next four years he lived in Northport with Memere. After *Big Sur* was published in 1962, (and sank to the bottom quickly) *Visions of Gerard* followed in 1963. This book also disappeared quickly. In 1965, *Desolation Angels* came out, and it was advertised as the final summing up of the Beat Generation. Though the idea of finality can easily be argued, the book does penetrate deeper into the characters of the people that lived on this Beat planet. Kerouac, himself, is focused more sharply than ever. But this book didn't sell either.

None of these aforementioned books were written during this

period, 1962-1965; they were from an earlier time and were published, like most of Jack's books, belatedly. Thus these years at Northport proved fallow in terms of Jack's literary productivity. It seemed as if at last the giant reservoir had been tapped out.

If he didn't write much at this time what *did* Kerouac do? He tried to live like most people — at home. He made some friends in the Northport community, notably the painter, Stanley Twardowicz. Yet the community thing would sometimes become too much for Kerouac, would stifle him; he had to get out. His declining literary image added to his pain. Relief would come with an occasional sortie into New York City catching up with any of his Beat buddies who happened to be around. What usually came out of these ephemeral escapes was a drink-shattered Kerouac who would return to Northport and would try to reassemble the pieces — until the next time.

Jack must have awakened one day and been shocked by the thought that he was a writer who hadn't written much of anything for some time. The shock must have intensified as he remembered his former days of floodtide creativity. But what would he write? The Duluoz Legend (both Lowell and Beat) appeared to have been all talked out. I remember Kerouac telling me one day: "A writer needs experience. Some writers need it more than others. I couldn't be a writer without it, because I couldn't sit down and make up fairy tales. I'd be a faker." He went on: "But then experience without the ability to write, without education that is, is no good either; because you couldn't write about your experience, and you'd be just a bash nosed drunk like any other bash nosed drunk who tried to express himself in a bar. Nobody would give a shit." He took one more shot at the idea: "But then again, if one could write but had no experience he'd be like Mr. Milktoast looking up anxiously from his tome, or waving his umbrella at butterflies."

So, in order to end the dry writing spell, Kerouac reached out for one more experience. He got on a plane and shot over to France for ten days. He was on a genealogical expedition which took him to Paris and on to Brittany. He sought out some library sources and came up with what he considered good evidence that his family tree had worthy roots in France. All this was not important really, because what was born of the experience was a thin volume entitled *Satori in Paris*. Satori, a sudden illumination; echoes of Kerouac's Buddhist phase.

A reading of the book will not convince the reader that Kerouac confronted a flash of enlightenment in France. What the book really comes to is a series of responses to French life; but then this was always Kerouac's writing strength: his all seeing eye, his all feeling psyche. The reading public couldn't care less, and *Satori in Paris* joined the growing stack of neglected published Kerouac books. They were beginning to collect dust — something they had learned to do well in their unpublished manuscript state. Another Kerouac irony.

When I asked Jack about *Satori in Paris,* he characterized the book as "a sentimental genealogical journey." He expanded briefly: "I went to Brittany and I went to Normandy, and though I'm not descended from kings, my blood was at the First Crusade."

"You gotta be kidding, Jack," I said challengingly.

He snickered. "Man, everytime I see a Saracen my blood begins to boil!"

In the Summer of 1965, the Kerouacs left Northport for good. They returned to Florida and once more were near the daughter, Caroline. They lived here quietly for the balance of the year. However, the new year brought tragedy. Caroline died.

There is disagreement as to the manner of Caroline's death. In her book on Kerouac, Ann Charters writes that Jack's sister shot herself soon after her husband told her he wanted a divorce. Tony Sampas, brother-in-law to Jack and one of his closest friends, told me that Caroline never recovered from the shock she suffered upon learning that her marriage was destroyed. (I confess that I have been unable to clarify the matter through the means of a death certificate.)

Following Caroline's death, Jack and his mother left Florida and settled in a comfortable home on Cape Cod, Hyannis, Massachusetts. They were back in their native state and Mrs. Kerouac especially was beginning to feel as if they had finally come home — though not exactly to Lowell. Yet they did have some Lowell friends visit them, among them Stella Sampas.

It was a fine summer on the Cape in 1966 and Jack culminated it by marrying Stella. The news media and just about everybody else were genuinely surprised. "Who is Stella Sampas?" was the question. I believe I have answered this question in an earlier segment of this work. Suffice to say that Stella proved to be the last link for Jack on this earth, the last link, that is, with devotion and love for him as an artist and as a man.

Jack Kerouac at the Jarvis home.
Lowell, Mass. May, 1967.

Left to right: Charles E. Jarvis, Jack Kerouac, James T. Curtis.

CHAPTER 16 - JACK COMES HOME

When the summer of 1966 ended, Jack made a somewhat surprising move. He took Memere and his new wife and settled in Lowell. Just prior to the move, Memere suffered a stroke. Thus 1966 proved one of personal tragedy for Jack: the death of his sister, the crippling of his mother. If there were any balance to it, it was his marriage to Stella Sampas.

Jack Kerouac had three more years of life remaining. The first two of these years he would spend in Lowell. Why he came back after years of peregrination, I am still not sure. He gave me a number of reasons, all poetically vague. The one I liked best was that he desired to re-enter the womb. "It's the only place where nobody can get at you," he said. "If Id'a known then what I know now, I never would've gotten the hell outta there!"

These last years in Lowell Kerouac apportioned between his house, writing, and Nicky's Cafe (a bar owned by a brother-in-law), drinking. Soon after he had returned to Lowell, I walked into Nicky's Cafe one night expressly to see him. He was dressed in his usual fatigue pants-lumberjack shirt outfit. Yes, he was drunk, stoned, smashed; but none of these words are really applicable. He told me once that this was "my liquid suit of armor, my shield which not even Flash Gordon's super ray gun could penetrate!"

When he spotted me, he let loose with a Shadow laugh and announced to everyone that I was Lamont Cranston and I had come to blast the underworld. The years that had intervened quickly fell away and Kerouac was at me once more, spattering me with "imponderables" as he called them.

As Kerouac settled deeper in Lowell (which he once described as a "vast collection of Christians") my friend Curtis and I would visit him occasionally. Early in our renewed relationship, I perceived an ill-disguised bitterness that had seeped into him. His outward image was still the same, still the liquored up, free talking, free wheeling exhibitionist. But at times, though infrequent, there would blink forth a sad light in his eye; he seemed to be waiting for something to happen. But then he would suddenly snicker as though he were playing a joke on himself.

One night he was complaining about the royalties from his books. He said that the outlets in foreign countries were short-changing him. *I* wondered about his royalties in the United States. I had no way of knowing whether his overall income was something more than adequate. He lived with his wife and mother in a comfortable, middle range home. Since his most popular book, *On The Road,* years before, he had not hit the mark again with a large audience. True his books appeared on college reading lists, but to what extent, I had no way of determining.

It was in the context of his complaint about foreign royalties that I suggested he come and lecture to one of my English classes at Lowell Tech. "We'll give you a hundred dollars," I blurted out, not sure whether I was treading on sensitive ground.

"Look, you salt and pepper haired old bastard," he admonished affectionately, "I'm asked to lecture at Oxford, Cambridge, Harvard and other hallowed, great seats of learning." (The last five words assumed an exaggerated rhetorical tone.) "Why should I bring my wondrous presence to Lowell Tech?" he added.

"Jack!" I asserted echoing his tone. "This is your own, your native city!" He laughed, and then made a face. "Besides," I went on, "I assign *On The Road* to my classes every year. What could be more ideal than to have the author interpret this classic for them."

He feigned a suspicious look. "Jarvis, screw you and your flattery. My book doesn't need anybody to interpret it. It speaks for itself."

"And so it does," I said. "But think of the impact of your divine presence!"

"Ah yess," he drawled a la W. C. Fields. "There *is* that to consider."

Kerouac did not give me a definite answer, but I was hopeful. My hopes seemed to bear fruit when he showed up at my office at Lowell Tech one day, unexpectedly. It was in the middle of a snowstorm and I was amazed to see that he wore no overcoat. Yet he did wear his "liquid suit of armor" and apparently this kept him warm enough. He was accompanied by a very young man whom he introduced as "Chico from Puerto Rico."

"He's come all the way from San Juan to talk with me about truth," said Kerouac. "And I've come here today to talk about the same thing."

I was pleased that he had come, but I confess that I felt uncomfortable and apprehensive. I had hoped he would give me advance notice; I had also hoped that he would come sober. I introduced him to some of my colleagues and he immediately launched into some obscene observations about professors of literature. They were amused. "You know," he said to one of them, "you remind me of John Updike. Unbutton your fly and let me check."

Kerouac did not speak to any of my classes that day, simply because I didn't have any. He lingered for awhile with his young companion, who by the way, yessed all of Kerouac's oral spendings. Just before Kerouac left, he said that he would contact me and make a formal appointment.

And he did. He called me at Lowell Tech soon after his snowstorm visit and said he would like to make a definite date on which he would visit my class. I was elated, of course, and immediately looked at my calendar and we agreed on a Monday of the ensuing month; that was three weeks away. I happily informed my colleagues and my class of the coming event and was delighted by their positive response.

I saw Kerouac at his house about a week after his phone call, and we enthusiastically talked about his coming lecture. He cackled at the prospect and said, "Jarvis, I'll juice up your students and we'll all get drunk and become holy degenerates!"

"And then I'll get fired," I said, "for corrupting the youth, and I'll be put on trial like Socrates was, and then I'll have to drink hemlock and that will be the end of that!"

"The only thing we're gonna drink will be booze, man. That stuff will kill, too," he said prophetically, "but it takes longer."

As we talked on about Kerouac's imminent Lowell Tech appearance the idea came on me that possibly he could become a more permanent part of the college's academic activity. "How about applying for a writer-in-residence job," I said. "No, I mean it. Here you are, an internationally famous writer, now living in

187

your hometown. You could hold seminars and have the students huddled around your feet classical style."

I immediately saw that the idea caught him, though he said, "Huddled around my feet? What's the matter, are Lowell Tech students paralyzed? Can't they sit up?"

"They can sit up, down, sideways, any way you want them, Jack. I think it's a great idea and there'd be nothing wrong with the money either."

"A writer-in-residence," he said slowly. "Hhmmm . . . that sounds wildly intellectual, Professor Jarvee." (Occasionally, he would gallicize my name.)

"All you have to do is give the word, Jack, and I'll start the ball rolling. I think Lowell Tech would look very kindly on such a prospect."

Though he seemed to be warming to the idea, he had doubts. "Does that mean I'll have to see the President of Lowell Tech, and have to put on a business suit, and go up there with my hat in my hand?"

"Hell no," I said, not really believing my own words. Maybe he *would* have to do all that, I thought, and I winced at the scene of Kerouac coming before the President and the Board of Trustees and letting fly with a cataract of pure, undiluted, uncensored Beatnik patois.

"I don't know, Jarvis," he said slowly. "I think you're trying to suck me into something." Then assuming a pose of mock pride, he asserted, "I'm not a meatball professor; I'm a writer. And the twain never shall meet — unless it's in a steambath!"

We left it there. But two days later I received a letter from Kerouac. It was postmarked Lowell. I thought it strange that he should write, when a telephone was so handy.

Dear Charley:

No, I'm serious about that Lowell Tech writer-in-residence job. Go right ahead for the second semester, and if it's too late for that, let me know. As I say I've had similar offers from other colleges round the country but to these seminars I could walk, over the Moody Street Bridge yet, and after the lecture I can always brood under the bridge or even jump in the river.

I can line up the lectures, brochures.

For the only experience I've had in teaching literature is teaching it, to thousands of kids already informally.

You can't learn how to write, but you certainly can learn why literature tells the truth of a given time.

I've got my haircut and I'se ready.

Yours affectionately,
you old bastard,
Jack Kerouac

P.S. I can write formal business letters if need be, and put in a phoney elymosynary initial, as witness: i.e., ect.
JLK:cej

Who's c.e.j.?

I was glad he had assented. It would be good for our English Department and it would also improve Kerouac's finances which by now I suspected needed improving. I did not anticipate any difficulty with the Lowell Tech administration; I assumed they would see the advantages of such a move.

I was never to find out whether my assumption was over-optimistic. Three days before Kerouac was to lecture to my class, I received a phone call from his wife, Stella.

"Charles," she said, "I must ask you to release Jack from his promise to speak to your class." She was pleading and I knew something had gone wrong. I waited. "Jack has become terribly upset over this thing. He told me he can't go through with it. Don't ask me why, but he's almost in tears thinking about it. He's been drinking more than ever and I'm afraid he's going to get very sick."

Certainly I was deeply disappointed. I wanted to ask Stella for reasons, but the emotion in her voice changed my mind. She sounded as distraught as her description of Kerouac. "Okay, Stella," I said. "Don't worry about it. Tell Jack that he's off the hook and tell him also to take it easy on the booze." I immediately regretted my term, off the hook. "Tell Jack I'll see him in a couple of days."

And for the next couple of days I thought about it. My disappointment gave way to curiosity. The idea of the Beat Prophet who had preached his philosophy all over America, both in his books and from the podium, getting cold feet, seemed absurd. I've seen Kerouac practically stand on a table in a quiet cocktail lounge and make like Dean Moriarty spewing holy goofball revelations. Yes, he was boozed up, but as I've said before, Kerouac's drunkenness was not a mind-numbing state; it was his norm.

I took another avenue. To my knowledge, Kerouac had never spoken, a la successful author, before a Lowell audience. The only speeches he had made in Lowell were in barrooms and his audiences were in a special category, to say the least; they were definitely not interested in literary philosophy. Now, he did not want to speak ex cathedra to a group of students at Lowell Tech. Why? I remembered a recurring thought in some of his letters — crossing the Moody Street Bridge. "Every time I cross the Moody Street Bridge I feel a weight of guilt," he had written in one letter. In his letter about the writer-in-residence job, he had said: ". . . to these seminars I could walk, over the Moody Street Bridge, yet, and after the lecture I can always brood under the bridge or even jump in the river."

The Moody Street Bridge (now called the Textile Bridge) spans the Merrimack River and is astride the area of Lowell in which Kerouac was born and raised. There is no doubt it was deeply interwoven with Kerouac's childhood fantasies. In *Dr. Sax* he writes:

> "By moonlight night I see the Mighty Merrimack foaming in a thousand white horses upon the tragic plains below. Dream: — wooden sidewalk planks of Moody Street Bridge fall out, I hover on beams over rages of white horses in the roaring low, — moaning onward, armies and cavalries of charging Euplantus Eudronicus King Grays loop'd & curly like artists' work, and with clay souls' snow curlicue rooster togas in the fore front. I had a terror of those waves, those rocks—." [31]

Thinking about his wife Stella's urgent, near-hysterical impor-tunings to me, I wondered if Kerouac had developed a "terror" of speaking at Lowell Tech, going before his hometown, stripping himself spiritually naked — for all his fellow townsmen to see. He talked about brooding under the bridge or even jumping in the river. If Kerouac were committing slow suicide by his cease-less, tragic drinking, maybe he was afraid of speeding up the process crossing the Moody Street Bridge.

The reader may recall that Kerouac visited me at Lowell Tech one snowy day and claimed he was ready to speak to my class then and there. Yes, he crossed the bridge that day; but in the midst of a howling snowstorm, I don't think Kerouac even *saw* the bridge.

The Moody Street Bridge: a psychoanalyst might have a bet-ter answer. He might call it "gephirophobia," a fear of bridges. Of course, Kerouac probably feared this *one* bridge and the flood of melancholia that would inundate him crossing it and remembering "The Night the Man With the Watermelon Died" and dwelling on child glooms.

When I saw Kerouac, soon after Stella's phone call, he tried to make light of the entire affair, that is, his change of heart about lecturing at Lowell Tech. "Man," he said, "the whole thing would be absurd. Why, I'd scare the hell out of them. I'd be Boris Karloff (and he stooped and grimaced) and I'd spook all those kids, and they'd run home to their mamas and say that a bad boogie man hurt their little souls." Despite his attempt at satire, humor, whatever, I could see an ill-disguised anxiety in his eyes. "Besides," he pressed on, "old Boris didn't need any juice but I'd have to have it man; it's the only thing that lasts."

He tilted his head and waited for my response. I could see he was now in pain; I decided to relieve him of it. "Why Jack," I said, trying to perpetuate his own feigned attitude, "you couldn't hurt anybody. Why, I've always pictured you as a *good* boogie man. However, you're absolutely right. Those kids wouldn't dig Boris Karloff."

He laughed hyena fashion and practically shouted, "Jarvis, despite the fact that you're a book-bound, hard cover at that, class imprisoned professor of bull excrement, you *do* make it, no question about that." He picked up his ever present bottle and swallowed an unusually long (for him) measure of booze. With those words, I knew that he had dismissed once and for all the whole plan of speaking to my students and pursuing the writer-in-residence position.

My students and my colleagues were disappointed when they learned that Kerouac wouldn't show up. When I tried to tell them why, I had trouble sounding coherent. I finally stopped in mid-explanation and simply said that he had changed his mind. I had assigned *On The Road* in anticipation of Kerouac's appearance. I now felt like an understudy, but a most unwilling one. The class discussion that followed seemed to me like an attempt to evaluate a copy of an original painting. The original was only a couple of miles away, though it might just as well have been in The Louvre in Paris.

In my class of about twenty students, only two or three had read *On The Road* before I assigned it. Moreover, only a few of the rest had ever heard of Kerouac prior to my course. In their comments, most of them reflected a subtle bewilderment. They attributed generous significance to the book, but they weren't quite sure why. Many confessed to having difficulty surmounting the first few chapters but then quickly admitted that once they succeeded in this, they latched onto Kerouac's coattails and really enjoyed the ride.

"Did he really do all that stuff that he writes in the book?" asked one student, and from the ripple that followed I knew that the question was important to them. Too bad, I thought, Kerouac isn't here to really sock it to them.

"You bet your life he did," I answered. "Dean Moriarty, Sal Paradise and all the rest of those mad saints were rolled up into one guy — Jack Kerouac. If Ernest Hemingway's books are partly autobiographical, Kerouac's books give you the whole man, the physical and spiritual marrow of him. This may sound wild to you, but there are passages in Kerouac's books that sound like *Saint Augustine's Confessions*."

"Is that why he claims that Beat stands for Beatitude?" came the question.

"That may be as good a reason as any," I practically shouted, though I couldn't recall ever hearing Kerouac claim Saint Augustine as a source of inspiration.

192

"I read somewhere that the Beatniks are considered the philosophical fathers of the Hippies," said another student. There was a challenging note to his voice.

"Don't let Kerouac hear you say that," I said. "Though he's not a violent man, he would at least spit in your face. In my talks with him about Hippies, he kept coming back to one term, 'loud mouthed fags.' He had no use for them; said they were assuming a stature they had not earned, said they were playacting, said they hadn't produced any real literature and never would."

"He sounds bitter to me," was the retort.

"Maybe he is. He's written some great books and few if any of these Hippies are aware of them."

"Maybe they don't say much to the Hippies."

"Maybe the Hippies don't have the capacity to receive much." This was exactly what I wanted to avoid: an apologia for Kerouac. "At least," I added quickly, "that's what Kerouac might think."

"Is it possible," asked someone else, "that *On The Road* and his other books are not with it today? Don't say much if anything about the social revolution, the many movements that are underfoot today?"

"To Kerouac," I answered, "the word, today, encompasses an eternity. Like any serious writer he's got an eye out for posterity."

"I don't see how he can ignore what's happening right now. That's part of posterity, too."

"Right you are," I said, "and I think that's where the answer lies. What's happening right now is too painful for him to dwell on for too long a time. He prefers a romanticized America which in the context of current events makes him an arch conservative. That's why I think he glares at the Hippies and I might say, other protesters. He sees them a threat to his beautiful America."

"Man, I think he's out of it," whispered someone.

I heard it. "I'm not so sure. Kerouac has never thought himself a reformist. As a matter of fact, he's never seen himself as belonging to any group — despite the Beatnik label — except that universal club we all belong to: the human race. What he writes in his books is what everybody longs to express and understand: life experience."

I picked up my copy of *On The Road* and read them the last paragraph:

"So in America when the sun goes down and I sit on the old broken-down river pier watching the long, long skies over New Jersey and sense all that raw land that rolls in one unbelievable huge bulge over to the West Coast, and all that road going, all the people dreaming in the immensity of it, and in Iowa I know by now the children must be crying in the land where they let the children cry, and tonight the stars'll be out, and don't you know that God is Pooh Bear? the evening star must be drooping and shedding her sparkler dims on the prairie, which is just before the coming of complete night that blesses the earth, darkens all rivers, cups the peaks and folds the final shore in, and nobody, nobody knows what's going to happen to anybody besides the forlorn rags of growing old, I think of Dean Moriarty, I even think of Old Dean Moriarty the father we never found, I think of Dean Moriarty." [32]

"Man, that's out o' sight," I heard one of my students say. I figured that was as good a time as any to dismiss the class.

If Jack Kerouac had not quite managed to bring himself as a speaker to Lowell Tech, (whatever the reasons) he succeeded in doing so at Lowell High. Yes, Lowell High, scene of his football and track glories, recurrent setting for some of his novels. The occasion of his appearance there could easily blend into an episode from one of his books; and had he lived long enough, he would have caught it in the netting of his far flung prose.

Greg Zahos, a friend of Jack's, is the man in the middle of this episode: "Jack Kerouac Returns to Lowell High." In the school year of 1967-68, Greg was a substitute teacher at Lowell High, being called sporadically to fill in for absent teachers. He taught English. On a late Autumn night, Greg and Jack were sitting in Nicky's Cafe. Jack was drinking, talking, dramatizing, incessantly — the Kerouac pose. Greg was drinking a little and listening a great deal. Around one in the morning, Jack insisted that Greg come home with him "for a couple of nightcaps." They went to Jack's house where they spent the rest of the early hours listening to tapes of Bach's music. Stella and Memere apparently slept through it all, or if they didn't, chose not to interfere.

When the sun began to show, Greg got up to leave; he was going to Lowell High for a day's teaching. It was then that Jack startled him by demanding that he go with him. "Man, I'll teach those kids a couple of things about English," he said. "I know a *little* about it, you know." Greg looked at Jack, drunk, dishevelled; he had a moment of misgiving — and decided to take him along.

When Greg reported to the school office to find out what his assignment would be, Jack followed him in. One look at Jack, and the staff, mostly women, got uptight. Greg, of course, noticed this, but he was into it too deeply now; he decided to push ahead. He introduced Jack as "the famous writer and an alumnus of Lowell High." Their reaction was to call up a couple of coaches from the athletic department. When they got to the office and saw Jack they got ready to bounce him. Greg was about to intervene, to explain, whatever, when Jack changed all that by launching into a reminiscence of his great days as a sports hero at Lowell High. One of the coaches remembered Jack, and what it all came down to was an ambivalence on their part as to how to handle the situation. They all finally moved out of the office; the coaches went back to their post and Greg headed for his first class followed by Jack.

Greg got into his classroom — still followed by Jack — and began speaking. As he spoke, the class listened, but not with full attention. It was diverted by the figure of Jack sitting on his haunches in a corner of the room. Soon, Greg introduced Jack to the class; the introduction was necessarily detailed because the students there, save for one or two, had never heard of Jack Kerouac. Jack got up, went to the front of the class and asked: "What is the White Whale?" A student responded and the moment became electric. "That's fantastic!" said Jack, and he took out a crumpled dollar bill and forward passed it to the student. His gesture was sincere and what followed was a genuine class discussion on Melville and his masterpiece, a discussion that was kept fired up by Kerouac's burning presence. If at first the students had been focusing part of their attention on Kerouac's

195

unlikely (raunchy, one might say) appearance, they aimed it all at Kerouac, the teacher, soon after the discussion began.

When the class was over, Greg headed for his next assignment, Jack still with him. On the way, the two coaches appeared again. They told Greg to continue on, and Greg remembers looking over his shoulder and seeing Jack engaging the coaches in enthusiastic conversation. Greg did not see Jack for the balance of the school day. That night, Greg was once more with Jack at Nicky's Cafe.

In the long night's Kerouac oratory, there was only a brief reference to his Lowell High visit; but the time alloted to it was in disproportion to the depth of its utterance. "I went to Lowell High today and I dug the kids there," he announced. "But as for the rest of them, they rejected me." Then he repeated softly, "They rejected me."

Greg Zahos ended his account of this episode to me with these words: "There were no tears rolling down Jack's cheeks, but there was a powerful lot of crying going on inside of him." Greg also informed me that he was never called again to do substitute teaching at Lowell High School.

Chapter 17 - On The Road — One More Time

Jack Kerouac had not ceased writing upon his return to his native city. Between almost daily visits to Nicky's Cafe, his restless, anguished pen bore on. Early in the Fall of 1967, he told me that he was finishing another novel. It was to be called *Vanity of Duluoz* and would be another chapter in the tragicomic legend of Jack Duluoz, better known as Jack Kerouac. "Those fink publishers," he complained," wouldn't let me use the name of Duluoz throughout all my books. I wanted to because they're all about Duluoz, that's me, Ti Jean."

We were in Jim Curtis's law office and we were about to go to lunch. "Well, Mr. Duluoz," I said, "you've already excited our literary anticipation of your latest epic. I'm on spiritual tenterhooks and look forward to an autographed copy." I knew this always amused Kerouac, my occasional deliberate lapse into a professorial manner and jargon. And I also knew that he always retorted with a cackling, obscene-tinged remark.

He bowed and addressed me as "Mon Professeur" in his best Canadian-French. "I will not only autograph my new book for you, but I will also write my immortal name on your academic, overeducated phallus. Then my name will wax and wane with your unacademic, unliterary passions."

Going to lunch (or anywhere) with Kerouac was no quiet affair. On that day we went to an elegant restaurant on the outskirts of Lowell. It's called The Speare House and looks on the Merrimack River. Its architectural motif is that of an Arthurian castle. Its entrance is a simulated drawbridge spanning a partial tiny moat. Once inside, you are surrounded by murals that blaze with scenes of King Arthur's Court. Four or five statues of knights in armor scattered about lend further credence to the scene.

The Speare House, I have no doubt, had worked hard and long to evolve its image as a classy emporium. Jack Kerouac wrecked that image (at least for the other customers that were there that day) in about one-half hour. He was in his usual state of booze-destroyed inhibitions.

As soon as we entered the place and sat down, Kerouac was up thirty seconds later announcing loudly that he was going to joust with the armored statue closest to him. "You know who that guy is, hiding behind that tin straitjacket? That's the top gun in King Arthur's mob. That's the one and only Sir Lancelot. He's skulking around here to latch onto Guinevere. Well I'ma gonna cross swords with him for the hand of Guinevere. She thinks he's got a groovy gun. Well, I'ma gonna show the Lady Guinevere that I've got a groovier gun."

Heads turned from everywhere to stare at our table. Curtis and I tried to shush Kerouac down, but did a poor job of it because we couldn't control our laughter. "Man, don't stop me now," Kerouac went on. "That Lancelot has been playing hanky panky with Guinevere behind the King's back. I'ma gonna shrive him, that's what I'ma gonna do." Kerouac's Western cowboy accent really broke me up. "Besides," he rambled on, "I've been looking for the Holy Grail, too. Lancelot ain't gonna find it because he ain't a holy goof. But *I* am. I've been holy all my life and I've been wearing a hair shirt clear down to my toenails."

One of the owners of the restaurant (whom Curtis and I knew very well) had come over now. He looked distressed. "Who the hell is that?" he demanded in suppressed rage.

I tried to placate him by saying, "Why that's the internationally famous writer from Lowell, Jack Kerouac."

He was far from impressed. "Fer chrissake, I don't care if he's Ernest Hemingway. Tone him down, will you? He's turning my place into a Gorham Street barroom." (Gorham Street is a rundown section in Lowell which he obviously considered beneath his dignity).

"He's very much impressed with your artistic atmosphere," I blurted for lack of something better to say.

"Well tell him to keep his impressions to himself," he came back to me. "He's disturbing my patrons." I was fleetingly amused by his term, patrons. He left. Kerouac hadn't even noticed him. He was too busy orating.

We managed to quiet him down, but only momentarily; and this was the pattern for the half-hour we were there. Curtis and I gulped down some food while Kerouac gulped down some liquor. He ate nothing. As a matter of fact, I find it difficult, even at this writing, to recall ever seeing Kerouac eating anything.

We had come to the restaurant in two cars, mine and Curtis's. Curtis left alone as he had an appointment out of town. Thus I found myself driving back to town with Kerouac next to me. "You know Jack," I said warily, "you really shook up that place back there. The owner almost threw us out."

"He wouldn't dare," he said in his best English accent,

On the way, we passed by the Franco-American Orphanage, a cluster of old but neatly kept red brick structures. Behind them is a grassy area that holds a series of religious statuettes. These represent the Stations to the Cross and culminate into a scene of the Crucifixion. "When I was a kid," I said to Kerouac, "my friends and I used to go behind that orphanage and walk the Stations to the Cross. I'm sure you must have done it, too, Jack."

Had I drenched him with a bucket of ice cold water, I would not have changed his mood as startlingly as I did with those words. "Walk the Stations to the Cross?" he said quietly. He brought his right hand to his forehead. He emitted a deep breath. "On Sunday afternoons," and his voice began to quiver, "when Spring would come around, my brother Gerard and I would go there. He would hold my hand, because he was my big brother, and we would walk, and he would explain every stop to me." I glanced at Kerouac and tears had already filled his eyes. "Gerard was little Jesus," he went on, his voice rising, "and I was his disciple. And I followed him through all those Stations to the Cross. And I have followed him ever since because I know he's up there guiding my every step." He was looking at me with the eyes of a child waiting to be reassured.

"I have no doubt of that, Jack," I said, and I was convinced then that the most meaningful person that Jack Kerouac had ever met had been Gerard — even though Kerouac, by his own admission, was only four when his brother died. Obviously, Kerouac had apotheosized his brother, and when one reads *Visions of Gerard,* he reads an elegy born of Kerouac's lifelong mourning for an idealized image. Months later when I happened to ask him which one of his books he favored, he told me it was *Visions of Gerard.* I think I knew the answer before posing the question.

199

The Franco-American Orphanage was far behind us now. I glanced at Kerouac and caught a rare image of him: silence in the presence of another human being. He had curled up into a Buddha mass. It didn't last long — about two minutes. Then he broke out into what he claimed was a Bob Eberle version of "The Breeze and I". Singing was not one of his talents.

I dropped him off at Nicky's Cafe after fending off his repeated attempts at persuading me to join him. I refused because I was exhausted; Kerouac had a way of doing that to people.

One night we sat with Kerouac in his house and watched him on the William Buckley T.V. Show. (It had been taped some weeks before). Two others were guesting with Kerouac on the show, a college professor and a Hippie. I personally feel that the show was a disaster for Kerouac. Besides Buckley, the professor and the Hippie did most of the talking, or I should say pontificating. Kerouac was in his "loose" state (which he made sure would endure by occasional nipping from a cup — at least that's what he told me) and he looked as if he didn't want to be there. I got the feeling that he was reining his wrath against his fellow guests. A few times he interrupted them in a muttering fashion which brought Buckley to the rescue. Buckley, himself, seemed greatly discomfited by the whole affair.

What did Kerouac actually say on the show? I honestly can't remember. Really, he said very little. All that has remained with me is his remark about the Vietnam War. He said the whole thing was a conspiracy by the Vietnamese — both North and South — to bring a lot of American Jeeps into the country.

Sitting there watching the show, I felt sad for Kerouac. I also felt frustrated and angry because I knew that of the three guests, the one that said nothing was the one that had the most to say. I amused myself in thinking what a different show it would have been, had it been taped in Nicky's Cafe.

When the show was over, I praised Kerouac (it was the humane thing to do) as did his wife, Stella, Jim Curtis, and a couple of other friends that were there. "You know," he said, "before the show, that Hippie followed me around like a puppy. Man, I had to tell him a dozen times to get lost."

"He admired you, Jack," I said.

He answered me with a lewd version of the concept of admiration. "Now Bill Buckley," he went on, "there's a guy that *I* admire. I know him from way back." If there were any doubt in my mind about Kerouac's political philosophy, it was finally dispelled.

The last year of Kerouac's residency in Lowell saw *Vanity of Duluoz* published. It was not a commercial success, and thus the years of arid reader appeal since *On The Road* mounted.

If Kerouac were deeply disturbed by this decline, he never directly expressed it — at least in my presence. I did venture once to remark to him about Allen Ginsberg's continuing popularity via television and public apperances. It was a mistake. "Look, you meatball!" he exploded. "I'm a writer, not a public exhibit!" It was the only time he was ever to show genuine anger towards me. I had no time to feel hurt, for he immediately broke in a cackle and said, "Jarvis, I like you, even though you *are* a professor. But if you're so concerned about my image, why don't you tell those Lowell politicians to take down that moldy Alan Ladd Monument in front of the city hall and put up a Zeusian statue of Ti Jean, Jack Kerouac, native son of Lowell. I'm even willing to pose for it, in the nude!" I grinned and we were back on comfortable ground.

The "Alan Ladd Monument" is a concrete memorial of nineteenth century vintage dedicated to two Lowell soldiers, Ladd and Whitney, who were killed in the Civil War. I grinned again at Kerouac's unique reference to it.

"Jack," I said. "Your *books* are your monument — if you'll pardon my cliché." He smiled — and kept on drinking.

I have no way of knowing when, if ever, the City of Lowell will officially recognize and honor Jack Kerouac. I do know, however, that a great segment of his literary output found its poetic wells in his early years in Lowell. And for anyone that desires to hear the "sad, tragic and beautiful strains" of those years, Kerouac's books will provide a wondrous symphony for him.

One of the closest friends that Jack Kerouac had during the last years of his Lowell life was Joe Chaput. Joe is a slim, fine looking man of about fifty; he works for the Lowell Courier Citizen, a large national printing firm. Joe was not a boyhood friend of Kerouac's, but became close with him when the latter returned to Lowell. The chemistry apparently was right for Joe and Jack Kerouac to become real buddies: Joe is a Lowell native, of French Canadian descent, an easy talking, sincere, comfortable man. Furthermore, Jack's mother "fell in love" with Joe Chaput—a rare distinction. Few people saw Jack's mother at this time; she was a phantom figure, an invalid living in a remote corner of Jack's household. But Joe Chaput saw her often and he obviously reached the old woman. He may have reminded her of those good French-Canadian boys she remembered in the old "Little Canada" days in Lowell. The Kerouac family — mother and son — loved Joe Chaput.

When Jack would go out drinking, Joe was usually there. (I was there a number of times, myself). If too many days would go by without Joe's presence, Jack would miss him. Disdaining the phone, he would send Joe postcards like the following:

Nov. 14, 1967

Dear Joe:

Where you been? What you been doing? Come on over and tell me what's up.

Jack Kerouac

Regarding a planned trip to New York City, Joe received the following letter from Kerouac:

Nov. 28, '67

Dear Joe:

I have to call off my proposed joining of you on this weekend's N.Y.C. trip, 'cause I got a story to write for Atlantic Monthly for next week, worse than that I'm not in shape any more after those last 2 days on the town — We'll get around to it sometime, maybe we oughta wait till my book (*Vanity of Duluoz*) is published this winter so we can be lionized at cocktail parties and you can meet fancy women with low-cut black gowns & long cigarette holders & apartments on Fifth Avenue, OO LA LA — Plus tard, s'il vous plais,

Ami Jack

Early in July, 1968, Joe Chaput pulled up in front of Kerouac's house on Sanders Avenue in Lowell. His car was ready for a nice long trip. Jack came out of the house, got in the car, and off they went. They had a mission — planned by Kerouac: go to Canada, the Town of Riviere du Loup in the Province of Quebec. Once there, Kerouac would research the town archives for evidence of his ancestry. (A few years earlier, he had gone to Britanny in France for the same purpose; no real proof was uncovered though *Satori in Paris* resulted.)

Joe pointed his car north, through New Hampshire and Maine. This was serious business — for the first hundred miles. Then for the rest of the distance and back, it became a beautiful experience wherein Jack Kerouac, Holy Goof, dug everything in sight — with Joe Chaput beside him. They didn't miss many bars and every night became a one-act play with Kerouac as the protagonist and the rest of the customers the supporting cast. Most of the time, it was joyous, free, rainbow-spectrumed dialogue. A couple of times, it bordered on grimness and a threat of violence against Jack as one or two listeners interpreted his myriad commentaries in a dark way. (Joe Chaput always came to the rescue with soft words).

It was a great ten-day trip: Jack never sought the archives once they arrived in Riviere du Loup; they never got to Quebec City and Montreal, destinations that Jack kept talking about enthusiastically on the way up; they never relaxed for one minute, a concept (to relax, that is) that was one of the reasons for making the trip.

"I really enjoyed it," Joe Chaput told me, "though I was exhausted by the time we got back."

Soon after the Canada excursion, Joe Chaput received a card from Kerouac:

July 18, 1968

Dear Joe:

All's well here, just got rid of the phone because too expensive. — All set later this year Florida move. — Hope you okay. —

Ti Jean

The Florida move involved Joe Chaput. He had promised Memere that he would drive them to Florida, a promise that he had extended out of love and concern for mother and son. Memere had had enough of the spectral New England climate; another winter would be unbearable.

A few weeks later (September, 1968), Jack Kerouac left his native city for the last time. The trip to St. Petersburg, Florida can be properly regarded as the epilogue to *On The Road*. The furniture was shipped south and a station wagon was hired in which they would drive down. Joe Chaput and another man were to be the drivers; Jack was to sit up front with them; the back of the wagon was carpeted with a mattress and this was the domain of Memere and Jack's wife, Stella. A covered wagon on rubber tires. On the way down, Jack filled in the long hours with booze-graced monologues and songs of crooners of an age gone by — the last trek, tragically echoing the final sad note of on the road —

Joe Chaput returned to Lowell and some weeks later, he received the following letter from Kerouac:

Nov. 15, '68

Dear Joe:

Well, just turned my typewriter ribbon over, in spite of the objections built into my Smith-Corona typewriter by the typewriter ribbon people who are in cahoots with the typewriter people, and old printers never quit. The only time an old printer should quit is when he gets itchy eyes and he should go to the bathroom and wash them (of lead). Then he should come and show the boss printer how to print.

I remember when my father was dead in his chair suddenly, I saw all that ink on his fingers.

Anyway, Joe, we made our move real good and you ought to see how nice this house and neighborhood is coming out. It's sleepy time down South, everybody ben sleeping, includin me, since you and Red and Dumphy left. My shinbone I cracked I had to pack ice on it and do extra headstands and I'm okay now. But the doctor, whom we visited remember in that office full of waiting people, he still hasn't shown up: emergency or no. So Memere is still waiting for her wheelchair and

I'm going to get a new doctor somehow and put that latter doctor in the hospital himself? The Mafia, doctors have become.

. . . As for you, you're my A number One man. I hope you can come down here this winter when you have your next vacation, and relax with a few Scotchcheshes and beer and a swim in the Gulf of Mexico, and grilled outdoor steaks black on the outside and red in the middle.

I've got my office-bedroom all fixed up and tho it's small it's cozy and I'se satisfied. I can step out this very second into the moonlight piney tree night where my cats are already making girls. I got some good money from Italy today and it will pay for my fence and a month's rent. My fence will be five foot tall and way in the back under the banyan tree. *I don't remember how the hell we ever got down here* . . . All worked out well, and your promise to Memere was fulfilled. I miss you, of course, but I know you'll come to see me once in a while: and I'm coming on annual trips to Lowell, anyway, praps on my way to Brittany with you next summer if we can get together on that with Youenn Guernic of Huelgoat, Bretagne (Finistère). See you anyhow: We called Tony collect as he instructed. Stella is all Gaga except she's worried about her mother, who is in good hands however.

I'm now going to undertake getting a good tan and reading Pascal again and getting set for a new book. I only hope you're as satisfied as I am with the way St. Christopher treated us and the way St. Joseph continues to treat us, that old Camel hobo.—
Ecrit!

Jean-Louis K.

A hopeful letter, indeed. A letter of looking ahead. But in less than a year Jack would be dead. This last brief period started out pretty well; he began to rework an old manuscript which ultimately would be named *Pic* and be published posthumously. It is not a very good book. It is a vague account of a young black

205

boy, circa 1948, heading north for an equally vague freedom. There are blurred scenes of Jim Crowism, jam sessions, and road dialogue. The book is a sad, faint memory of Kerouac's once awesome power of blasting a human emotion to smithereens.

Not much longer after his letter to Joe Chaput, Jack Kerouac began his final descent. The move to Florida had only changed the scenery; the libretto remained the same: long hours in a bar, uninterrupted drinking, endless monologues and serio-comic dialogues with anybody who happened to be around. Stella and Memere remained at home, Stella as much the widow as the mother. Kerouac's descent into the shadows began to accelerate; Stella, the final faithful one, tride to slow the fall. But it was too late, years too late.

Shortly before he died, Kerouac spoke in his prose one more time. He wrote an article entitled "The Bippie in the Middle," a series of observations on the immediate rebellious scene. At worst, the article appears ill focused; at best, it flickers with one last protest by Kerouac that he's always been for God and country and that nobody has the right to attack them. The misunderstood man protesting, "That is not it at all, That is not what I meant, at all." [33]

Perhaps the final indignity was a bad beating Kerouac absorbed a few weeks before his death. It was in a bar, a black bar, where Jack's utterances were interpreted as untimely, unholy. Time had played its final irony on Jack Kerouac — Angel Goof. He passed away on October 21, 1969.

EPILOGUE

One is tempted to divide Kerouac's works into two broad categories: Beat and Lowell. *On The Road, The Dharma Bums, Big Sur, The Subterraneans* — these books scream out Kerouac's ecstasy of search. In this search he created a new language, a kind of onomatopoetic glossary of pain, an E.S.P. set to words. These novels are really long essays that try to record (without benefit of musical instruments) the true cadence of life. Whether or not a reader of these novels thinks they do is almost irrelevant. What *is* relevant is that Kerouac offers, to those who dare to look, some explosive flashes of life's terror. True, a character like Dean Moriarty comes through most of the time as a no-good bastard, an animal whose only concern is drinking, goofballing, and sleeping with women. Man still regards these activities as a dear portion of his waking moments.

When Kerouac wrote *On The Road*, LSD was unheard of. Jim Curtis claimed that after reading this book, he felt like a man who had taken A Trip without benefit of hallucinatory drugs. If Kerouac's Beatnik reflects volcanic desperation, how different really is he from Thoreau's man and his quiet desperation? They both sweat, but in varying degrees.

Kerouac's Lowell novels may be regarded as the other half of his spiritual schizophrenia. Here, he's the romanticist. His characters are seen silhouetted against a twilight sky. They move about with a rugged, honest innocence and Kerouac seems to weep for them because death will sweep them all away. French, Greeks, Irish, Portuguese, Poles — these are the late immigrants and the sons of immigrants that populate Kerouac's Lowell. They are a microcosm of larger U.S. cities; but because of this smaller dimension, they offered Kerouac a sharper focus of man struggling to put meaning into his life. If they were crude, hard working people, Kerouac ennobled them because they were not afraid of life. Yet, in books like *Maggie Cassidy* and *Dr. Sax,* there is a melancholy background theme suggestive of futility and death. And death is what Kerouac tries to understand in *Visions of Gerard.* He doesn't, of course. He mourns; yet in mourning, he resurrects Gerard and reaffirms his love for him. In an essay entitled, "Once God Moves the Hand, You Go Back and Revise, It's a Sin!" by Paul Jarvis (who happens to be my son), the concept is advanced that there were always three main themes that intruded into Kerouac's consciousness. I quote:

> *Inspiration,* from heaven (Gerard, really), which Jack believed was responsible for his fame as a writer. *Death,* that ambivalent state, which he was continually aware of and saw as the equalizer to redeem himself of guilt on the one hand, and reunite him with his brother, on the other. And finally, *Drinking,* the means to accomplish this end and soothe him in the meantime. [34]

Yes. Death, indeed.

I spoke of the temptation to separate Kerouac's works into two all embracing areas. And I have, temporarily, succumbed to this temptation. While in this frame of mind, may I go further and introduce one Robert Herrick, seventeenth century English poet. He belonged to the "Tribe of Ben" (Jonson), a literary group that would meet at London's wildest taverns and devote their wit and energy to paganistic feasts. Their poetry sang of the "good life" and the gathering of rosebuds before Autumn's deadening hand reached out. Robert Herrick was a major contributor to this poetry of pleasure. He was also a parish priest, and for every pagan poem he wrote, he practically matched it with a fervently religious verse. Thus the same man that created "To the Virgins To Make Much of Time" and "Upon Julia's Clothes" wrote "His Prayer for Absolution" and "Litany of the Holy Spirit". The pagan was incessantly at war with the priest.

Jack Kerouac was no priest (though generally considered the High Priest of the Beatniks). But he *was* a man at war with himself. If his Beat novels shriek for the desire to burn, burn, burn, his Lowell novels lament for a lost innocence, an unfulfilled grace. Despite his monumental travels in the world of the id (with side journeys into Zen Buddhism and other credos), Kerouac in the end professed the belief of his childhood saints.

In the final analysis, however, it must be said that the two-type Kerouac novel concept must live precariously. All his

208

novels are deep throated fugues, that sing of a rare figurine, a satyr one might say, in which the Beat artist and the wide-eyed youth were inextricably sculptured together. There was always about him, amid the wild flood of words, an unmistakable beat or rhythm of gentility, a hint of caution, a soft, recurring note of concern.

In the middle of the avalanche of existence in *On The Road,* Jack Kerouac comes to a screeching halt and writes:

> And for just a moment I had reached the point of ecstasy that I always wanted to reach, which was the complete step across chronological time into timeless shadows, and wonderment in the bleakness of the mortal realm, and the sensation of death kicking at my heels to move on, with a phantom dogging its own heels, and myself hurrying to a plank where all the angels dove off and flew into the holy void of uncreated emptiness, the potent and inconceivable radiancies shining in bright Mind Essence, innumerable lotus-lands falling open in the magic mothswarm of heaven. I could hear an indescribable seething roar which wasn't in my ear but everywhere and had nothing to do with sounds. I realized that I had died and been reborn numberless times but just didn't remember especially because the transitions from life to death and back to life are so ghostly easy, a magical action for naught, like falling asleep and waking up again a million times, the utter casualness and deep ignorance of it. I realized it was only because of the stability of the intrinsic mind that these ripples of birth and death took place, like that action of wind on a sheet of pure, serene, mirror-like water. I felt sweet, swinging bliss, like a big shot of heroin in the mainline vein; like a gulp of wine late in the afternoon and it makes you shudder; my feet tingled. I thought I was going to die the very next moment. [35]

Jack Kerouac died in the month of October — Autumn's most beloved. I think he always lived in an Autumn dream watching the tree leaves take sad flight.

Allen Ginsberg at the funeral of Jack Kerouac
Lowell, Mass. Oct. 24, 1969.

Appendix: The Beginning and the End

Dec. 27, 1949
91-21 134th St.
Richmond Hill, N.Y.

Charles G. Sampas
c/o the Lowell Sun
Lowell, Mass.

Dear Charley:

I'm sure you remember me, Jack Kerouac, and even more your old cry for a novel about Lowell by a native LOWELLIAN (or Lowellite). In three years of work, from 1946 to 1949, during which time my father Leo died of cancer, I wrote a long novel about Lowell — and about New York City — entitled "The Town and the City."

It was accepted by Harcourt, Brace & Co., by editor-in-chief Robert Giroux, and will appear on the bookstands all over the country on Feb. 23, 1950. One of the heroes is Sammy, whose name is Alex Panos in the novel. It covers the period from the 30's on through the war and after.

It's not strictly autobiographical, since I used various friends and girl-friends, and my own parents, to form a large family, the Martin family, whose in an old Victorian house on Galloway Road (which is actually Varnum Avenue). So that at one point, when the hero Peter Martin meets Alexander Panos, he realizes that all his life he has seen an old ramshackle house across the river, the Panos house (which I recall could be visible from Varnum Avenue), without knowing that a great friend of his life lived there.

The first lines of the novel read: "The town is Galloway. The Merrimac River, broad and placid, flows down to it from the New Hampshire hills, broken at the falls to make frothy havoc on the rocks, foaming on over ancient stone towards a place where the river suddenly swings about in a wide and peaceful basin, moving on now around the flank of the town, on to places known as Lawrence and Haverhill, through a wooded valley,

211

and on to the sea at Plum Island, where the river enters an infinity of waters and is gone. Somewhere far north of Galloway, in headwaters close to Canada, the river is continually fed and made to brim out of endless sources and unfathomable springs. The little children of Galloway sit on the banks of the Merrimac and consider these facts and mysteries. In the wild echoing misty March night, little Mickey Martin kneels at his bedroom window and listens to the river's rush, the distant barking of dogs, the soughing thunder of the falls, and he ponders the wellsprings and sources of his own mysterious life.

"The grownups on Galloway are less concerned with riverside broodings. They work — in factories, in shops and stores and offices, and on the farms all around.

". . . If at night a man goes out to the woods surrounding Galloway' and stands on a hill . . ." . . . And it begins this way, going on for 512 pages, and dealing with everything I could think of about Lowell life and the war, and the City, and death. The last chapter is the funeral of the father, George Martin, printer, in "Lacoshua, N.H." when the entire large Galloway family is reunited after the war and sad scatterings, at the site of their true life & origin . . . New England.

I'm having a review copy sent to you at the Sun, and only hope you will enjoy it. The book is slated for some success, if indications of advance sale (20,000 copies), advertising outlay ($7500), and the fact that an English publisher, Eyre Spotteswood, accepted it in proof, means anything. Several advances and a Guggenheim fellowship also came my way. I'm the last to deny amazement at this strange success.

So this brings us by a "commodius vicus of recirculation past river Eve and Adam" back to the nights when we'd all bump on the Square — Sammy, Ian MacDonald, Mike Largay, Conny Murphy, Eddy Tully, yourself and others like Jim O'Dea and John Koumantzelis and so many others, and chat about what we all felt . . . an enriching background for all of us. Strange, dark Lowell. And the night I talked to you at your table in the Moody street club, only four years ago, and you advised me to stay out of Lowell. I understand that too. But it's all the same, and Lowell, like Winesburg Ohio or Asheville North Carolina or Fresno

California or Hawthorne's Salem, is always the place where the darkness of the trees by the river, on a starry night, gives hint of that inscrutable *future* Americans are always longing and longing for. And when they find that future, not till then they begin looking *back* with sorrows, and an understanding of how man haunts the earth, pacing, prowling, circling in the shades, and the intelligence of the compass pointing to nothing in sight save starry passion . . . strange, is strange, how we be-dot infinity with our thoughts and poor prooftops, and hometown, then go away forever.

Where is Michael Largay these days? I hear no more from Ian. The invisible strings got tangled in the night. Sammy — I have all his letters and many poems, an scoured them for his speeches in The Town and the City. I wonder about his kid brothers and sisters who, in those days, sat on the porch singing like Saroyan children. And how, when the munitions plant was built near the foot of Stevens, Sammy said, "How green was my valley."

Hoping to hear from you soon, Charley, and that you will enjoy my contribution to the general lore and that all is well with you & yours.

Sincerely,
Jack K.

p.s. Whatever happened to Bill Sullivan, formerly of the Leader, later Notre Dame publicity? If you know, please insert info whenever you have time to write.

JACK KEROUAC NEVER LEFT LOWELL
By Charles E. Jarvis

When he first saw that French-Canadian light in Lowell,
He must have said: "Man, look at all the truth roiling everywhere!
"Jean," his mother must have called, "come see the river."
And when he ran to the window, he saw the Merrimack easing by
Then "broken at the falls to make frothy havoc on the rocks."
"Man," he must have thought, "that has to be eternity."
So he set out with Gerard, his saint, to know the river.
They baptized themselves in its holy waters, a prelude
To the holy goofiness that he would elegize.
Beyond the river, he saw them: solid immigrants
Who had come to Lowell to sweat in the fever of its trackless spine
He saw their eyes sparkling in the fever,
And beneath the flame, a facet of fear.
The New England seasons seared deeply into him,
Though in the Lowell grayness, he saw them all
As sad voices lamenting the simple death of people.
But there were other voices: Maggie Cassidy, G. J.
The high school football idolaters, Alexander Panos,
And Gerard—whose voice from the grave never ceased,
Like an organ ever playing in the wondrous dawn light
Seeping through the windows of Saint Jean Baptiste Church.
"Gadzooks!" Jack said one day. "I'll never leave Lowell,
But I've got a lotta living to do!"
So he went to the Big City and dived into the sewer.
"Mon Dieu," he gurgled, "this ain't no Lowell canal!"
But the canal and the sewer became The Town and the City.
Later, he was to say, "I used violins to play that melody,
But I knew there was another beat somewhere."

So he took to the Road and followed the Western sky,
On the way, he thrilled to every sunrise and sunset,

He reached out for every atom of meaning,
And the route was from the weed to the chalice of love.
San Francisco! The Mecca of Beatitude!
He thought: "All the holy goofs after the holy grail are here!"
And they were: Ginsberg, Corso, Burroughs, Ferlinghetti,
And the unforgettable, holiest of them all—Neal Cassady.
North Beach never got over it; all those fiery madmen
Running around shouting, "Burn it all off,
Burn every conceivable atom of untruth off me.
What's left after the fire might be worthwhile."
A kind of spiritual nihilism, one might say.
But after the hours, days, months, eons it seemed,
Of screaming for the Mithraistic Light,
They discovered that it was more like
The General Electric Light Bulb: it has to be replaced.

So they scattered and Jack put on his roller skates once more.
L. A., Denver, Gallup, New Mexico, Mexico—you name it,
He was there. But skating wasn't all he did.
He wrote, too. He wrote with the panic of a man
Who's been told he has a terminal disease.
Life is a disease, someone said. I guess
That's what Jack had; the pain at times was unbearable.
He took all the pain killers imaginable,
But he had one old standby; that old devil nectar.
In the end, it worked great—and the pain stopped.

When Jack said he'd never leave Lowell, he meant it.
For in his last years he brought back the flesh
To mate once more with his spirit,
One that had never left the Autumn banks of the Merrimack.
He was forever the little boy holding Gerard's hand,
The two of them ranging along the river's leafy shores,
Always with the look of thrilling innocence,
Expecting around the next bend to see Little Jesus.

215

Funeral of Jack Kerouac
St. Jean Baptiste Church - Lowell, Mass. - Oct. 24, 1969

WHO CONCEIVED JACK KEROUAC—
FAMILY OR AMERICA?

by PAUL C. JARVIS

Much has been said in this biography about the early family dynamics and Catholic influences on Jack Kerouac. The impact of Gerard's death has been a major premise of this book, especially as it portrays Kerouac's tragic vision of reality, his need to find a continued renewal in the relationships with Sammy Sampas and Neal Cassady, and, finally, Kerouac's guilt feelings regarding his success as a recognized author. In addition, this biography has made numerous references concerning the irony of Kerouac's apparent neurotic dependency on his mother as contrasted with the lifestyle reflected in his Beat Books. However, I feel that in order to understand Jack more fully, further clarification ought to be made regarding his response to both parents, which would include more information concerning his father's relationship and the bearing this had on his expression. Finally, this essay will attempt to explain the seeming paradox of Jack's political perspective which leads many to conclude erroneously that he had a conservative orientation towards social issues and thus did not live up to the spirit of the Beat Generation.

There is no doubt, developmentally, of the influence of the idealized memory of Gerard lingering mystically throughout Jack's life. We may infer that both parents encouraged this awe, especially during times of enforced discipline when Jack was compared to his brother in heaven: "Why can't you, Jackie, be a good boy —— like Gerard?" This could be confusing to any child, since to be good in this case also meant to be dead and in heaven. Nevertheless, up through high school, Gerard, from Jack's perception, would have been pleased (as would his parents) that Ti Jean was indeed a good Catholic boy.

However, the period of time from graduation day at Lowell High School in 1939 till just prior to the cancer illness and death of Jack's father in the spring of 1946 marks a period of search and conflict which needs to be understood further. This phase covers ages eighteen through twenty-four and for most people these years ought to involve a period of growing autonomy and independence from one's family as a healthy response rather than conformity and dependence on values that parents might impose on their child. It is unfortunate that the latter process is more prevalent in our society and is the basis of how conventional middle-class values are transmitted if one is not allowed within the family to be different. No wonder that a book such as *On The Road* appeals to this age group and all libertarians who seek to define their own essence rather than by means dictated by conventional institutions of our society.

Yet prior to Jack's going on the road in 1947, it seems that he was well on his way to pleasing his father by becoming a football athlete-scholar and, hopefully, a graduate of an ivy league college. His father was a printer, a short, loud pugnacious man who seemed to have no inhibitions about taking on the world. Thus Jack was apparently trying to satisfy the machismo need of his father who wanted a football hero for a son; although coming from a working class background, a football scholarship was the only way to afford college. Jack's mother was a religious woman who instilled the fear of God into him; she also encouraged him to associate with kids from well-to-do families. Thus both parents ingrained in Jack a sense of pride about being a Kerouac.

When Jack left Lowell to go to prep school and then to matriculate at Columbia University, a string of events and some choices by Jack created tension and conflict which threatened to alienate him from his family. It was the first time he was on his own, away from the control of his parents. Eventually, he decided to drop out of Columbia. During this time, Jack told his friend, Sammy Sampas, that he really wanted to be a writer and not a football jock. He was only in football to please his father.

Following a brief stint in the merchant marine, he joined the service; but within three months, he was out on a psychiatric discharge. Although Jack at times tried to compensate and prove his patriotism consciously, it is clear that he was an anti-authoritarian personality unable to carry out the absurd orders of commanding officers or the orders of his father for that matter. What Jack couldn't admit was the conscious declaration of independence from his parents. His sense of honor and Catholic respect

218

and reverence in Gerard's name made it difficult. Yet he was able (outside the family) to defy social control from convention which is the crux of the Beat counter-culture ideology.

In addition, this period is marked by his association with the future "holy degenerates" who gave each other substance and encouragement—something that Jack in his later years missed. These friends occupied much of his time as he sought to be away from his parents, and long arguments (especially with his father) were frequent about whom he should have as friends. It seems that Jack never resolved telling his parents off or holding anger towards them. Instead, he idealized them in his writings. Jack saw something noble and pure about the blue collar work that Leo and Gabrielle were involved with as he contrasted it with the affairs of upper class establishment people. In the final analysis, Jack's parents had a hold on him emotionally, one that was capable of making him feel guilty. The climax of this distance with his father prior to his father's cancer suffering is best characterized by the cold rejection Jack got when he called from jail asking for $5,000 bail money after his implication in a murder case. His friend, Lucien Carr, had killed a homosexual assailant and had gone to Jack for help. Jack was jailed as an accessory after the fact for failing to report the homicide. Jack later claimed that he wrote nothing but truth in his novels; yet, this episode of murder is conspicuously altered in his first novel, *The Town and the City*, and the killing is depicted as a suicide. Thus what is forgotten by "memory babe" about his feelings of rejection from his father says much about this relationship.

All this soul searching or rebellion during these years from constrictive, prudish parents came to a temporary, screeching halt because Jack's father was now going through the agony of dying from cancer. This episode is described poignantly and remorsefully in *The Town and the City*. Jack's guilt, or as I see it, love and concern, would not allow him to challenge his father any longer. This moratorium centered on only trying to prove to his father that he was serious about a writing career. Interesting to note that his father was a printer who, one would think, would have encouraged his only son to become a writer rather than put him down.

The critical point here is that at a time when Jack was be-

219

coming his own person and recovering from the mourning of his brother who had died twenty years earlier, he had to stop dead in his tracks and promise a dying father he would do what was expected. I wonder if Jack's mother ever said: "See what you are doing to your father, you are killing him by not listening to him." This leads to the promise he made on his father's deathbed to take care of memere—forever. Gerard and dad would have wanted it so. Thus the behavior of the subsequent episodes of so-called oedipal fixation with memere can only truly be understood within the context of this *social contract* that Jack felt obsessed and compelled to carry out.

It was as though he chose to carry out this promise rather than reap the ravages of anxiety over abandoning her. This meant that, although he would go on the road temporarily to experience the fits and bursts of life and grow as a writer, he would always return dutifully to her, never getting involved with any one person. This allegiance towards his mother was also based on the stark reality that she worked in shoe factories to support her unemployed son, "the writer," waiting for him to become recognized as a great author. Jack felt he must repay her with kindness. He did not have the luxury of an upper-class background that would support his habit as a writer—such as Burroughs did. Moreover, when the establishment rejected Jack, memere was always there to love him.

This context thus provides a more accurate backdrop of his lifelong relationship with his mother. It should also be pointed out that with the trauma of Gerard's death, when Jack was four, she had let Jack sleep in bed with her to deal obviously with their nightmare. She had just lost one son, and she was not about to lose another, and thus her protective attitude, towards Jack especially, accelerated with the loss of her husband. Jack's father died at 57; at the time, Mrs. Kerouac was 50 and Jack was 24. Mrs. Kerouac had had even more losses in her childhood: she had never known her mother and lost her father when he was 37. At the age of 15, she began working in a shoe factory.

So during the year of illness and death of his father, Jack was concerned with atoning for his previous years of "recklessness and wanderings" (a thought not suggested by his writings), staying put, taking care of memere while finishing his first novel that he had begun in that mournful year. But something happened that proved too great a temptation. In that year, 1946, Jack was introduced to Neal Cassady and the chemistry was just right. Jack had somebody to believe in and respond to since Gerard and Sammy Sampas. This marks the beginning of the Beat experiences which would end with the belated publication of *On The Road* in 1957, finished seven years earlier. The final phase in Jack's life begins with that publication date and ends with his death. This time is characterized by his rejection of the role and image that he was cast into because he could not allow himself to feel good or responsible for a counter-culture movement due to the personal image he felt he had to maintain within his family.

But back in 1947 it seemed clear that Jack would be the kind of writer that needed life experiences on which to base his art. Thus a year after his father's death, the somber, repentant side of Jack is suppressed as he takes off with Neal Cassady, on the road, to "burn, burn every atom of untruth off." *The Town and the City* was begun and finished as a sentimental romantic attempt to explain himself to his dying father. Now he had a lot of living to catch up on and this would mark the period of the Beat lifestyle. Yet, when Jack ventured too far off the road, he always returned to his mother. Or, if he tired of the Beat scene, he would regress back to the nostalgic past and rework his lingering childhood and adolescent memories. *Visions of Gerard* was thus written during the apogee of his Beat years. He considered this book his favorite work, while every one else was responding to the fury of *On The Road*.

There is further irony towards the end of these Beat years. Jack had sought recognition and fame as a true recorder of the American social reality including the Beat responses to it, but when it finally, belatedly, came in 1957, it was a letdown. Or, more accurately, Jack ultimately could not allow himself to deservedly feel comfortable about accepting the honor of being the principal author that forged a new consciousness of America. (But then, the literary establishment gave him reason to feel dejected). Moreover, he had trouble feeling worthy since his personal identity ate away at him. How could he end up famous when Gerard was dead? He claimed that Gerard was behind his creative energy. *"He's* the one that is doing all this . . . Once God moves the hand, you go back and revise, it's a sin!" But the drugs and determination and the need to tell it like it was made him speed on as the athlete of the typewriter.

Yet the theme of unworthiness was present in 1957 as well, when he felt shameful with the recognition over the publication of *On The Road.* He felt he had reached fame by capturing every atom of movement from his "blood brother," Neal Cassady. This was probably Jack's need to debase himself; because if this is true, then Jack exploited Gerard as well in *Visions of Gerard.* It is more accurate to say that both Gerard and Neal were captured by a labor of love. Nevertheless, there was also a social base to the feeling with Cassady because soon after the publicaton of *On The Road,* Cassady was busted for allegedly carrying grass; some claim the police framed him for being the degenerate hero of the Beat novel. Neal spent about two years in jail. Again we have the theme of the brother suffering and giving substance to Jack who ends up prospering; too much to bear—followed by self-flagellation with alcoholic nightmares. Gerard and Jack's father had innocently suffered; Sammy Sampas and childhood friends were killed in action during World War II; and now Neal Cassady is imprisoned. Jack's repentant side would never allow him to feel famous or prosper as Ginsberg has. He once claimed: "There are one thousand guys in Lowell who know more about heaven than I do."

It is interesting to speculate what would have happened to Jack if he had been spotted in grammar school as a quiet, sad, dejected child (as many children are today) by mental health professionals and helped to work through the imposed guilt from Gerard's death. He might have ended up a "well adjusted" cog in the wheel. It seems that the artist has a sense of pain and anguish that drives him on to find meaning and purpose in his art, as he brings closure to his emotional needs; but the price is great —to let oneself feel.

Consequently, although Jack obviously contributed monumentally towards the counter-culture movement in the 1950's, which found fruition by the end of the 1960's, he could not allow himself to consciously feel a part of it. The political solidarity he might have felt with other Beats was avoided as he remained the "lonesome traveler" suffering alone rather than be branded a Communist as Snyder and Ginsberg were. It would have seemed unpatriotic to his father to have taken a political stand per se. Thus the *personal* obscured a defined political orientation. It seems that if one is never allowed to get angry with one's parents, it then becomes difficult to show anger directly towards one's government. Moreover, Jack was concerned more with the absurd of the cosmic void rather than the specific, mundane, political issues of the day—such as the McCarthy hearings.

Both of Jack's parents were middle America; to reject their value system would have meant to reject them. That is why Jack tried to appear, at times, *neutral* when he wrote "The Bippie in the Middle" reflections on his political views. It is interesting to contrast Jack's mother with Naomi, Ginsberg's mother, who was a leftist and ended up in a psychiatric facility. We can see how Allen had an easier time actualizing his political identity.

However, it is important to realize that the sense of truth and justice about America did not escape Jack's sense of social analysis. One thing the remembrance of Gerard had taught Jack was to be sensitive toward hurt innocence coming from oppressive sources. Yet, it appears that Jack's political profile has been misunderstood, unfortunately, based on what he said to friends or what he didn't do, rather than what he actually wrote. It is apparent to this reader of Kerouac, that writing was his media for his message and true persona. There is no doubt of the radical perspective and overview he has about the nature of social reality in America as he acts as a visual social documentary focusing in on the foreground of specific lives and the larger context to educate us towards the sights, sounds, smells and everyday existence of Americans in their element.

In some ways it is misleading to suggest he was the father of the Beat generation (Kerouac himself felt he wasn't) and subsequent Hippie counter-culture. I feel it is more accurate to say that the social conditions themselves that are America conceived a strong and accurate response from Jack. This response from Jack and the other Beats could only come from someone in touch with their personal pain to allow them to be able to reach out and empathize with the hurt of the oppressed. Witness the commonality of the childhood socialization of other Beat authors.

Jack had begun early to respond with sensitivity and awareness initiated and fostered by Gerard, who could feel the suffering perpetrated on the innocent. A perfect teacher to model oneself after. Thus Jack transferred this ability nobly and accurately to describe the effects of the "Moloch" oppression on its victims.

This focus ranged over the total political spectrum of oppressed groups. Look at any of Jack's books and you'll find that numerous references are made regarding class oppression: the noble mill workers stretching from the railroad earth of his mill-town Lowell to California; the racist imperialism of the white man as Jack describes (in *The Subterraneans*) Mardou Fox's father, the half-breed Black-Indian. In *Pic*, Jack writes through the point of view of the sad and hurt eyes of a twelve year old black boy. In other books, Jack delineates migrant workers, hoboes and the junkie offspring of society. In addition, when it was not fashionable, Jack parodied his machismo male conditioning as he sought to find a true meaningful dialogue of love and sweetness with the women he came to know intimately. He had disdain for the brute sexist force in most men and although he did not accept homosexuality for himself, understood and accepted it in his friends. This kind of tenderness and empathy towards the social underdog found expression in his love for lower class non-white women: the migrant woman and her son in California, Tristessa, and Mardou Fox. In *The Subterraneans*, could Mardou Fox's psychotherapist have understood Mardou's family·dynamics and social pain and suffering as Jack did, regarding the devastation of her half-breed hobo father at the hands of racist imperialism? Moreover, Jack's political tone is a more global sadness than just the immediacy of responding to the egocentric complaints of a subterranean girl and his trying to figure out how to get her to stop talking and make her. Jack responds as usual to the greater issue:

> "I kept imagining that Cherokee-halfbreed
> hobo father of hers lying bellydown on a
> flatcar with the wind furling back his rags
> and black hat, his brown sad face facing all
> that land and desolation . . . I saw the vision
> of her father, he's standing straight up,
> proudly, handsome, in the bleak dim red

light of America on a corner, nobody knows
his name, nobody cares . . .

Her father the founder of her flesh and
predecessor terror-ee of her terrors and knower
of much greater flips and madness than she
in psycho-analytic-induced anxieties could ever
even summon up to just imagine, formed just
the background for thoughts about the Negroes
and Indians and America in general but with
all the overtones of "new generation" and
other historical concerns in which she was
now swirled just like all of us in the Wig
and Europe Sadness of us all, the innocent
seriousness with which she told her story . . .

I'd been out there and sat down on the
ground and seen the rail and steel of America
covering the ground filled with the bones of
old Indians and Original Americans.—In the
cold gray fall in Colorado and Wyoming I'd
worked on the land and watched Indian hoboes
come suddenly out of brush by the track and
move slowly, hawk lipped, rill-jawed and
wrinkled, into the great shadow of the light
bearing burdenbags and junk talking quietly
to one another and so distant from the
absorptions of the field hands, even the
Negroes of Cheyenne and Denver street, the
Japs, the general minority Armenians and
Mexicans of the whole West that to look at a
three-or-foursome of Indians crossing a
field and a railroad track is to the senses
like something unbelievable as a dream . . .

And only with a great amount of effort
you realize "But they were the inhabitors
of this land and under these huge skies they
were the worriers and keeners and protectors
of wives in whole nations gathered around
tents—now the rail that runs over their
forefathers' bones leads them onward
pointing into infinity, wraiths of humanity
treading lightly the surface of the ground

so deeply suppurated with the stock of their
suffering you only have to dig a foot down
to find a baby's hand.—The hotshot passen-
ger train with gnashing diesel balls by,
browm, browm, the Indians just look up—I
see them vanishing like spots . . ."³⁶

This radical perspective to identify with the underdog is
seen again in Jack's novel, *Pic*, which was published after his
death. In this work what is interesting is that Jack brings closure
to his personal and political identity. Pic (Jack), a young Negro
boy from the South, is taken on the road by a wiser, older brother, Slim (Gerard, Sammy, Neal—take your choice) and rescued
from a controlling family as he travels through a racist America
towards freedom.

If actions speak louder than words, it's difficult to say that
if Jack had marched and protested in the 1960's he would have
done more in focusing and raising the social consciousness of
millions. As a result, the works of Kerouac do not reflect red-
neck conservatism. It is inconceivable that someone of the right
politically could write as Jack did. His are the concerns and out-
rages of a man at war with the "Moloch" monster and those of
the establishment who go about their lives without any fuss and
strain; and that if they only knew about "IT", they would want
to burn, burn all the untruth off.

As a result, Jack's vision of America is one indignant with the
injustice and suffering of the oppressed. The Duluoz legend
transcends the personal life of the author's own ego needs (that
he was working through) and comments on the very fabric of
our society. It is no mistake that he was perceived as corrupting
the values of youth in our society. Had Jack not been revolutionary in challenging the middle class lifestyle, he never would
have been branded by the smug upper class intellectual critics as
corrupting the youth of the land by suggesting hedonistic, amo-
ral pursuits in his Beat books. It is clear that it is this elitist group
that Jack had contempt for all his life; this group could never
really see what it meant to be *beat* by the system, because they
are the defenders of it with their intellectual rationalizations. His
allegiance was with the beatitude of the working class people.

Consequently, with the beginning decalcification of the

straight world, there was in the 1950's a vendetta launched by the protectors of the establishment. Jack was not the only one hit hard and rejected for having the courage to *speak out.* The poem, *Howl,* by Allen Ginsberg was suppressed as obscene along with Lenny Bruce who was shattered and crushed by the system, because he dared to point out the hypocrisy via comedy. It's even ludicrous that a bland Dr. Spock would be seen as a threat and blamed for creating a permissive generation because of his child-rearing methods which advocated love and tenderness rather than hitting a child. The real tragedy, however, was all those Beat women who got mad about the straightjacket of conventional expectations and roles and thus fared more poorly than their male counterparts by finding themselves incarcerated more often in insane asylums. What the straight world never wants to acknowledge even though it understands the truth, is that it is not a demon or a medical illness or the brainwashing of communists that causes a person in this society to rebel, but the actual choice to defy the values of a corrupt way of being.

Thus, middle American values began to be shaken with rebels with due cause in the 1950's and Jack was part of this new force. By the 1960's this movement became a threat to our capitalistic economic system not to have all those mindless consumers buying new underwear, clothes and deodorants, let alone being "anti-American" for not supporting those dirty little wars, (what does it mean to be American then?) and not wanting to get married in a church and live in suburbia like everyone else. Yet, by the 1970's the Madison "Moloch" Avenue mentality has managed to delude many into the illusion of freedom based on appearances; a danger to personal freedom that Jack saw coming in *The Vanishing American Hobo,* in which the surveillance of society prevents one from just dropping out from a crazy rat race, to just be.

Consequently, youth of the 1970's face exploitation and mystification based on looking free with their denim outfits with already sewn on patches with flowers and peace signs largely manufactured by exploited labor from Mexico, Taiwan and South Korea, while American workers are laid off.

If Jack were living today, I'm sure he would continue even more strongly to point out the sham of the sophisticated subliminal thought police who seek to mystify us into non-awareness and non-choosing in order to fit in and accept the spiritual wasteland around us, known today as the "plastic" straight world.

Jack faced many obstacles, the greatest of which was the establishment that actively invalidated his depiction of social injustice. Ironically, even working class people that Jack felt akin to and eulogized in his writings were caught in a bind themselves, certainly aware of their exploitation while at the same time having been successfully socialized not to show anger at the government per se. To do so would be unpatriotic. Yet the outlet for this political frustration all too often was directed to more disadvantaged lower class people, as we see today the outrage of working class people misdirected towards welfare recipients.

This error Jack never made or would have made politically as he described with compassion the victims of our system. The personal responsibility and obligation to his family caused Jack much guilt and anxiety but more importantly contributed to Jack's awesome empathy and pain for the true Americans. Thus, he managed to describe reality and give us his legend, not merely of Duluoz but documentary visions of America as well; a legend that is truly revolutionary in its consciousness raising. Let's hope that those who need to *Dig* him, do so.

NOTES

1 Jack Kerouac, *Dr. Sax* (New York: Grove Press, Inc., 1959), pp. 16-17.

2 Jack Kerouac, *Visions of Gerard* (New York: Farrar, Straus & Giroux, Inc., 1963), pp. 7-8.

3 *Ibid.,* p. 64.

4 *Ibid.,* p. 129.

5 *Ibid.,* p. 132.

6 *Ibid.,* p. 129.

7 Ted Berrigan, "The Art of Fiction LXI," *The Paris Review,* No. 43 (Summer 1968), pp. 85-86.

8 Kerouac, *Dr. Sax,* p. 4.

9 *Ibid.,* p. 64.

10 Jack Kerouac, *The Town and the City* (New York: Harcourt Brace Jovanovich, Inc., 1950), p. 84.

11 Jack Kerouac, *Vanity of Duluoz* (New York: Coward, McCann & Geoghegan, Inc., 1967), p. 151.

12 Berrigan, *The Paris Review,* p. 72.

13 Kerouac, *The Town and the City,* p. 82.

14 Kerouac, *Dr. Sax,* p. 54.

15 Kerouac, *Vanity of Duluoz,* pp. 85-86.

16 Kerouac, *Visions of Gerard,* pp. 13-14.

17 Kerouac, *Vanity of Duluoz,* pp. 119-120.

18 *Ibid.,* p. 149.

19 *Ibid.,* p. 151.

20 *Ibid.,* p. 172.

21 Kerouac, *The Town and the City,* p. 446.

22 Berrigan, *The Paris Review,* p. 77.

23 *Idem.*

24 Kerouac, *Visions of Gerard,* pp. 14-15.

25 Allen Young, "The Life and Loves of Allen Ginsberg: An Interview," *The Real Paper* (March 28, 1973), p. 8.

26 Jack Kerouac, *The Subterraneans* (New York: Grove Press, Inc., 1958), pp. 64-66.

27 Kerouac, *Dr. Sax,* p. 64.

28 Kerouac, *Vanity of Duluoz,* p. 13.

29 Jack Kerouac, *Desolation Angels* (New York: Coward, McCann & Geoghegan, Inc., 1960), p. 238.

30 Dan Wakefield, "Jack Kerouac Comes Home" *The Atlantic,* Vol. 216, No. 1 (July 1965) pp. 69-72.

31 Kerouac, *Dr. Sax,* pp. 8-9.

32 Jack Kerouac, *On The Road* (New York: The Viking Press, Inc., 1957), pp. 309-310.

33 From the poem, "The Love Song of J. Alfred Prufrock" by T. S. Eliot.

34 Paul Jarvis, Essay, "Once God Moves the Hand, You Go Back and Revise, It's a Sin!" (March 1972), p. 6.

35 Kerouac, *On The Road,* p. 173.

36 Kerouac, *The Subterraneans,* pp. 26-29.

BIBLIOGRAPHY

Beaulieu, Henry. "Letter to Pertinax," *The Lowell Sun,* (April 17, 1973).

Berrigan, Ted. "The Art of Fiction LXI," *The Paris Review,* No. 43 (Summer 1968), 60-105.

Burroughs, William S. *Naked Lunch.* New York: Grove Press, Inc., 1959.

Cassady, Neal. *The First Third.* San Francisco: City Lights Books, 1971.

Charters, Ann. *Kerouac.* San Francisco: Straight Arrow Books, 1973.

Ciardi, John. "In Loving Memory of Myself," *Saturday Review,* 42 (July 25, 1959), 22-23.

Cook, Bruce. *The Beat Generation.* New York: Charles Scribner's Sons, 1971.

Corso, Gregory. *The Happy Birthday of Death.* New York: New Directions, 1960.

Feldman, Gene and Gartenberg, Max, eds. *The Beat Generation and The Angry Young Men.* New York: Dell Publishing Co. Inc., 1958.

Ferlinghetti, Lawrence. *A Coney Island of the Mind.* New York: New Directions, 1958.

Ginsberg, Allen. *Howl and Other Poems.* San Francisco: City Lights Books, 1956.

Holmes, John Clellon. *Go.* New York: Charles Scribner's Sons, 1952.

Jack Kerouac Symposium. Professor John W. P. McHale, Moderator. *Salem State College,* (April 5, 1973).

Jarvis, C. E. and Curtis, J. T. "Dialogues in Great Books," Kerouac Interview on Radio Station WCAP, Lowell, Massachusetts (September 1962).

Jarvis, Paul. "Once God Moves the Hand, You Go Back and Revise, It's a Sin!" Essay, (March 1972).

Kerouac, Jack.

    On The Road. New York: The Viking Press, Inc., 1957.

    The Town and the City. New York: Harcourt Brace Jovanovich, Inc., 1950.

    The Subterraneans. New York: Grove Press, Inc., 1958.

    Doctor Sax. New York: Grove Press, Inc., 1959.

    Maggie Cassidy. New York: Avon Publications, Inc., 1959.

    Tristessa. New York: Avon Publications, Inc., 1960.

    Mexico City Blues. New York: Grove Press, Inc., 1959.

    The Scripture of Golden Eternity. New York: Totem Press/Corinth Press, Inc., 1960.

    The Dharma Bums. New York: The Viking Press, Inc., 1958.

    Big Sur. New York: Farrar, Straus & Giroux, 1962.

    Visions of Gerard. New York: Farrar, Straus & Giroux, 1963.

Desolation Angels. New York: Coward, McCann & Geoghegan, Inc., 1960.

Vanity of Duluoz. New York: Coward, McCann & Geoghegan, Inc., 1967.

Pic. New York: Grove Press, Inc., 1971.

Book of Dreams. San Francisco: City Lights Books, 1961.

Lonesome Traveler. New York: McGraw-Hill Book Company, 1960.

Visions of Cody. New York: McGraw-Hill Book Company, 1973.

Satori in Paris. New York: Grove Press, Inc., 1966.

"The Bippie in the Middle," *The Boston Sunday Globe* (October 5, 1969).

"October in the Railroad Earth," *Evergreen Review,* Vol. 1, No. 2, pp. 119-136.

"The Origins of the Beat Generation," *Playboy,* Vol 6, No. 6 (June 1959).

Sports Report on a Basketball Game. *The Lowell Sun.* (February 19, 1942).

Krim, Seymour, ed. *The Beats.* New York: Fawcett Publications, Inc., 1960.

Krim, Seymour. *Shake It for the World, Smartass.* New York: The Dial Press, Inc., 1970.

Lipton, Lawrence. *The Holy Barbarians.* New York: Julian Messner, Inc., 1959.

Manville, Bill. *Saloon Society.* New York: Dell Books, 1960.

Parry, Albert. *Garrets and Pretenders.* New York: Dover Publications, Inc., 1960.

Snyder, Gary. *Riprap.* San Francisco: Four Seasons Foundation, City Lights Books, 1959.

Wakefield, Dan. "Jack Kerouac Comes Home," *The Atlantic.* Vol. 216, No. 1 (July 1965), 69-72.

Wolfe, Tom. *The Electric Kool-Aid Acid Test.* New York: Farrar, Straus & Giroux, Inc., 1968.

Young, Allen. "The Life and Loves of Allen Ginsberg," *The Real Paper,* (March 28, 1973).

Sculpture of Jack Kerouac on front cover by Mico Kaufman

Photographic art work on front cover by Peter Schell

Cover design by Cynthia Fowler

Printed by PICKEN PRINTING Inc., North Chelmsford, Mass.

232

Index

233